YES, LORD CHANCELLOR
A BIOGRAPHY OF LORD SCHUSTER

Permanent Secretary to
10 Lord Chancellors

Printed by: EntaPrint Ltd, Cranleigh, Surrey

YES, LORD CHANCELLOR
A BIOGRAPHY OF
LORD SCHUSTER

Permanent Secretary to
10 Lord Chancellors

by

JEAN GRAHAM HALL
LLM (London), FCIArb, Retired Circuit Judge

and

DOUGLAS F. MARTIN
ISO, LLB (London)

Barry Rose Law Publishers
Chichester, West Sussex

Also by the authors:

Haldane - Statesman, Lawyer, Philosopher, 1996
A Perfect Judge - Cases and Reports of Lord Sterndale,
    Master of the Rolls, 1999

www.lawpublications.co.uk

Contents

Acknowledgements

We gratefully acknowledge the help and kindness shown to us in different ways by many people and institutions.

In particular we wish to thank:

Lord Croham
Dr Stephen Cretney
The Librarian of the Supreme Court
Mrs E. Thompson
Rev. Christopher Turner
Staff of the Fawcett Library
Staff of Gray's Inn Library
The late Sir Paul Osmond
Officials of the Lord Chancellor's Department

Introduction

On December 11, 1934, a calm gentlemanly debate was proceeding in the House of Lords. In a monotone a noble Lord had been speaking on an unimportant bill about osteopaths. Speeches in the Lords rarely displayed emotion - never anger. Many of the noble Lords were having their post-prandial doze. They were rudely awakened when a chubby red-faced little man rose from the cross benches to interrupt the Lord Chancellor, Lord Sankey. Obviously he was angry about something. Starting in cold fury he became almost incoherent with rage. His tone was menacing and the words tumbled out. He spluttered and shouted about "a hidden hand", a "despotic power". His language became stronger. There was, he said, a dark design; the words "evil" and "odious" were repeated; he claimed that there was a sinister plot. For the first time in years all the noble Lords were awake; some even sat up in their seats. According to this angry man, there was an insidious assault on the Constitution, with the object of forming a Ministry of Justice along continental lines.

Who was this man who felt so strongly that our institutions were being threatened? To most of the noble Lords he was a stranger and many did not understand what he was talking about. The lawyers in the House knew him well as Lord Hewart, the Lord Chief Justice of England, and that he was attacking Sir Claud Schuster, the Permanent Secretary to the Lord Chancellor and to six of his predecessors.

Schuster had become one of the most powerful permanent secretaries ever, and he was to serve four more

Lord Chancellors.

Sir Arnold Lunn, travel agent, was the editor of the *British Ski Year Book for 1957*[1] in which he wrote an obituary for Lord Schuster and concluded it with these words:

> "No Englishman in this century has exercised greater influence on the mountain brotherhood than Claud Schuster, an influence which was partly due to his wisdom and judgment in the many executive positions he held in mountaineering and skiing clubs and partly to the felicity with which, in his writings, he interpreted the chief things of the ancient mountains and the precious things of the lasting hills."[2]

This is the story of the life of that extraordinary man, the position in which he found himself and how he used that position to influence the government of the country.

He was also a man who loved mountaineering and the Alps. When as Lord Schuster he chose a motto for his coat of arms it was *Levavi Oculos* - "I raised my eyes".

---

1. *British Ski Year Book*, vol.xvii, no.38, p.293.
2. *Ibid.*

Foreword

Lord Croham, GCB

The television series "Yes, Minister", a title echoed in this biography of Lord Schuster, "Yes, Lord Chancellor", was about the domination of a weak Minister, Jim Hacker, by the permanent secretary of his department, Sir Humphrey Appleby. Many people still believe that the events in the series are a realistic description of what went on in Whitehall and still continues. One reason for this belief is that British ministers change their departments so frequently that their knowledge of details of their department's work is assumed to be limited and that in contrast the senior civil servants, especially the permanent secretaries, have years of experience in the same area. It might therefore be expected that Claud Schuster, who was permanent secretary of the Lord Chancellor's Office for no less than 29 years, serving in that time 10 Lord Chancellors, would have been the Sir Humphrey par excellence, treating his ministers as mere puppets.

Yet this biography, while emphasising the very great influence that Schuster exercised over the work of the Lord Chancellor's Department, illustrates the entirely proper relationship he had with his ministers. The Department, when he became permanent secretary in 1915, was small. It differed in several ways from the generality of Whitehall departments of that time and remained so for most of Schuster's tenure of office. It had a high degree of independence from Treasury control, its permanent secretary was always a lawyer, and there was a great deal of flexibility about his retiring age. The powers and duties of the Lord Chancellor were very extensive, although the borderlines between his duties and those of the other lawyers in government were not always clearly drawn. In particular, the Lord Chancellor not only had a major role in the whole of the legislative programme of the government but his agreement was required for a large number of public appointments in the courts system and in the administration of the law. Most Lord Chancellors found that they had insufficient time to reach a personal view of all the potential appointees for that wide range of posts and were prepared to rely very heavily on the advice of their officials.

It is part of the duties of a permanent secretary to ensure that the minister is adequately briefed on all the questions that fall to the department, and to add his or her personal advice. Schuster's ability and depth of experience meant that his advice was always powerful though it was not always followed in policy issues. That reflected the proper constitutional relationship that he would never have questioned. Civil servants do not possess statutory powers; those lie with ministers. But on issues that they consider matters of executive detail, busy ministers may entrust a senior official to take decisions in their name. It is usual for instance to leave to the permanent secretary the detailed organisation of a department and the training, development and posting of the staff. It is clear in Schuster's case that he not only ran the Department but that he also, by virtue of the information he cultivated about individuals, had a dominating influence over many appointments in the court system and in committees set up with the authority of Lord

Chancellors he served. In this role he considered himself filling a gap in the system that would be likely to result in bad appointments. That his views often determined what appointments were made was widely known and sometimes resented. In many of the arguments that arose Schuster's views were very advanced for his time, especially in relation to women's rights, and in general his influence on appointments would appear to a modern audience to have been beneficial.

As a consequence of the extent of his influence and his long period of office, Schuster was certainly not an anonymous figure in government circles. Today many would question whether a civil servant should ever be conceded so much influence. They may however be assured by the fact that for many reasons it is virtually impossible for a civil servant to acquire anything approaching the degree of influence that Schuster possessed. There have been many changes both in the way public appointments are made and in the environment in which civil servants now operate. Top posts are more open to competition and are sometimes for fixed contract periods. It is therefore most unlikely that any permanent official would remain in place for anything approaching Schuster's period of service. Nor could any individual play a decisive role in such a wide range of public appointments, since appointments in all areas of public life are now covered by rules to make them more open, and thus less subject to most forms of patronage.

In addition, while the basic duties of permanent secretaries in terms of responsibility for the running of their departments have remained basically the same since

Schuster's day, the balance of power in Whitehall in relation to policy has shifted considerably. Policy advice to the minister no longer goes along a single pathway controlled by the permanent secretary; departments have politically appointed temporary civil servants as policy advisers operating close to ministers. Their influence is extensive over most aspects of policy, and has been dominating over news reporting and comment. The long-term experience of permanent civil servants is less regarded than it used to be because both social and economic changes have become more rapid. Nonetheless the principle of a politically neutral civil service supporting ministers remains an important element of our constitution. It is a principle that guided Claud Schuster during his long working life as a public servant, during which he constantly gave excellent advice on the legal and constitutional problems of the day.

Family Tree - Samuel Judah Schuster (know as Julius) 1747-1805

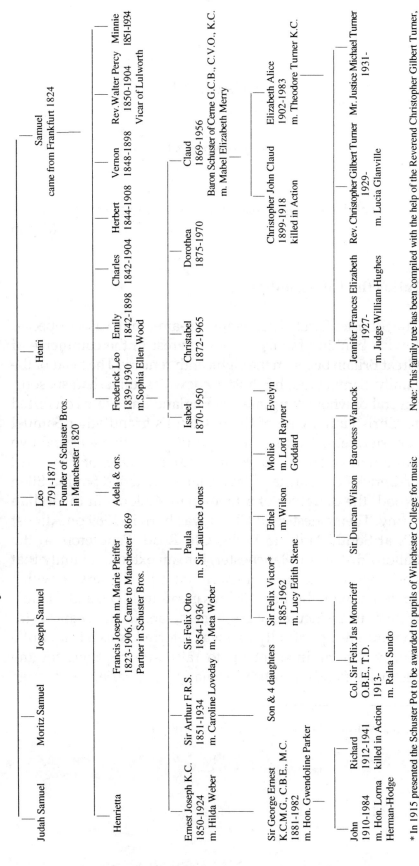

Samuel
came from Frankfurt 1824

Henri

Leo
1791-1871
Founder of Schuster Bros.
in Manchester 1820

Joseph Samuel

Moritz Samuel

Judah Samuel

Henrietta

Francis Joseph m. Marie Pfeiffer
1823-1906. Came to Manchester 1869
Partner in Schuster Bros.

Adela & ors.

Frederick Leo
1839-1930
m.Sophia Ellen Wood

Emily
1842-1898

Charles
1842-1904

Herbert
1844-1908

Vernon
1848-1898

Rev. Walter Percy
1850-1904
Vicar of Lulworth

Minnie
1851-1934

Claud
1869-1956
Baron Schuster of Ceme G.C.B., C.V.O., K.C.
m. Mabel Elizabeth Merry

Isabel
1870-1950

Paula
m. Sir Laurence Jones

Christabel
1872-1965

Dorothea
1875-1970

Ernest Joseph K.C.
1850-1924
m. Hilda Weber

Sir Arthur F.R.S.
1851-1934
m. Caroline Loveday

Sir Felix Otto
1854-1936   m. Meta Weber

Ethel
m. Wilson

Mollie
m. Lord Rayner
Goddard

Evelyn

Christopher John Claud
1899-1918
killed in Action

Elizabeth Alice
1902-1983
m. Theodore Turner K.C.

Sir George Ernest
K.C.M.G., C.B.E., M.C.
1881-1982
m. Hon. Gwendoline Parker

Sir Felix Victor*
1885-1962
m. Lucy Edith Skene

Son & 4 daughters

Sir Duncan Wilson

Baroness Warnock

Jennifer Frances Elizabeth
1927-
m. Judge William Hughes

Rev. Christopher Gilbert Turner
1929-
m. Lucia Glanville

Mr. Justice Michael Turner
1931-

John
1910-1984
m. Hon. Lorna
Herman-Hodge

Richard
1912-1941
killed in Action

Col. Sir Felix Jas Moncrieff
O.B.E., T.D.
1913-
m. Ralna Sundo

Note: This family tree has been compiled with the help of the Reverend Christopher Gilbert Turner,
Headmaster of Dean Close 1968-1979 and Headmaster of Stowe School 1979-1989

* In 1915 presented the Schuster Pot to be awarded to pupils of Winchester College for music
(It was won on one occasion by the Reverend Christopher Gilbert Turner)

Note: Hilda and Meta Weber were the daughters of Sir Herman Weber, physician to Prince Albert

CHAPTER 1

Claud Schuster

The childhood shows the man, as morning shows the day.

Milton

Julius the Paterfamilias

The Schuster family from Frankfurt-am-Main was a respected Jewish banking family whose interest in the commerce of Great Britain began in the eighteenth century. The head of the family, Samuel Judah Schuster known as Julius, had six sons, several of whom emigrated to England and were converted to Christianity. One of them, Claud's grandfather Samuel Schuster, settled in Manchester in 1824. His five sons and two daughters were all born in England. One of his sons, Frederick Leo Schuster, Claud's father, married Sophia Ellen Wood, the daughter of a Lieutenant-Colonel in the Indian Army. Their eldest child Claud was born in 1869 on August 22, at South Bank, 15 Eccles Old Road, Pendleton, in the Salford district of Manchester, into an extended family that had a strong tradition of charity and public service which continues until this day. Claud's great-uncle Leo and Claud's father, in particular, were benefactors to the Manchester community. Specifically Leo was referred to as a leader of a German committee set up to raise subscriptions for the victims of floods in South Germany.[1] The variety and range

---

1. Bill Williams. *The Making of Manchester Jewry*, p.43.

1

of his charitable works were not restricted by religion. Local church records show that on December 10, 1833, Marianne, the daughter of Leo Schuster, was baptised at a chapel in Mosley Street, Manchester, described as "Presbyterian or Unitarian". It follows that by then his branch of the family at least had taken the Christian faith. *The Jewish World* of September 7, 1877 was pleased to claim Leo Schuster's Jewish origin, although he was described as a "conversionist".

Claud's father, Frederick Leo Schuster was, like Leo, prominent in the public life of Manchester. A newspaper report of that time describes him as being of the firm of Schuster, Fulda and Company, shipping merchants, of Sackville Street. It lists the public bodies with which he had connections. He had been a member of the Board of Manchester Royal Infirmary for 38 years and a leading member of the committees of the Barnes' Convalescent Hospital, the Barnes' Samaritan Charity, Maye's Charity, the Bishop of Manchester's Fund and the Manchester and Salford Savings Bank of which he had been Trustee and deputy-chairman since 1898.

The tradition of public service continues in Claud's three grandchildren, Jennifer Frances Elizabeth Turner; the Reverend Christopher Gilbert Turner - Headmaster of Dean Close and then of Stowe School from 1979-1989; and Mr Justice Michael Turner, a High Court Judge.

Numbered among the descendants of Julius Schuster are five knights, a baroness and one baron (Claud). They are not the only members of the family who have served this country with distinction. Altogether the family can boast of many who have achieved high office in various fields including finance, the law, the church, science, education and the army.

St George's School, Ascot

The young Claud attended the same preparatory school as Winston Churchill, St George's School, Ascot. Schuster, five years older than Churchill, was there from 1876-1883 and Churchill from 1881-1883. Schuster's grandson (the Reverend Christopher Turner) says that his grandfather was reluctant to talk about his preparatory school but the family knew that conditions were as Churchill had described them in his book *My Early Life*.[2] It was one of the most fashionable and expensive preparatory schools in the country. Its object was to prepare boys for Eton and it had all the facilities a school could wish for at that time including the new invention of electric light. However, the regime was harsh in the extreme. As at Eton punishment meant flogging with the birch. Churchill says that he felt sure that no Eton boy and certainly no Harrow boy in his day ever received such a cruel flogging as was administered by the headmaster upon the little boys in his care and power. It was the practice to produce delinquents before the assembly and then take them to an adjoining room where the headmaster would first flog them until they bled while the assembled pupils and staff listened to their screams. The Reverend Christopher Turner describes the headmaster, H.W. Sneyd Kynnersley, as "a truly terrible man - but he did give sumptuous prizes".

---

2. Winston Churchill. *My Early Life*. Leo Cooper. 1989, pp.23-26.

He must have found some consolation for the harshness in the holidays. When he was 10 he accompanied his father, with whom he was on good terms, to Switzerland. It was his first experience of the Swiss Alps and the beginning of his life-long love affair with mountains, which is more fully described in Chapter 6.

In *Men, Women and Mountains,* published in 1931, he paints a vivid picture of the impression that visit made on him.

"To me as a boy, Chur was the gateway to the land of dreams which had occupied me all the winter; and the great roads to the south and the south-east were the highways to the capital of that enchanted country. Chur, or at least the centre of the town, has perhaps not changed much since then in outward appearance. It has the same crooked, narrow, inconvenient streets and the same air of being an illustration to a German fairy story. But the spirit and the smell are different. It then smelt of horse. When you had left the train and had a bath at the best hotel in the world, you went to look at the horses and their drivers. You talked to the drivers for hours, and inspected the carriages and thumped the cushions to see whether they were soft enough and, when the long hot day had gone and it was time for dinner, you made your bargain for the drive to Engadine. Next morning you set off with a great clatter. The driver was a gallant fellow with an enormous watch-chain, a pheasant feather in his hat and a whip with a long lash which he cracked in sheer swagger to get an echo from the narrow street. There were four or five horses, each with feathers in his headstall and a fox's brush dangling from the bridle. The pace was sedate enough, whichever route you took, you had two passes to cross before you reached the inn, and the custom of the road was to take two days on the journey. But it was all a delight. In the first place you were 'abroad'. I don't know whether anyone 'goes abroad' nowadays. Personally I still have the same thrill,

4

in no way diminished in intensity, when I feel under my feet the station platform at Chur or Interlaken. Then there was the broad road, dustier and hotter as the day wore on, sometimes gleaming miles ahead on the hill-side before us; sometimes hemmed in between rock and precipice with a surprise round every corner. It led through villages, between wonderfully neat houses with barred windows and crimson carnations in window-boxes and the large plates which announced the particular company in which each was insured for fire; and over all hung the omnipresent, all-pervading smell of horse. We made it a point of honour, as far as we could, to choose a different combination of roads every year and to make the night's halt at a different inn."[3]

Several years later, in 1886, again with his parents whose object was to drink the waters of the Engadine, he observed the curious crowds from every nation who shared this peculiar exercise - German princelings, occasionally an Indian Rajah and many Germans and Austrians. On August 23, 1886, he ascended the Piz Lnaguard, 10,000 feet high. From then until 1913 no summer passed without his climbing some mountain or other.[4]

In the same book he writes about his father's love of the mountains and how that love had passed from father to son. Father and son must have been alike in stature and probably in manner. Schuster describes him as being small and spare, walking with rapid short steps which should have tired him out in an hour but he seemed insensible to fatigue. Schuster

---

3. Claud Schuster. *Men, Women and Mountains*. Nicholson and Watson. 1931, pp.100/101.
4. *Ibid.*, p.105.

had accompanied him on several mountain walks and learnt that toil and sweat, hunger and thirst, cold and heat are all part of mountaineering and he says that his father "... implanted in me that desire, which, when once it catches the heart, can never be eradicated ... He taught me the delight in labour and in the cessation of labour. Above all he delighted in my delight of them."[5]

His father loved all men individually, though he detested great numbers of them in the mass; and he was, Schuster says, a most amusing travelling companion, for he would fall into talk with anyone whom he met and he never tired of meeting new men seeking new valleys and new viewpoints.[6]

Winchester

At the age of 14 Claud became a pupil at Winchester, then, as now, one of the foremost public schools in the country. According to the Wykehamist Society he did not achieve great fame at school. He spoke occasionally in debates and played the local brand of Winchester football sufficiently well to get into the XV a-side team representing half the school.

Winchester in the 1890s was the most academic and intellectual of the major public schools and even then had a reputation for producing men for public service. However, it was notoriously lacking in comfort. One pupil's view were that the food was "execrable, badly cooked and inconceivably

---

5. *Ibid.*, p.73.
6. *Ibid.*

monotonous" and the boys "cold, dirty and a little savage ... we had a tremendous zest for life and enjoyed it; above all we were not soft and we were not prigs".[7]

The hardship young Claud endured at his preparatory school prepared him for discomfort. He loved Winchester, was immensely proud of being a Wykehamist and retained his interest in the school throughout his life.

His interest in climbing, already aroused by his visit to Switzerland with his father was further encouraged at Winchester. In *Men, Women and Mountains* he described his housemaster Frederick Morshead and revealed a little of his school at Winchester:

"At school we all knew that he was a great climber and had ascended Mount Blanc at a speed which in another man would have been incredible ... When in the cold of the morning a shivering junior issued from the house-yard, still hastily adjusting his garments and wondering how fast he must run to be in time for Chapel, he heard, sometimes - alas - before, a swift and measured tramp. It suggested doom, as it came on, inevitable, unhurrying, unwearying. One did not need to pause to realise that it was Frederick Morshead. He moved like the man he was, with body and limbs perfectly adjusted to his task. One would have called him stark and grim but for the kindliness that seemed to lurk in the half-smile between his closely trimmed moustache and beard. His clothes were simple and formal, and the mortarboard and gown emphasised the athletic lines of his figure, so that he seemed to have cast away every encumbrance and to be prepared to run the race that was set before him. So he was

7. Euan O'Halpin - *Head of the Civil Service, a Study of Warren Fisher.* Routledge. 1986, p.4.

in life, and he might be taken as the best type of Wykehamist of his age as the Wykehamical tradition of the time would have had him - sane, strong, a Liberal in politics, hopeful, determined, a man who knew his job and meant to do it."[8]

The Wykehamist Society have a letter written by Sir Claud Schuster about the most appropriate method of commemorating the dead in the War Memorial Cloister. His only son, Christopher, also a Wykehamist, was killed in action in 1918 and he and others, must have felt strongly about the commemoration. The letter to the Warden (Lord Selbourne) began with the words "At the risk of being tedious ..." and ended 11 pages of typed foolscap later!

At Oxford

Like many Wykehamists and some of his relatives Schuster went from Winchester to New College, Oxford. In common with many others of European descent he was becoming steeped in English tradition. He remained at Oxford from 1888 to 1892 when he obtained a second class degree in history. He was not an outstanding student perhaps because he found time to enjoy himself as well as to study. After retirement in 1944, he was invited to give the Romanes Lecture, an honour bestowed only on the most eminent. In the lecture he related an experience which showed he was not afraid to break the rules at Oxford. It was reported that:

---

8. Claud Schuster. *Men, Women and Mountains*, p.73.

"Mr Gladstone delivered the Romanes Lecture in the Sheldonian Theatre. Crowds of undergraduates arrived to see him. Schuster could not get through the gate so he climbed the railings. At the top he either slipped or someone pulled his leg and he sat on one of the spikes. He disengaged himself, came down inside the railings and found his way to the highest gallery in the theatre. He was sitting uncomfortably and felt compelled to leave his seat. He stumbled and fell down the stairs but somehow managed to get home where he examined his wounds with a looking glass. It was subsequently reported, presumably by the scout, that he had been taken home in a dying condition and bleeding 'orribly."[9]

Marriage

In 1896 just after he had been called to the Bar, Claud Schuster married Elizabeth Merry, the daughter of the Reverend William Walter Merry (1835-1918) the Rector of Lincoln College, Oxford. Claud described him as:

"Pious and grave, massive in body, brilliant in conversation. Went to the Alps just after taking his degree, saw not only the Matterhorn but also knickerbockers. He wrote:

'Some sporting young tourists we see
Wear trousers that end at the knee
T'would be better by half
To cover the calf
Or the place where the calf ought to be.'"[10]

---

9. *The Romanes Lecture.* Clarendon Press. 1984, p.4.
10. *Men, Women and Mountains*, p.75.

Merry was another of Schuster's associates who was passionately fond of mountaineering. He was also a renowned classical scholar, a leading authority on Greek and Latin literature. He had edited editions of the *Odyssey* and the plays of Aristophanes. His writing was described as sufficiently erudite, full of sound learning and spiced with congenial humour. A great preacher, he was awarded the perpetual curacy of All Saints Oxford from 1880 to 1910 and was the public orator of Oxford University. In addition to the lucidity of his Latin, aided by his delivery, he had a lively wit and great qualities as a host. As Vice-Chancellor of the University from 1904-6 he maintained the tradition of hospitality associated with that office.[11]

Schuster met Merry while at Oxford and no doubt enjoyed his hospitality. He had much in common with his father-in-law. He admired Merry's learning and developed the same love of language and mountaineering as Merry. When he asked Merry for his daughter's hand in marriage it was willingly granted. Mabel Elizabeth Schuster died in 1936. That loss and the death of his son were the two tragic events in a highly successful life.

Schuster was also influenced by his uncle, the Reverend Walter Percy Schuster, who was curate of Corfe Castle and later Vicar of Lulworth. As a boy the young Schuster used to stay with his uncle and so acquired such a love of Dorset that he made his country home there at the Manor House, Piddletrenthide. In 1941 he was appointed High Sheriff of the

---

11. Information from *The Times*, March 7, 1918 and the *Oxford Magazine*, March 15, 1918.

county and when he was awarded a barony in 1944 he became Lord Schuster of Cerne in the County of Dorset.

At the Liverpool Bar

Having obtained a second class degree in history in 1892 Schuster unsuccessfully applied to be a Fellow of All Souls, Oxford. In view of his age his failure was not surprising. He was called to the Bar by the Inner Temple in 1895. Thirty years later he became a Bencher of that Inn and in 1947 the Treasurer. On being elected to the Northern Circuit Bar on March 14, 1895, he was proposed by J.C. Bingham, QC (later Lord Mersey) and seconded by J.A. Hamilton (later Lord Sumner). The latter was to become one of his climbing companions. On occasions he devilled for both of them in court.

He joined the Chambers of William Pickford, who later became Lord Sterndale, Master of the Rolls.

As a boy Claud was interested in hunting and would have met Pickford, then a leading member of the Northern Circuit Bar whose pastime was following a pack of beagles in Cheshire. The two men had a close friendship and a mutual interest in mountaineering.

A few months after being elected to the Circuit Bar he was appointed the Circuit Junior. That is an important and onerous position in the nature of a General Secretary and general factotum. His time of practice at the Liverpool Bar was brief and not very successful but evidently he had progressed from the lower courts to the old Liverpool Crown

Court (which was equivalent to Quarter Sessions at the time).[12]

At Oxford the young Claud was not a wealthy undergraduate and to some extent had to fend for himself. When required to go to London, to dine at the Inner Temple, for example, he cycled there and back to save the train fare. When he was called to the Bar in 1895 he could not count on his father's support during the difficult early years of a young barrister. Moreover, his marriage in 1896 meant that a reasonable income became a priority. Although his start at the Bar was slow he continued to practise until 1899 when a good dependable salary was offered as an alternative.

There may have been other reasons for his change of career. He may have realised that he was not likely to reach the heights at the Bar. In appearance he was small in stature (5ft 7ins in height); handsome enough with piercing blue eyes said to have come from his mother's Irish ancestry, and he certainly had a dynamic personality. But he did not have the commanding presence of men he later came to admire, eg, his close friend Lord Sterndale, and Lord Maugham. They were both tall and handsome with the look of steady impartiality appropriate in ideal representatives of British justice. In addition his love of the English language and knowing that he was "good on paper" may have been other reasons which persuaded him that the Civil Service was a more suitable career for him than the Bar.

---

12. *Hansard*. House of Lords. March 23, 1950, col.490, vol.166.

A Public Servant

In order to start on the ladder leading to the position of a Permanent Secretary at the turn of the century it was necessary to pass the Higher Division Examination, but Schuster, having entered the service as a lawyer did not have to sit the Examination. For that and other reasons, although he had close relationships with his contemporary Permánent Secretaries, he was regarded as being "different".

His career in government service began as secretary to the Chief Commissioner of the Local Government Act Commission, the report of which led to the formation of the London County Council. His appointment was recommended by a certain H.W. Orange who wrote to Schuster's mother (July 28, 1899) expressing confidence that her son would be successful at the Bar and that the Commission contained several barristers who meant to return to practice, "It will at any rate give him an opportunity of exercising his talents and making them known to a wider circle which is not always possible to achieve if one has nothing else to do but to sit in Chambers and wait."

When the Local Government Act Commission had completed its report Schuster was for a while secretary to the Great Northern Railway and then an employee of the Union of London & Smith's Bank Ltd. He was then noticed by Sir Robert Morant, the Permanent Secretary of the Board of Education who employed him as a temporary legal assistant in his department from February 12, 1903. Morant wrote to Schuster (April 20, 1903) to the effect that the post would be transformed into a permanent and pensionable one "at the earliest possible moment". That moment did not arrive for almost four years and in the meantime Schuster worked temporarily in the Parliamentary Counsel's Office. The experience he gained there was to prove very valuable in his later career when he frequently concerned himself with the drafting of Bills. On January 28, 1907 he wrote to his mother:

> "You will be surprised to hear that I am back to the Board of Education permanently, I am offered a certainty at £1,000 a year with a pension instead of uncertainty and don't feel that I can refuse, especially at this coming year as the Parliamentary Counsel's Office looks like being very lean. I was only offered the thing on Friday last and I begin work (nominally) on Friday next. I am a good deal upset and flurried at this sudden jump."

He now had a permanent post as legal adviser to the Board of Education and by 1911 he was promoted again to be a Principal Assistant Secretary. In the same year Sir Robert Morant was appointed chairman of the English Commission under the National Insurance Act of 1911. Schuster was appointed Chief Registrar of Friendly Societies which made him an *ex officio* member of the Insurance Commission. By February 1912 he had given up being Registrar of Friendly Societies to be Secretary of the English Insurance Commission and soon after that he became legal adviser to the Commission. About this time a newspaper report stated that he had had three promotions in two months. Much of this rapid advancement was undoubtedly due to Morant's high opinion of his protégé.

CHAPTER 2

A Galaxy of Future Whitehall Stars

After years in a stagnant office, I had tasted the joys of a new, adventurous, constructive task, and of the camaraderie it brings.[1]
Lord Salter

The burgeoning of Schuster's career had begun with Sir Robert Morant in the Board of Education. Morant was the elder by six years but both men had been educated at Winchester, and New College, Oxford. Schuster's six to seven years in education, working with the greatest civil servant of his day, gave him experience of administration which served him well. The two continued to work together in the National Insurance Commission. It was a great achievement of the Liberal Government of that period to have put the National Insurance Act of 1911 on the statute book despite all kinds of opposition, and opened up a new chapter in the life of Schuster and of the country. The prime movers of the quite revolutionary system of administration which followed the Act were to have much influence on Schuster, giving him access to the wider field of government in Whitehall.

The First National Insurance Act 1911

Lloyd George, Chancellor of the Exchequer, like Haldane and

---

1. Lord Salter. *Memoirs of a Public Servant*. Faber and Faber, 1981, p.72.

others at the time, was an admirer of German organisation. He had visited Germany in 1908 to see how the Bismarkian system of state insurance operated. He determined, as he later put it in a speech in Birmingham, to join "The Red Cross". "I am in the ambulance corps. I am engaged to drive a wagon through the twistings and turnings and ruts of the Parliamentary road."[2] The enterprise thereafter became known as "Lloyd George's Ambulance Wagon" (it became the title of Braithwaite's memoir).

At the end of 1910 the Chancellor sent W.J. Braithwaite (a classically trained Wykehamist who lived at Toynbee Hall, the East End settlement which nurtured the social conscience of many others including Morant and Attlee), on a fact-finding mission. Lloyd George received Braithwaite's report with typical panache on the pier at Nice where he was holidaying.[3] The report was just what he wanted to introduce social insurance by the State.

The First National Insurance Act reached the statute book in 1911, after a difficult passage through Parliament. This success of the reforming Liberal Government was due largely to the dynamic energy of Lloyd George. Under the Act the administrative machinery was set up in February 1912 consisting of four Commissions - for England, Scotland, Wales and Ireland. They were composed of members representing friendly society, trade union and medical experience. Each Commission had a woman as a member. The chairman was of general administrative ability. As had

2. P.J. Grigg. *The People's Champion*, p.335.
3. Peter Hennessy. *Whitehall*. Fontana Press, 1990, p.58.

been expected the English Commission took the lead and the others followed.

The English Commission (subsequently referred to as "the Commission") had the job of launching and setting up the operating machinery for Lloyd George's complicated insurance scheme. This affected such ministries as Labour and Health: and there were also financial problems implicating the Treasury and the Inland Revenue. The Commissioner's Report (1914, Cmd.7687) had to use most of the civil service departments to bring the Act into operation and thereafter to administer it. The chairman of the Commission, Sir Robert Morant, insisted on taking Schuster with him as secretary to the Commission. This move determined the course of Schuster's career. After the limited nature of his work in the Board of Education, the Commission gave the alert Schuster the opportunity to understand the machinery of government. Moreover, he had the good fortune that his colleagues were exceptional.

Sir Robert Morant

As Morant's protégé Schuster learnt much from whom he acquired his dynamism, mental agility and perception. Morant was a man of magnetic presence, tall, and with a great leonine head of white hair; he combined dynamic energy with an excitable and nervous temperament.[4] Moreover he was to become a great force in Whitehall. His

---

4. Lord Salter, p.57.

career was remarkable and a summary of it shows the influence he had on Schuster.

After a first class degree in theology at New College, Oxford, Morant became a teacher, briefly in England and then in Siam (Thailand) where he was the tutor to the King's nephews and then the Crown Prince. He founded a system of public education in Siam and acquired a position of great influence. This caused some jealousy and he was forced to leave in 1894. On his return to England, he undertook some social work at Toynbee Hall, Whitechapel, and in 1895 he joined the Board of Education where - as described in the *Dictionary of National Biography* (1912-1921):

> "His achievement as a relatively junior officer, in mobilizing and marshalling the political, municipal and educational forces of the country for the not unhazardous enterprise of constructing an orderly and comprehensive system of public education out of incoherent and antagonistic elements, is one of the romances of the Civil Service. The passing of the Education Act 1902 was largely due to his vision, courage and ingenuity. His promotion ... to the substantive post of Permanent Secretary, was not only appropriate but inevitable. Until 1911 he worked on education showing his exceptional ability as an administrator - revolutionary at times, conservative at others but an opportunist who knew when to make the right moves."

Morant's success as chairman of the National Insurance Commission inevitably led to further promotion. He became Permanent Secretary to the new Ministry of Health, and in 1917 he was asked to serve on Lord Haldane's Machinery of Government Committee. In 1915 Schuster had been appointed Permanent Secretary to the Lord Chancellor on Morant's recommendation. By 1917, in a position to influence the membership of committees, Schuster was repaying a debt.

The Dictionary of National Biography concludes with this tribute:

> "His premature death on March 13, 1920 left the civil service with the feeling that their order had lost one of the greatest figures it had ever produced - great by both character and achievement."

The Staff of the Commission - a Corps of Talent

Morant had great achievements to his credit in the field of education but foresaw complications in the National Insurance Commission and prophesied a complete breakdown. A strong Cabinet Committee including Lloyd George, Lord Reading and Lord Haldane decided that Morant must be persuaded to get on with the job. They authorised him to strengthen his staff by picking the best brains available from any government department. The result was the assembly of the most talented body of civil servants ever concentrated on one project. This corps of talent outshone the original members of the Commission. It consisted of mainly young men all of whom were to have subsequently brilliant careers in various departments. They included Warren Fisher, Arthur Salter and John Anderson who replaced Schuster as Secretary in 1913 (Schuster was knighted in the same year). Salter described Schuster as "a brilliant lawyer". He continued:

> "Schuster had for a time served as Secretary of the Commission,

where his capacity for lucid and luminous exposition (exceeding his knowledge either of insurance or of the institutions and organizations through which it had now to be administered) gave him at first an undue influence in decisions on administrative policy until he was transferred to the more appropriate post of legal adviser."[5]

That comment seems to suggest that a true mandarin was putting an outsider in his place.

In John Anderson's biography the author comments: "... apart from the general recognition that the ablest man among them had got the job, there was a consensus of opinion, perhaps in part unconscious, that John (Anderson) could team up with and control the volatile genius of Morant, in a way that Schuster had not done ..."[6]

In addition to the brilliant Morant, the Commission "... boasted no less than four Fellows of All Souls and was a veritable *Who's Who* of future Whitehall stars. Warren Fisher (*infra*); John Swanwick Bradbury - Joint Permanent Secretary to the Treasury from 1913-19, who had, by the end of his period of officer there, reorganised the Treasury; John Anderson (prematurely grand and as pompous as ever).[7]

Other members of the Commission were Ernest Gowers, barrister (and editor of *Plain Words*); Alfred Watson, a actuarial expert; Maurice Gwyer, a skilled draftsman and later Treasury Solicitor.

Another member who did not appreciate the camaraderie

---

5. Lord Salter, p.59.
6. J.W. Wheeler-Bennett. *John Anderson, Viscount Waverley*. MacMillan, 1962, p.35.
7. Peter Hennessy.

of this coterie of stars was the unfortunate Braithwaite - the pioneer of the whole scheme. Lord Salter contrasts him with Schuster:

> "In rather tragic contrast with him [Schuster] at this period, was W.J. Braithwaite who had so little of Schuster's particular gifts but an almost unrivalled knowledge of what Schuster knew so little ... Unhappily as so often happens with overworked able men, he did not realise soon enough that extra help and further delegation were essential ... The consequence was, not a nervous breakdown, but a nervous exhaustion, which made co-operation with the able and critical new men, brought in by Morant, both difficult and irritating."[8]

John Anderson (later Lord Waverley) Permanent Secretary Home Office 1922-32

John Anderson replaced Schuster as Secretary in 1913, and Schuster was made the Commission's legal adviser. Anderson, who became Lord Waverley in 1950, had served in the Colonial Office and the Ministry of Shipping when Morant spotted his talents. As was the case with several other members, his secondment to the Commission gave him the opportunity to shine. The result was another glittering career. From Permanent Secretary in the Home Office, he became Governor of Bengal in 1932. On leaving the civil service for politics, in 1938 he was elected MP for the Scottish Universities and the same year was appointed Lord Privy

---

8. Lord Salter, p.59.

Seal. In 1939 he became on the outbreak of war Home
Secretary [the Anderson air-raid shelters were named after
him]. He ended his extraordinary career as Chancellor of the
Exchequer in 1945 having introduced the "Pay-As-You-Earn"
system of collecting income tax. *The Dictionary of National
Biography* describes him as possessing "... a readiness to
delegate, unflurried and objective judgment on issues of
policy together with an air of pontifical authority - one of the
giants of Whitehall."

Warren Fisher - Permanent Secretary to the Treasury 1919-1939

In 1919 John Bradbury (also a member of the Commission)
had reorganised the Treasury. Instead of three joint
Permanent Secretaries, there would be one. That one turned
out to be Warren Fisher, "another peculiarly obsessional
bureaucratic animal ... who was to leave a permanent mark
on his profession and British central government thanks to
his 20 years headship of the Treasury ... Henceforth the
Permanent Secretary to the Treasury became the Permanent
Head of the Civil Service."[9] In that capacity, Warren Fisher
with his ideas of tidy and centralised organisation, created
the profession of higher bureaucrats - the administrative Civil
Service.

Fisher was a liberal with a belief that the State had a

---

9. Euan O'Halpin. *The Head of the Civil Service - a Study of Sir Warren Fisher*.
Routledge, 1989, p.12.

positive duty to promote for the common good. He succeeded in all that he did and became a driving force in the Commission.

In appearance he was not unlike Schuster, small, slim and spry. He was interested in sport, being responsible for funding the Civil Service Sports Association and for his part in arranging the purchase of the Civil Service sports ground at Chiswick. One would have expected Fisher, by virtue of his education at Winchester and the position he achieved to be a conservative with a small "c", uncontroversial and traditional. He was not. Politically liberal in his outlook, he was unconventional, eccentric almost. He had a habit of addressing men as "love" and "darling", his personal letters contained inappropriate endearments. He addressed the First Sea Lord, Lord Chatfield, as "Ernie Dear".

Although, according to a contemporary, he resembled a woman in his likes and dislikes, he was essentially masculine in his personal relationships. He clearly liked women and had said that he believed in the innate superiority of woman to man. He had many women friends and in the civil service he had the reputation of being a ladies' man. His contemporaries agreed that he was a very unusual man; one of his critics said he had a mind like a quick-witted clerk. Another referred to him as a bureaucratic magpie - a pundit on every sort of question. Certainly his position gave him the opportunity, if not the right, to offer his opinion on almost every kind of government activity.[10]

Historically it is a mystery how, as soon as he was

---

10. *Ibid.*

appointed Permanent Secretary, Warren Fisher had got himself designated head of the Civil Service and as such the official adviser of the Prime Minister (the First Lord of the Treasury) on all civil service matters. It was not until 1968 that the Civil Service Department was formed separate from the Treasury and responsible to the Prime Minister - a department subsequently abolished by Mrs Thatcher in 1981, when the Civil Service reverted to the Treasury. Fisher laid down that no head or deputy head of a department and no accounting officer should be appointed or removed without Prime Minister's concurrence. The object of this was not, as has been so often said, to make the Secretary to the Treasury superior to departmental Ministers in choosing their senior officials, but to ensure that all suitable candidates from the Civil Service as a whole should be reviewed before any such appointment was settled. This meant a great unifying of the Civil Service, for the promising members of it were not thenceforward to be confined to their original departments for advancement. It meant also that the Secretary of the Treasury made it his business to stimulate a search for talent wherever it could be found.[11]

Sir Warren Fisher's aim was to weld a team spirit into the Civil Service. One means was the use of the telephone to promote informality. Before the First War, Sir Thomas Heath, Joint Permanent Secretary, had opposed the introduction of the telephone at the Treasury on the ground that it would impair the ability of officials to write concisely.[12] In order to

---

11. P.J. Grigg. *Prejudice and Judgment*. Jonathan Cape, 1948, p.51.
12. Euan O'Halpin, p.128.

encourage the idea of a single service with team spirit, Fisher arranged a Civil Service dinner at the Connaught Rooms in 1926. The diners were representatives of all grades and departments of the Civil Service. There were guests from the Royal Family, the armed services and politics and there was an address from a Cabinet Minister. But this innovation was not continued. Fisher had always held informal discussions with other heads of departments to decide who should be chosen to fill senior posts. On July 27, 1931 he arranged for all heads of departments to meet to decide on what action to take on the 1929 Report of the Royal Commission on the Civil Service.

He had always insisted that the head of a department must also be the chief accounting officer. One result of that policy was that responsibility for the accounts of the County Courts Branch was transferred in 1922 from the Treasury to Sir Claud Schuster as Permanent Secretary to the Lord Chancellor's Department.

When he was 60, Fisher decided to retire from the Civil Service. He had become something of a prima donna and there was general relief when he left.

The Forcing Ground of Future Reputations

Sir John Anderson's biographer, J.W. Wheeler-Bennett, describes how a galaxy of stars gathered around Morant to assist in the gigantic task of getting the National Insurance Act working within a few months (by April 1, 1913). Three of Anderson's colleagues (John Bradbury, Arthur Salter and

Claud Schuster) later received peerages in addition to himself and a fourth (Warren Fisher) might have had one if he had wanted it;[13] no fewer than 20 others received knighthoods.

In is memoirs Salter refers to the camaraderie which developed between members of the Commission's staff:

> "Morant, Bradbury, Schuster, Braithwaite, Watson were all men of strong personality, skilled in argument and fortified by great administrative experience. They would discuss a problem ... with a brilliant and metaphysical subtlety which both dazzled and confused ..."[14]

They were

> "... a congenial team absorbed in a common and constructive task, which submerged personal rivalries and ambitions. There are few joys in life to excel those of such a camaraderie, and no better basis for enduring masculine friendship."[15]

For Schuster this was a fortunate environment. As a lawyer rather than a mandarin, coming from a department which was regarded as different from the others, he was almost an outsider. Being a member of this select team gave him experience and connections which he was to use to the full in his subsequent career. In particular his association with Fisher and Anderson caused the three to be referred to as the triumvirate who ran Whitehall during the thirties.[16]

---

13. *Ibid.*
14. Lord Salter, p.63.
15. *Ibid.*, pp.65/6.
16. Robert Stevens. *The Independence of the Judiciary*. Clarendon Press, 1993, p.32.

CHAPTER 3

The Office of Lord Chancellor

*All Lord Chancellors respect the law, but some are more
respectful than others.*[1]

The power of a Permanent Secretary is derived from the
functions of his Minister. But the Lord Chancellor's place in
the Constitution puts his Permanent Secretary in a unique
position. From that position Schuster built his exceptional
power and influence.

He gave a lecture to students attending a course for foreign
lawyers in July 1949 at Cambridge University.[2] Its theme was
a consideration of Montesquieu's theory of the Separation of
Powers in the British Constitution illustrated by the position
of the Lord Chancellor. Schuster began with the accepted
history of the office which is summarized below and described the British Constitution as an enigma. Whereas
modern democracies have written constitutions based more
or less on Montesquieu's theory of the Separation of Powers,
Britain has merely a collection of ancient statutes and con-
ventions, the provisions of which are virtually unenforceable.
Foreigners do not understand how it works; but it does. The
proposals to enact a written constitution which are made from
time to time, so far have made no progress.

---

1. Lord Devlin. *The Judge*. OUP. 1979, p.53.
2. Lord Schuster. "The Office of Lord Chancellor." 10 *Cambridge Law Journal No.2*,
   1949, p.175.

The office of Lord Chancellor is the oldest ministerial office in our unwritten Constitution, being at least a thousand years old. One view is that it could have existed from 615 AD, but Edward the Confessor (1042-1066) was the first English King to have had a Great Seal and a designated Lord Chancellor to keep it. It is an office of great dignity. In writing to Lord Buckmaster the future Lord Chancellor Maugham, described it thus, "Your post is one of almost absurd eminence, the sort of uncanny position that my instinct tells me no friend of mine ought to occupy ..."[3]

The Lord Chancellor has precedence in the Royal presence and at public functions over all peers and commoners in the land except for the Royal Dukes and the Archbishop of Canterbury. Originally the holder of the office was the keeper of the King's conscience. In that capacity he had his own court, the Court of Chancery, in which he could exercise his influence over the law by issuing Chancery writs which would correct grievances for which the Common Law had no remedy. From that jurisdiction the Lord Chancellor acquired a special responsibility for wards of court, infants generally, trusts, the property of married women and persons of unsound mind.

A Flexible Separation of Powers

As the Constitution developed over the centuries it is as if the

3. R.F.V. Heuston. *Lives of the Lord Chancellors*. Clarendon Press. 1885-1940, 1964, p.268.

office of Lord Chancellor had become superimposed on the three powers of Montesquieu. There is no clear division as in the United States, but what could be called a flexible separation. The result is an outstanding anomaly personified in the Lord Chancellor. He holds the highest judicial appointment in the land and as such, is Head of the Judiciary. As Speaker of the House of Lords he is a member of the second chamber of the legislature. As a member of the Cabinet and as Head of the Lord Chancellor's Department he is a member of the Executive.

Lord Haldane's view of the Lord Chancellor's duties is expressed in the *Report of the Machinery of Government Committee.*[4] The Report makes much of the amount of work a Lord Chancellor was expected to do.

> "Its nature is such that while it includes functions of a judicial, an administrative and a legislative character, it does not readily lend itself to rigid classification under these separate heads. We therefore proceed to enumerate the duties of the Lord Chancellor and his Department as they operate in practice, in order to indicate clearly the pressure which at present falls upon the Chancellor personally and his staff."[5]

The multifarious duties of the Chancellor have changed little since Haldane's time but for the sake of brevity the following is an account of the present duties under the heading of the three powers.

---

4. Jean Graham Hall and Douglas F. Martin. *Haldane - Statesman, Lawyer, Philosopher*. Barry Rose, 1996, p.329.
5. *Report of the Machinery of Government Committee*, cd 9230 HMSO 1918, p.64, para.3.

Judiciary

The Lord Chancellor is the Senior Lord of Appeal in Ordinary and as such is President of the House of Lords as the Supreme Appellate Court for England and Wales, Scotland and Northern Ireland and President of the Judicial Committee of the Privy Council which was formerly the Supreme Appellate Tribunal for the countries of the British Commonwealth and remains so for those countries which have chosen to retain the jurisdiction. By statute he is also the President of the Supreme Court of Judicature under the Acts of 1873 and 1875 and can sit there as a Judge. Lord Mackay, when Lord Chancellor, for example, never sat as a Judge. In practice the sitting of Lord Chancellors as Judges has decreased in recent years.

Legislature

Although in practice the Attorney-General's Department deals with everyday matters, the Lord Chancellor is nominally the chief legal adviser to the Crown. It is his duty to defend Government policy in the House of Lords and to initiate such legislation as may be required relating to the administration of the law, legal practice and procedure. He has further responsibility for all bills which do not concern legal procedure, etc., where he is appealed to on points of law and interpretation.

As Speaker of the House of Lords he takes his seat on the Woolsack as President of that House discharging its legislative function. Unlike the Speaker in the Commons he does not call members to order. He takes part in debates and when doing so he moves to the left of the Woolsack thus becoming a statesman or politician instead of having the impartiality of the Speaker. When the House is in Committee the chair is taken by a Lord Chairman and the Lord Chancellor takes his seat on the front Government Bench and debates like any other member of the Government.

The Lord Chancellor is the President of the Rule Committee of the Supreme Court. The rules form a code of procedure which require frequent amendment in view of the rapid changes taking place in society. The Committee consists of judicial personages, appointed by the Lord Chancellor and empowered to make subordinate legislation. He is also required to appoint members of the County Court Rule Committee and the Magistrates' Courts' Rules Committee and to approve the rules made by the committees.

Executive

The role of the Lord Chancellor has developed over the last century from a predominately judicial one in which the Lord Chancellor was very much the bridge between the judiciary and the executive, to its modern one which involves administration of the courts, policy and criteria for access to justice.

In recent times the Lord Chancellor has always been a member of the Cabinet, of which he is the highest paid. Conflicts between members inevitably arise from time to time and his role can help to resolve them. His position in the Cabinet was well set out by Schuster in a memorandum written in 1943, in which he stated:

> "The advantages which accrue to the Cabinet from the presence of a colleague who is not only of high judicial reputation but who can represent to them the view of the judiciary and to the judiciary from the fact that its President is in close touch with current political affairs are enormous. In a democracy, whose legislature may be advancing, or at least moving rapidly, and where the judiciary remains static, there is always a serious risk of collision between the two elements ... Even in England, with an unwritten Constitution and an unwritten common law, unless there is some link or buffer (whichever term may be preferred) between the two elements the situation would be perilous."[6]

In addition to being a member of the Cabinet the Lord Chancellor is also the Head of a Department of State with many and varied executive responsibilities. Many are delegated to his Permanent Secretary and staff but ministerial responsibility rests with him. Lord Haldane was not the only holder of the post to complain that his workload was too heavy. The present Lord Chancellor's responsibilities include:

> The appointment (and removal) of Judges, District Judges, Recorders and High Court Mastership. High Court Judges are appointed by the Crown, on the recommendation of the Lord Chancellor.
> The appointment of justices on the advice of advisory committees.

---

6. LCO 2/3630.

The appointment of lawyers to administrative tribunals.

Advising on the appointment of Privy Counsellors.

The training of Judges via the Judicial Studies Board.

Dealing with applications for "silk" (about half those applying to be Queen's Counsel are approved).

Legal Aid and publicly funded legal services.

Law reform via the Law Commission.

Responsibility for the Constitution and procedure of the Judicial Committee of the Privy Council and of administrative tribunals.

Administrative responsibility for the Supreme Court, the county courts, magistrates' courts (since 1993), Northern Ireland Court Service, Land Registry, Public Records Office, and the Public Trust (formerly the Public Trustee).

Relations with the Bar and the Law Society.

Representing the Monarch as a Visitor to Colleges, eg, Trinity Hall.

Acting as a Trustee of the British Museum.

Responsibility for about 20 ecclesiastical presentations every year. The number of these has been diminishing since Schuster's time owing to pastoral reorganisation linking parishes together in large benefices under one incumbent. The Lord Chancellor now has the right of presentation of 12 canonries and approximately 250 livings in his own right. He shares the right of presentation in a further 250 livings with other patrons including the Prime Minister. Since 1964 the Lord Chancellor's Ecclesiastical Office has been located in 10 Downing Street.

He is also responsible for ensuring that letters patent and other formal documents are passed in the proper form under the Great Seal (see below) of which he is the custodian. The work in connection with this is carried out under his direction by the Clerk of the Crown in Chancery (see next chapter).

Furthermore, under the Labour Government of 2001, the Lord Chancellor's Department has acquired responsibility for constitutional issues, in particular human rights, freedom of information, data protection and devolution.

The Appointment of Judges

This is probably the most important function of Lord Chancellors and it is now under active consideration. The present position is as set out in the Fulton Report on the Civil Service:

> "Judicial appointments in the United Kingdom are a matter for the executive. The Queen's Judges are appointed on the advice of the Queen's Ministers. There is no formal machinery, such as a Judicial Service Commission, to insulate judicial appointments from executive control. Appointments to the House of Lords and to most senior judicial posts in England (including Lord Justice of Appeal, Master of the Rolls, President of the Family Division and the Lord Chief Justice) are made by the Crown on the advice of the Prime Minister. High Court Judges, Circuit Judges and Recorders are appointed by the Crown on the advice of the Lord Chancellor" [Supreme Court Act 1981, s.10].[7]

In practice the Prime Minister always consults the Lord Chancellor before giving his advice. According to Schuster such advice was never influenced by political services given to the party in power. He believed that some politicians

---

7. *Fulton Report on the Civil Service.* Cmnd. 3638, 1968, Appendix A, p.375.

should reach the Bench, that was desirable, but very few had ever become High Court or Appeal Court Judges.

Schuster's Opinion of Judges

Schuster was well aware that appointment to the Bench could change a man. He had, during his career, experienced Judges whose omnipotence in court had given them delusions of grandeur. "High office, no doubt separates a man from his fellows" he said in a lecture during his retirement, "and the office of Judge, who is in his own court omnipotent, may tend to lead a man to think that by his unaided genius, he should be considered omnipotent everywhere. But in truth Judges, and even the Lord Chancellor, do not live in isolation ..."[8]

This sense of omnipotence was frequently manifested by interference with the administration of the courts. The administrative input by Judges was largely achieved by "influence, irritation and obstruction".[9] While in office Schuster was not backward in giving his opinion of the Judges, albeit less publicly than when he was retired. In a memorandum dated March 25, 1929 he insisted that the management of the court system should be the responsibility of administration - not Judges.[10]

Not surprisingly some Judges deteriorate with age so that what seemed to be good appointments when made turned

---

8. Lord Schuster. "The Office of Lord Chancellor." *Cambridge Law Journal*, vol.10, no.2, 1949, p.179.
9. Robert Stevens. *Independence of the Judiciary*. Clarendon Press, 1993, p.80.
10. LCO 2/1133.

out badly. Mr Justice Charles, appointed by Lord Cave against Schuster's advice is an example. He was described by Mr Justice Birkett when he was on circuit with him in 1942, "he smokes in the [Assize] procession, belched from beer in his Assize sermon" and in Birkett's view he was "a domineering, vulgar, unjust and decrepit old man, who is a blot on the administration of justice."[11]

Ironically when Mr Justice Charles died *The Times*, in his obituary, described him as "the embodiment of genial good sense and straight dealing."[12] During the running feud between Schuster and Lord Chief Justice Hewart (see Chapter 17) the latter had proposed a candidate for the Rule Committee which had not been accepted. Hewart had then proposed Mr Justice Charles knowing that such a derisive suggestion would infuriate Schuster.

Judges have failings and idiosyncrasies as do all human beings but there is still a reluctance in legal and government circles to publicly criticise living Judges. Moreover from the memoirs of many of the leading members of the judiciary one would think that the judicial system and all Judges are perfect. The process for the selection of Judges, obscure as it is, tends to choose the traditionalist conventional candidates. Once appointed the majority become congealed into the system and develop a parochial outlook. Consequently, with notable exceptions, few initiatives for change or reform come from Judges.

---

11. "The Diary of a Judge." *The Sunday Times*. April 7, 1963.
12. *The Times*, May 4, 1950. Quoted by Dr Patrick Polden. *Guide to the Records of the Lord Chancellor's Department*. HMSO, 1988, p.89.

High Court Judges can only be removed by resolution of both Houses of Parliament but none have been removed in the past 250 years. Circuit Judges can be removed by the Lord Chancellor and in recent times several have been asked to resign.

Ceremonial of the Lord Chancellor

The time taken by every Lord Chancellor on ceremonial duties is considerable and many would say wasted. The argument for its preservation is that it is a part of the fabric of our Constitution which has gained strength and permanency by reason of its age. To dispense with the ceremonial would mean a break with tradition and therefore a weakening of our mainly unwritten Constitution. The ceremonial starts with his appointment which is made by the Sovereign delivering the plates which form the Great Seal to the recipient. The plates are six inches in diameter and weigh 18 lbs. The Sovereign just touches the plates on the table so that the delivering is notional. The Lord Chancellor then kisses hands just like any other Cabinet Minister when receiving the seals of his office. The Oath of Allegiance and the Official Oath are then administered by the Clerk to the Privy Council. The Lord Chancellor then leaves Buckingham Palace for the Palace of Westminster, a messenger carrying the Great Seal.

Usually, a few days later the Lord Chancellor takes the judicial oath before the Master of the Rolls in his court. The President of the Family Division and the Lord Chief Justice are also present. This ceremony serves to demonstrate that the Lord Chancellor is the senior Judge in the land. He enters the court in the full black and gold robes with his train-bearer and preceded by his mace-bearer and his purse-bearer. When the oaths have been taken the Attorney-General moves that the proceedings be recorded by the King (or Queen's) Remembrancer. There is also another ceremony when the Lord Chancellor is introduced to the House of Lords. The overseeing of these occasions is the responsibility of the Permanent Secretary assisted by the Clerk to the Parliaments.

On formal occasions such as the opening of Parliament or the beginning of the legal year (the Lord Chancellor's Breakfast), the Lord Chancellor is attended by a procession of five persons. First comes the Tipstaff, then the Permanent Secretary who is also the Clerk to the Crown in Chancery; then the Mace-bearer (the mace is five feet long and weighs 22 lb); then the Purse-bearer, and the Lord Chancellor himself followed by his Train-bearer and, on the opening of Parliament, by Black Rod.

Several Lord Chancellors (including the present one, Lord Irvine) have found the ceremonial, particularly wearing the robes, tedious and time-consuming.

The Lord Chancellor receives the Lord Mayor of London-elect on behalf of the Sovereign in October at the House of Lords prior to the Lord Mayor's admission in November. The Lord Chancellor conveys the Monarch's approval of the appointment. On the second Saturday in November, the Lord Mayor in colourful procession halts his famous gold coach at the Royal Courts of Justice where he is presented to the Lord Chief Justice and the Judges of the Queen's Bench (who are the successors of the Judges of the Court of Exchequer) and he or she swears allegiance to the Sovereign.

In the early 2000s moves continue afoot to alter, denude, if not abolish the office of Lord Chancellor. Would-be reformers regard as out-of-date and undemocratic the concentration of so much power in the hands of one, unelected person.

"Truly he is a remarkable Officer of State and it is scarcely surprising that on occasion he found difficulty reconciling the claims made upon him in these different capacities."[13]

Perhaps we shall see some changes, although the issue may carry too little political and popular weight for the pressure to be affective. Considerable thought will have to be concentrated on the possible alternatives. In the meantime - Sir Alan Herbert's description of the office still sustains:

The Lord Chancellor
If you have seen upon the street
a man who absolutely beat ...
... a multitude of drums and things
by simply pulling strings -
you knew it not, but that is what
the Chancellor is like.

Poor gentleman - he has to mix
with barristers and lords
he is in charge of lunatics;
and coroners and wards;

---

13. Dr Patrick Pollen.

and what with listening to Earls,
and looking after orphan girls,
and imbeciles of every kind and judges of the County Court
and all that kind of thing;
he gets extremely little sleep
and then, of course, he has to keep
the Conscience of the King;
and sometimes at the close of day
he gives a Vicarage away;
the reason why is dark to me,
but anyhow, he has to be
a most religious man ...

But round his neck the GREAT BIG SEAL
is permanently tied;
he wears it for the common-weal
by night, by day, at every meal;
it is a source of pride ...
... and by a rotten chance
it's not allowed to leave the land
and so, of course, you understand
he cannot go to France.[14]

---

14. A copy of this poem is in LCO 2/3632.

CHAPTER 4

The Role of the Permanent Secretary

Eminence Grise

Up to 1885, Schuster's predecessor, Sir Kenneth Muir MacKenzie, had been Principal Secretary in the Lord Chancellor's Office. From that date he became the Permanent Secretary and, as the Crown Office became a part of the Lord Chancellor's Office, he also became the Clerk to the Crown in Chancery. The two offices have been held by one person ever since. This change was largely due to Lord Selbourne who was Lord Chancellor at the time, and commented in 1884:

> "I have for some time contemplated a rearrangement of the subordinate offices in the Lord Chancellor's Department ... as necessary for the public service ... The Lord Chancellor, though Minister of Justice for almost every purpose unconnected with the Criminal Law, had no assistance of the kind given to the other chief Departments of State, either of permanent secretaries or under secretaries. The officers attached to him were personal and liable to change with every change of Government ... but on each change of Government the lack of continuity was more or less felt; and as the Lord Chancellor's Department work had a constant tendency to increase, the pressure of that lack increased with it."[1]

In referring to Lord Selbourne's statement Schuster made a

---

1.   LCO - 2/262.

point of commenting that it did not mean that the Lord Chancellor was a Minister of Justice in the continental sense; neither did it mean that the Lord Chancellor had no connection with the criminal law. He had always appointed magistrates (although not in the Duchy of Lancaster) and was responsible for the Summary Jurisdiction Rules. Now of course he is responsible for the administration of all courts save the Coroners' courts, although he has the power to remove a coroner for inability or misbehaviour (Section 3, Coroner's Act 1988).

Until the Courts Act 1971 the Lord Chancellor's Office was a very small department. In 1960 it was still called the Lord Chancellor's Office and it had a staff of only 13 qualified lawyers plus some typists and subordinate staff. Nevertheless - as R.F.V. Heuston put it, "Whether the Office was small or large, its efficient operation would depend on the civil servant in charge of it - the Permanent Secretary. Here fortune has favoured the Great Seal. There have been only six holders of the Office since 1885 and each was a man of quality fully comparable to his fellow Whitehall mandarins in charge of larger establishments ..."[2] Heuston also suggested that the holders of the Office came from backgrounds somewhat "grander" than the background of other Permanent Secretaries.

Notwithstanding the "grander" background of the Lord Chancellor's Permanent Secretaries and of their power and influence, there is no doubt that they and their department

2. R.F.V. Heuston. *Lives of the Lord Chancellors 1940-70*. Clarendon Press, 1895. Introduction, p.32.

were regarded by the mandarins as outsiders - as one has said, Schuster was - "... never regarded as quite 'one of us' by other Whitehall Permanent Secretaries."[3]

Sir Kenneth Muir MacKenzie

Schuster's predecessor as Permanent Secretary had, in over 30 years in the post, made it one of power and influence. It was said that he *was* the Lord Chancellor's Office. His background was "grander" than most public servants. He was the son of a Baronet and his wife was the aunt of the late first Lord Hailsham. This, and a powerful personality, put him on terms of equality with Judges and politicians and he was able to ensure that all communications to the Lord Chancellor came through him. He called himself "the Lord Chancellor's postman".[4]

In a confidential memorandum of January 31, 1943, Schuster described his predecessor as "an advanced radical in politics"[5] although his enthusiasm for reform had waned towards the end of his career. He was, however, very conservative in some ways. Schuster wrote that he "detested the use of either shorthand or of typewriting ... he wrote his letters himself and kept no copies, and he directed the letters himself and stuck them up" (the Office only had one typewriter when Schuster arrived there). He only employed

---

3. Letter from Lord Croham, GCB, to Jean Graham Hall, March 14, 1998.
4. R.F.V. Heuston. *Lives of the Lord Chancellors 1885-1940*. Oxford, Clarendon Press, 1964, p.502.
5. LCO - 2/3630, January 31, 1943, pp.4-5

those who would not oppose him and he was unwilling to delegate. In a letter to Coldstream (Schuster's successor) of July 12, 1955, Schuster said that Muir MacKenzie was "... completely unscrupulous in interpreting a statute and disregarding its provisions if they did not suit him".[6]

So it was that Schuster inherited the mantle of an autocrat which gave him considerable status amongst the judiciary, politicians and other government departments. For the alert Schuster this was an ideal base on which to build and consolidate his position and influence.

The Appointment of Claud Schuster as Permanent Secretary

In 1915 when Lord Haldane had been Lord Chancellor for almost three years, Muir Mackenzie was due to retire and a replacement secretary was required. Haldane's experience as Lord Chancellor led him to believe that the duties of the position put an intolerable burden on one man. He had ideas of dividing the duties between a Lord Chancellor and a Minister of Justice to be appointed after the war. He wanted a Permanent Secretary who was a lawyer with administrative ability who would assist him in setting up a Ministry of Justice when the time came. Sir Robert Morant, the most influential civil servant of the time, recommended Schuster, who indeed seemed to be the ideal choice - but with one drawback - this was wartime and Schuster's German-Jewish

---

6. LCO - 2/5233, July 12, 1955.

ancestry might well have disqualified him in the face of the prejudices of the time. Therefore, his appointment caused some surprise and it showed some courage on the part of Haldane in making it and on the part of Schuster in accepting it. It is a tribute to Schuster's abilities that he appeared to overcome quite easily any antipathy towards him as the following opinion shows:

> "... Schuster rapidly established himself as the dominant force in the Lord Chancellor's Office and a power in the wider professional and political arena. The size of the Office increased somewhat, but perhaps the most significant aspect was that within a few years, Schuster was seen as the alter ego of the Lord Chancellor and a moving force in Whitehall."[7]

Haldane, on the other hand fared badly. He had been partly educated in Germany and was an admirer of German culture but in spite of a fine record as War Minister from 1906-1912, he was forced to resign in May 1915 on the grounds that the public and his political opponents regarded him as pro-German. Schuster did not take up his appointment until July 2, 1915, consequently the two men did not work together until Haldane became Lord Chancellor for the second time in 1924. However, Schuster was not the right man to promote Haldane's ideas for a Ministry of Justice; indeed Gavin Drewry, in an aptly entitled article "Lord Haldane's Ministry of Justice - Stillborn or Strangled at Birth" has expounded a convincing argument that Schuster during his time, killed all

---

7. Robert Stevens. *The Independence of the Judiciary*. Clarendon Press, 1993, p.24.

ideas for such a ministry.[8]

The Lord Chancellor's Office

In his 1943 memorandum Schuster described the Office as it was when he arrived in 1915. He explained why Haldane had found the burden of work too much for one man, although Schuster himself did not believe that it was greater than that of any other Minister:

> "Lord Haldane came to the Office after having served for years as a Secretary of State in a highly organised department (the War Office) with a proper allowance of private secretaries and with all such conveniences as are naturally attached to a modern office, such as shorthand, typewriting, a properly organised registry and an established course of business. It was therefore not unnatural that he should have felt himself overwhelmed when he came to the Woolsack, and should have been struck not only with the lack of method for the discharge of the ordinary business of the Department, but with the complete absence of any organisation for a continuous examination of the functions which the Department supervised and for laying plans for the future."[9]

The Duties of the Permanent Secretary

On July 16, 1917, Vaughan Nash, secretary of the

8. Gavin Drewry. *Lord Haldane's Ministry of Justice*. Public Administration, vol.61, winter, 1983, p.396.
9. LCO - 2/3630.

Reconstruction Committee, wrote to Schuster asking him to provide a memorandum (with eight copies) describing the functions of the Lord Chancellor's Office. Schuster, confident and cavalier in the knowledge that his department was unique, replied somewhat curtly the following day to the effect that he had a small staff, it was the busiest time of the year (just before the Long Vacation when most of the staff went on leave) and that he was too busy to prepare a memorandum.[10] Nevertheless a comprehensive memorandum was prepared. This has no file date, but was probably prepared after the Long Vacation.

This memorandum included the information that the Lord Chancellor had £600 a year with which to provide a Secretary of Commissions (for appointing Justices of the Peace), a Secretary of Presentations of Ecclesiastical Livings and a private secretary. The Permanent Secretary had £150 a year to provide himself with a private secretary. It also referred to the Lord Chancellor's responsibility for lunatics which meant that they could write letters to him; some did every day. These had to be read and answered.[11]

A summary of that memorandum appeared in the Machinery of Government Committee's Report chapter X.[12] Paragraphs 23 to 28 of the Report focus on the duties of the Permanent Secretary and Clerk of the Crown in Chancery.

Paragraph 23 of the Report describes Schuster's relationship with his Minister perfectly. One can detect

---

10. LCO - 410.
11. *Ibid.*
12. 1918, Cd 9230.

Schuster's phraseology in the drafting:

> "From the nature of the responsibility which the Lord Chancellor bears, but for physical reasons cannot to a great extent discharge by his own person, the duties of the Permanent Secretary bring him into peculiarly close relations with his Minister, and require for their proper performance an unusual degree of ability, energy and tact."

The Crown Office

The functions of the Clerk of the Crown in Chancery are set out in para.28 of the Report. There have been few changes since 1918. It is difficult to separate his duties from those of the Permanent Secretary. As they are the same person it is academic. The following duties are those not included above. Some are patronage, some legislative and some ceremonial:

Sealing and issuing grants of honour and dignities, offices, charters, etc, which were required to pass under the Great Seal as prescribed by the Great Seal Act 1884.

Preparing warrants for issue of letters patent conferring peerages and baronetcies.

Making out commissions and patents for officers of the Crown when appointed to posts such as:

The Army Council, Commissioners of the Treasury, Post-Master-General, College of Heralds, Principal Heralds (Queen's-at-arms), Lord Lieutenants, Pursuivants, Constable of the Tower of London, High Court Judges, Companions of Honour, Master of Trinity College Cambridge, various authorities of the Royal Family, Clerks of the Parliaments, Privy Councillors, Chairmen of

Committees, Speakers and Deputies, etc.

Schuster chaired a committee which resulted in the abolition of Peers for many of these appointments. The Crown Office also makes proclamations of states of emergency, issues commissions for the opening and proroguing of Parliament and writs summoning Peers to Parliament. As the Clerk to the Crown in Chancery, Schuster was entitled to sign all such documents for which he was responsible with the word "Schuster" as if he was a Peer. He had a close relationship with the Clerk to the Parliaments, Jack Badeley (later Lord Badeley), and he kept a close eye on the arrangements for the business of the House of Lords. In that House he was entitled to sit on the steps of the throne. He also had the title of Registrar of the Court of Claims and that entailed much work when there was a Coronation.

The Crown Office is also responsible for issuing writs for elections and by-elections and dealing with any questions arising. It has many ceremonial functions such as arranging the Lord Chancellor's Breakfast preceded by the service at Westminster Abbey at the opening of the legal year. Disputes between Peers over precedence at various occasions have to be settled. The Clerk to the Crown or his deputy must perform some ceremonial duties personally such as: the swearing in of Lord Chancellors, Lords Justices of Appeal, Judges of the Supreme Court and Queen's Counsel. He is also required to recite the names of Acts of Parliament when the Royal Assent is given.

The Great Seal

A new Great Seal is required for each Lord Chancellor and it is forged by the Royal Mint. Differences as to the design has on occasion caused friction between LCO and the Mint. Hailsham described one as looking, "like the Pope in the family way"[13] and Schuster at another time, "... was preparing myself for a supreme struggle ... if at any time a proposal was made that the Seal should be prepared by (the *avant garde*) Eric Gill."[14]

Peculiarities of the Lord Chancellor's Department

Until 1992 the Department had no Minister to speak for it in the House of Commons; parliamentary questions were answered by the Attorney-General. The Department was also exempt from scrutiny by the 12 Parliamentary Select Committees set up in 1979. The argument for these singularities was that the independence of the Judiciary must be preserved and judicial appointments should not be criticised. Consequently the Department was isolated from the rest of government and less open to criticism than other departments.

Following the Courts Act of 1971, which set up the Crown Court, many changes have taken place. By 1995 the Department as a whole had a staff of 11,500 and has since

---

13. LCO - 2/1440.
14. LCO - 2/905.

Lord Schuster when a young man

In the Alps with a friend

Last photograph of Lord Schuster aged 86 April 1 in Greece with his nephew Rev. Christopher Turner

Celebrities and Signatures from Winter Sports Land.

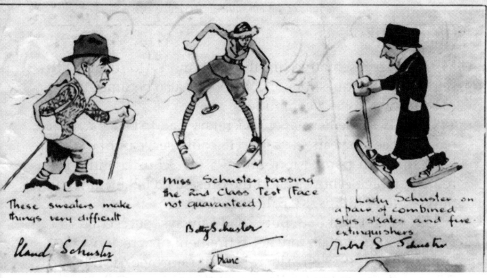

The Sketch. January 31st 1923
(Betty Schuster later to become Mrs. Betty Turner)

From: The Chief.
The Biography of Gordon Hewart.
Lord Chief Justice of England 1922-1940
Robert Jackson
Harrap 1959

1992 a representative in the Commons to deal with parliamentary questions, etc. In 1990 it also became subject to scrutiny by select committees.

Until 1990 the Permanent Secretary had to be a barrister of at least seven years standing. He could serve until the age of 72 or with permission, until 75 (as Schuster did). The retirement age is now 62 and the present (2002) incumbent, Sir Hayden Phillips, KCB, is not a lawyer.

Up to 1990 the deputy had always succeeded the Permanent Secretary on his retirement. There is written record that in 1953 Sir Albert Napier informed Sir Edward Bridges (head of the Civil Service) that George Coldstream would succeed him.[15]

The Power of Permanent Secretaries

The senior civil servant within a department is the Permanent Secretary. According to the Fulton Committee of 1968 he has four functions:

1. He is the Minister's most immediate adviser on policy.
2. He is the managing director of the day-to-day operations of the department.
3. He has the ultimate responsibility for questions of staff and organisation.
4. As the Accounting Officer (in nearly every department) he also has the ultimate responsibility for all departmental

---

15. LCO - 4/23.

expenditure.[16]

Until the Fulton Committee Report the Home Civil Service was fundamentally the produce of the 19th century philosophy of the Northcote-Trevelyan Report of 1854. In the opinion of the Fulton Committee that philosophy had encouraged the cult of the amateur in the process of administration. Paradoxically this cult prevailed more in the administrative class than at the lower levels of the service. It was common for high-flyers to move rapidly from department to department irrespective of their previous experience. In the 1970s this philosophy began to change. Since then higher posts have frequently been filled from commerce and industry. Civil servants can no longer expect a lifetime career in the service. Short contracts of service are becoming more common. The cult of the amateur has been weakened but still exists. Schuster as a lawyer in a legal department well before 1970 was not affected by these movements. He was able to consolidate his position and augment his influence, well knowing that he would not be transferred to another department.

Nevertheless he was in the same relationship with his Lord Chancellor as other Permanent Secretaries. According to Sir Warren Fisher:

"The relationship between Ministers and civil servants is conditioned by the recognition that the position of the latter is in the wings and that the foot-lights are the monopoly of the politician who is constitutionally the sole responsible

16. Cmnd. 3638, p.298.

authority."[17]

Schuster found himself in a position with all the advantages. As a lawyer in a legal department he was not an amateur. He had security of tenure with a retirement age of 72 or possibly 75. When appointed at the age of 46 he knew he had at least 26 years before him in the same post. That did not deter him from losing no time in making his presence felt, as we shall see. He already appreciated that, like all Permanent Secretaries he must not, as a member of the Executive, be seen to influence the Legislature or the Judiciary.

To the outside world Permanent Secretaries must appear to be just secretaries; they do not reveal their real power. There are circumstances when their authority becomes more public. When an election is announced and electioneering begins, a Cabinet group - the Election Business Committee - comes into being. It consists of the Lord Chancellor and one or two other Ministers who are Peers and therefore do not have Constituencies in which to campaign. They are there to look after the shop while the Ministers are away. The Permanent Secretaries then come into their own. Ministers are only recalled to Whitehall in the case of serious emergencies and it is said that the departments run better when they are away. The Election Business Committee, chaired by the Lord Chancellor, would give his Permanent Secretary, already responsible for the writs for general elections and for receiving the election returns, a stronger position than most.

---

17. Euan O. Halpin. *Head of the Civil Service: a biography of Sir Warren Fisher.* Routledge, 1989, pp.220-1.

After the elections there would normally be a new Minister full of enthusiasm to implement the relevant promises in his party's manifesto. His first contact with the department would be with his chief civil servant, the Permanent Secretary. The latter's first duty is to discuss the practicalities of the new policies with great tact and diplomacy. Some of the policies are possible to implement, some difficult and some impossible. The last are dealt with by being amended, side tracked, substituted, shelved or whatever.

Permanent Secretaries to Cabinet Ministers are in a special position. They have to brief their Ministers for Cabinet meetings in which there may be competition between departments for funds and resources. They need to know what is going on in other parts of Whitehall and for this information they depend on others such as the Private Secretaries of Ministers. Referred to as "spies", these young, up and coming civil servants keep their Ministers informed about protocol and the workings of Whitehall. In Schuster's time, the Private Secretary to the Chancellor was inevitably a young barrister. Lord Birkenhead for example depended heavily on Roland Burrows who devilled for him, did research and drafted his judgments.

There is a network between Permanent Secretaries and it is possible for them to cooperate in order to thwart a policy they do not like. It has become the practice during the latter half of the last century for the Secretary of the Cabinet to convene meetings every Wednesday morning to which all Permanent Secretaries are invited. Most of them attend regularly. There are also *ad hoc* meetings all the time for some of them, and occasionally all, as well as frequent other contacts in the course of business. There is also a good deal of social meeting and communication such as when there is a retirement dinner for one of their number or a memorial service. Occasionally there may be social dinners and lunches but these are now far less frequent than in Schuster's time. He was often a guest at Haldane's house in Queen Anne's Gate where politicians, writers, academics, etc, would meet to discuss the problems of the day. In those days, Permanent Secretaries had more time than they do now. They were invariably members of one or more of the West End clubs and these were convenient for them to meet socially.

The BBC's "Yes Minister", satirical though it was, portrayed the archetypal Permanent Secretary. Indeed, the authors could have modelled the character of Sir Humphrey on Schuster. Characteristics common to both are an art of conversation, including subtle hints, suggestions, silences and pauses at the right time. They were always courteous, instructive rather than informative, with the object of moulding their master's opinion to their own.

Schuster and his Lord Chancellors

During his 29 years as Permanent Secretary Schuster served 10 Lord Chancellors. Their periods in office varied from six years in the case of Lord Sankey to eight months for Lord Caldecote. Lord Cave served for four years and seven months in two sessions and Lord Hailsham served for three years and 11 months in two sessions. Thus, as with other Ministers of State, a Lord Chancellor usually had little time to make a real impression on the running of his department. It has been said that because the tenure of a Ministers is so short, all want to make their mark. One Minister said to his Permanent Secretary, "You are running a marathon; I am in a 100 metre sprint" (Sir Geoffrey Holland in a lecture to the RSA, May 3, 1995). Schuster was certainly running a marathon; his tenure of office of 29 years is a record for this century, and his power and influence increased with time.

There is an influential power which Schuster certainly had and used which is not specified in any list of his duties. When a lawyer was required to be a member of an inter-departmental committee, a Royal Commission or to be the chairman of an inquiry, the Lord Chancellor would be consulted. He in turn would consult Schuster who was always able to give advice difficult to reject.

According to Professor Drewry:

"Schuster, himself an autocratic and long-serving Permanent Secretary in a small department, effectively personified the Lord Chancellor's Office in all that it did."[18]

That was surely the situation of 70 years ago when the Lord Chancellor's Office consisted of a small group of lawyers with Schuster heading a very small Office with a limited management charge. It should be understood that today the Permanent Secretary is the chief executive of an organisation with nearly 12,000 staff directly employed, another 10,000 indirectly employed, nearly 1,000 buildings overall (the

18. Gavin Drewry. "Lord Haldane's Ministry of Justice - Stillborn or Strangled at Birth." *Public Administration*, vol.61, winter, 1983, p.401.

largest civil estate of any Department), a budget of £2.4 billion a year and a judiciary many time bigger than before the Second World War.

Nevertheless in spite of his huge management responsibility, the Permanent Secretary to the Lord Chancellor, like other Permanent Secretaries, should always be, and normally is, in a position to advise his Minister on all significant official matters. On matters affecting public expenditure it has been from Gladstone's time, mandatory that a Permanent Secretary must be heard.

In another respect there has been a change since Schuster was in post. He concerned himself with the drafting of any legislation which affected the courts, the judiciary, law reform and related matters. He was frequently in contact with the parliamentary draftsmen. For example, there are records which show that he was responsible for the wording of the first Infanticide Act in 1922.[19] A modern Permanent Secretary, probably not a lawyer, will be interested in legislation which affects the management role but will leave the drafting to counsel.

---

19. LCO - 2/1329.

CHAPTER 5

"The Very Battlements of Heaven"

Schuster never lost his love of high places. When as Lord Schuster he chose a motto for his coat of arms, it was, Levavi Oculos - *I raised my eyes.*

The social environment of the Alps in the long vacation coupled with the opportunity for outdoor activity in dramatic scenery was exactly the right kind of relaxation for Schuster. Any high-powered executive needs a break and for him mountaineering provided a complete contrast to his work. In 1921, at the age of 52, he took up skiing and became President of the Ski Club of Great Britain from 1932-4 and of the Alpine Club from 1938-40. He was the first person to have been president of both clubs.

As an example of Schuster's executive ability, Arnold Lunn credits him with effecting the change in the method of electing members to the Alpine Club. The usual method for London clubs was election by secret ballot with one black ball in 10 excluding an applicant. As the ordinary attendance at the Alpine Club was about 100, a clique of 10 could exclude anyone from the club. Several great climbers had been blackballed; Arnold Lunn himself was blackballed as a young man because he was the director of a travel agency. Presumably that was an example of the Victorian class prejudice against persons engaged in trade. Schuster was aware of this; he refers to his time at the turn of the century as "The Golden Age of British exploration in the Alps". The

Grand Tour of Europe had become commonplace for wealthy Britons and something more demanding became fashionable. During the Long Vacation and the recess of Parliament, the Alps were accessible for lawyers, politicians, etc. Mountaineering then was a pastime for the "upper classes". Arnold Lunn says that his father, Sir Henry Lunn, the original founder of the well-known travel agency, tried to compete with Cooks. He failed, and only succeeded in the travel business when in 1903 he founded the Public Schools Alpine Sports Club for taking abroad winter sportsmen "who were glad to carry with them to the Alps the social environment in which they had been born and bred".[1]

Writing in *Men, Women and Mountains*, Schuster refers to the social environment and describes some of his climbing companions. He regrets the passing of an age:

> "They form, taken together, an epitome of a phase of English life, now passing or already passed; a Judge [Lord Sterndale], an official [Sir Edward Davidson], two dons, two schoolmasters, a banker, a merchant, a manufacturer, a brewer. One and all, they are oddly different from the picture of the typical middle-class Englishman which the modern journalist likes to draw. All of them could laugh, all had blood in their veins, all had some zest for adventure, all had a cheerful thought and voice for youth. To look back upon them must needs stir regret. But when 'I have the days of old and the years that are past,' I call to remembrance my song."[2]

---

1. Quoted by Piers Brandon in Thomas Cook, Secker and Warburg, p.245.
2. *Men, Women and Mountains*. Nicolson and Watson, 1931, p.75.

Arnold Lunn said that Schuster,

"... was not a guileless climber or an acrobat, but a sound mountaineer with an intimate knowledge of the mountains in their many moods. He had known the founding fathers of the sport, and as an Alpine gossip he was in a class by himself."[3]

But climbing can be dangerous, and skiing more so, even for a sound mountaineer. On one occasion Schuster was stranded on the Bernese Oberland with nothing but melted snow to drink. In 1935 while skiing, he fell against a rock and having his penknife in his pocket it broke his hip. Nevertheless his climbing achievements were noteworthy. He had climbed Mont Blanc four times by different routes and had recorded against him 33 climbs of more than 4,000 metres. The Zermatt Valley and the Engadine were his favourites, but by 1911 his high climbing had ceased. After 1921 he was often accompanied by his daughter Betty Turner. By 1925 his relatives were trying to persuade him to stop mountaineering of any kind, but he continued nevertheless. His last summer in the Alps, 1937, in Zermatt, was spent with his grand-daughter Jennifer aged 10.

A Graphic Literary Style

It was not just the physical activity that he enjoyed. He loved the natural beauty and wild grandeur of the mountains and having a sense of appreciation of literature and a fluent

---

3. *British Ski Year Book*, vol.XVII, no.38, p.283.

command of the English language, he loved to write about them. Lord Sankey greatly admired Schuster's literary style and in the foreword to *Men, Women and Mountains* he quotes the following as an example of one of many fine passages:

> "The clear heavens were thick with stars. There was no wind or even motion in the air. Suddenly there came into vision a great light from the Eiger. Beyond it was the risen moon and the stars in that quarter of the firmament paled in their fires, 'touched to death with diviner eyes'. But to us it was as if we gazed from without at the very battlements of heaven and as if, on the further side, were its illumined courts."[4]

There are many such examples in the same book of Schuster's vivid use of words when describing mountain scenery, eg:

> "The clouds hung low on the pass, veiling the graceful forms of the summits on the north, and giving an air of mystery to the glaciers emerging from them, while to the somewhat formless hills on the south they imparted a savage grandeur."[5]

Although his real love was for the Alps, he wrote in the same enraptured vein about the vistas of the Pyrenees:

> "... Either, if it be enclosed by mightier ranges, some graceful or majestic form to which it is a footstool, or, if by accident of position it commands a gap in the chain, an arrangement in colour and form leading your eye across great spaces to the very

---

4. *Men, Women and Mountains*, p.VIII.
5. *Ibid.*, p.6.

ramparts of heaven ..."[6]

His account of an incident in the Alps in which Lord Sterndale was concerned shows how much he admired his great friend and regarded him as the ideal Englishman. The occasion was in 1906 when Lord Sterndale was 58 years of age and making his last climb.

Sterndale's Last Climb

Schuster tells how five amateurs including one lady, Sterndale's daughter, with four guides, were gathered at Tête Rousse to celebrate in the fashion of a wake, the last climb of their senior member and leader, William Pickford, KC. He was then a highly respected member of the Bar who was to be appointed to the King's Bench Division the following year and who subsequently became Lord Sterndale, Master of the Rolls. He was regarded by many as near perfect a Judge as a human being could be and it is not surprising that Schuster admired him.[7]

Schuster's fine description of his friend shows the kind of Englishman and lawyer he regarded as ideal:

"His eye, indeed, was not dimmed, nor his natural force abated. His magnificent presence, his erect form, his calm and regular features (the index of his mind), bore witness that the vast frame of his body was still full of vigour and proclaimed his unshaken

---

6. *Ibid.,* p.31.
7. See Jean Graham Hall and Douglas F. Martin. *A Perfect Judge.* Barry Rose, 1999.

constancy of soul; while a certain light in his eyes, a certain pucker which came and went in the corner of his lips, relieved what might have seemed austere, and made clear why he was then beloved in his profession, and was to be, when he ascended the Bench, acknowledged as the incarnation of British justice, equal, mild, but firm. He could still breast the hill path, and was as steady on ice or snow and as agile on rocks as in days gone by. But a knee, tried by many descents, could no longer carry his weight downhill without pain, and he had decided that the time has come to say farewell to high mountains by his first ascent of the monarch of them all [Mont Blanc]."[8]

Schuster went on to describe how, after spending the night in a hut, they had roped themselves into two parties, led by a guide from Saas, followed by the "hero of the day" [Sterndale]. Then came his daughter followed by another guide. Schuster was in the second group of roped climbers. He wrote vividly of the dangers and difficulties of the ascent, the steepness of the climb, the danger from falling stones. They were approaching the top with only a pleasant but lengthy stroll ahead of them when suddenly something happened. There was a shout and a crash. The leading guide had surmounted some obstacle when a huge boulder detached itself from the mountain wall. Sterndale managed to hold it for a while but in spite of his great strength he had to release it and it fell straight at his successor - his daughter. Her fate was certain for she could move neither up nor down. But the second guide caught her round the waist and swung her out of the track of the stone on to another pinnacle. The

---

8. Claud Schuster. *Men, Women and Mountains*, pp.18/19.

climb continued and Schuster's party eventually found the first group stretched out on the summit of Mont Blanc "reclined like gods together, careless of mankind".[9]

The descent proved to be more difficult than expected. This was due to the effect of the autumn heat on the convergence of two glaciers. The prospect of spending a night on a glacier loomed; they had neither food nor drink. At last they found a gully to get them through and some water to drink. They rested a while and then descended to a small restaurant where they met up with the other party. A guide was sent ahead to the hotel at Chamonix to order hot water for baths and cold champagne. The day ended with a meal and Schuster sought the silence of his bed, over 20 hours after setting out that morning. He wrote that the scene as he left it for bed was memorable:

> "The bottles on the long table were arranged in a curious order. One represented the Judge; one the plaintiff's counsel; one the defendant's; as many more as were available stood for the jury. With their aid a well-known junior [Edward Davidson] - since Solicitor-General for England - was instructing a somewhat better-known King's Counsel - since Master of the Rolls [Sterndale] - how to conduct an action at *nisi prius*."

He concludes his account of this episode with some of his own elegant verse:

> "What did we get from it all?
>   Smiles broke from us and we had ease,

---

9. *Ibid.,* p.21.

> The hills were round us, and the breeze
> Went o'er the sun-lit fields again,
> Our foreheads felt the wind and rain,
> Our youth returned, for there was shed
> On spirits that had long been dead,
> Spirits dried up and closely furl'd
> The freshness of the early world."[10]

The Virtues of Mountaineering

In his valedictory address to the Alpine Club on December 9, 1940 Schuster, retiring as President, expounded the virtues of mountaineering:

"... But the world can never be safe, nor is it for safety that we should aspire. We are not, nor is the common kindly race of man, heroes, nor should their aspiration be for a land, like some Mohammedan paradise, in which they should lie unmindful of mankind, of its labours, its disappointments, its toil and its dangers. Mountaineering is not life in the round, but it is a very fair emblem of life as it should be considered and as it should be lived, to aspire to and to attempt great achievement and yet to set out on the adventure after forethought, with due care and with a due adjustment of ends to means; to endure toil and fatigue, and to find the reward rather in the performance than in the accomplishment; not to court danger for her own bright eyes, but not to shrink from her unduly when she bars the path; and above all and in all to preserve a high serenity of mind. These surely are the distinguishing marks of a happy mountaineer, as of a happy warrior. Thus tempered and thus attuned, he can go

---

10. *Ibid.*, p.25.

on his way to whatever fate attends him.[11]

Climbing does induce, at times and in some men, a sense of withdrawal from the things of the world, leading to an almost trance-like absorption into something outside the world. This seems, at first, strange, for in no other form of bodily activity is there a greater or more continuous call on the active physical functions. It is desperately necessary not to slip, to make good your hold and your footing, to advance up the ice slope, and for these purposes to beat down fatigue and fear and carelessness, to sharpen every faculty, to compel the will to conquer your weakness. But, for these very reasons, the antinomy between body and spirit seems to increase ..."[12]

Tyndall as a Mountaineer

In 1945 a book was published entitled *Life and Work of John Tyndall* by Eve and Creasy. Lord Schuster wrote a chapter of the book, "Tyndall as a Mountaineer". Professor Tyndall was also a scientist and philosopher of some eminence. This was obviously written for aficionados of the pastime. It shows Schuster's comprehensive first-hand knowledge of the peaks and glaciers in the Eastern Alps. He obviously relished being in challenging situations; physically challenging that is, in contrast to the mentally challenging problems he had to deal with as a Civil Servant. In the chapter about Tyndall he wrote: "... But the mountain, from whatever side it is taken, will always remain a long and arduous business, requiring great care, even when it is at its easiest, and, if the expedition

---

11. Claud Schuster. *Postscript to Adventure*. Eyre and Spottiswoode, 1950, p.192.
12. *Ibid.*, p.210.

is to be enjoyed, calling for aptitude and proficiency. Thus it is when the rocks are quiet. When the rocks have a film of ice, when snow is blown before a cutting wind, and the mountain itself seems to be astir with stones that fall from above, or quiver beneath the feet, life there is brutish and miserable, and may probably be short."[13]

The Romanes Lecture

In 1948 he gave the Romanes Lecture in the Sheldonian Theatre at Oxford. This was published by Clarendon Press in a 32-page booklet under the title *Mountaineering*. It was prepared for a mixed audience and was much more revealing of Schuster's own feelings. He refers to the "intermingling of the physical and spiritual forms" as being one of the principal charms of the exercise. The nail in the boot chafing the heel, the tired muscles, the anticipation of food and the thought of relaxation - all those contrast with the joy of arriving at the crest of a ridge to see "... the Italian plain across a fantastic tangle of foothills stretched out in amethyst and silver, a final overcoming and the late return into the shadows of the valley - these make up your day. You hardly know why you chose to undergo the cold, the heat, the hunger, the thirst, the slight indications of danger. But, taken together, it has all been very good!"[14]

In the Romanes Lecture Schuster related the history of the

---

13. Eve and Creasy. *Life and Work of John Tyndall*. 1945, p.386.
14. *Mountaineering*. Clarendon Press, 1948, pp.3/4.

exploration of the Alps by mountaineers who were mainly but not entirely British, aided of course by guides from the Alpine countries. He developed this historical account into the theme of "Why Do Men Climb?"

Describing the wonderful views from various vantage points and the feeling of a climber on the summits of Mont Blanc for example, "... in the long dark tramp of morning, as the sun illumines the world with a myriad lights and colours, in his sharp struggle and his overcoming, his eyes have seen sights and his spirit has been refreshed with a loveliness unknown to those who have not sought and fought for them."[15] He described the pleasure of physical exercise in the open air. Air that is at 10-to-15-thousand feet above the surface of the earth. More than that is the sense of overcoming. "You are, perhaps, a little weary. You have mastered the last pinnacle on the ridge and, lo and behold here are two more. Your fingers are a little sore and the straps of your knapsack gall your shoulders a little. It is a long time since you ate or drank, but it is hardly worth while now to make a halt ..." He continued expressing his feelings, "when the pain and the discomfort became acute there were the thoughts of a soft bed in an inn - wine, food and tobacco ... or even the hay of a cowshed with milk and cheese from a herdsman. No matter, it is the achievement that counts."

Finally he elaborated on the ancient idea that the mountains are nearer to God. How the sense of beauty and exhilaration from the clear air coupled with fatigue produce a feeling of other-worldliness. Some men have their faith

---

15. *Ibid.*, p.29.

heightened, others like Tyndall ask themselves questions without answers. The ambitions of the Nazi and Fascist climbers to show their superiority led, Schuster said, to dangerous extravagances and loss of life.

"But the Alps are not a theatre for the display of hysterical frenzy, nor a battlefield for the exercise of frantic nationalism. We cannot say exactly what we found in them, nor how we ourselves were transformed in them. But we know that, after our struggles, our defeats and partial successes, we found rest and peace in the evening."

Why Do Men Climb?

In 1950, *Postscript to Adventure* was published when Schuster was 80. It was a series of reminiscences interspersed with some Schuster philosophy about mountaineering and skiing. There are many ways of getting hungry, dirty and weary, he says, which are not as perilous or expensive as the Alpine sports. He poses the question - why do we do it at all?

> "Hundreds must have asked themselves the question as they panted and sweated up a path to a hut with the afternoon sun on their back, or froze in the shade of a steep slope with ice from the steps cut above them falling down their necks, or tossed sleepless on a straw bed amid bites of their ancient inhabitants and the snores of more recent invaders."[16]

His answer is in two parts. First, there is the pleasure in

---

16. Claud Schuster. *Postscript to Adventure*, p.13.

physical exertion; in climbing the arms are brought into play and it demands the employment of more parts of the body at once than other forms of exercise. Coupled with this is the need to exercise the mind in deciding the strategic or tactical problems of a climb. The second part of his answer is philosophical. Mountaineering, he says, satisfies two of the most deeply-seated instincts of man - the desire to get to the top and the appetite for a little mild discomfort. Both atavistic, like the child who wants to stand on the top of a sandcastle and cover itself with dirt. He personifies the desire to get to the top, explaining his enjoyment in reaching the top and looking down on to a strange land, a new valley, and descending down into it, "to come out on the other side of the moon, to slip behind the looking glass, to penetrate through the city gate." All these reasons set in a scene of peculiar beauty, amid mountain forms of fantastic delicacy, of stupendous grandeur, with every range of colour and every lovely effect of light.[17]

He regrets the passing of the years: "For myself the sword has outworn the sheath and 'I go no more a roving'. I must content myself with a comfortable armchair." He describes the younger mountaineers leaving the hotel in the early morning, in stocking feet, boots in their hands so as not to waken the "cripple and the sluggard". He watches them as they ascend higher and higher; black spots on the snow, and then they disappear swallowed from sight in the great hollow of the mountain, "I hope that I shall welcome them as they reach the hotel again, and perhaps they will allow me to

---

17. *Ibid.*, pp.13/14.

toddle about and get drinks for them; or perhaps I shall not be there."[18]

---

18. *Ibid.,* p.29.

CHAPTER 6

Lord Buckmaster -
May 27, 1915 to December 11, 1916

Son of an Agricultural Labourer

One might assume that during the first half of the 20th
century the highest legal office in the land would be occupied
by a son of a wealthy aristocratic father. That was not the
case. Most Lord Chancellors came from middle-class
backgrounds. Maugham and Caldecote were sons of
solicitors; Finlay the son of a doctor; Sankey's father had a
draper's shop and Cave's father was a farmer who had
business interests in the City. Buckmaster's father was an
agricultural labourer who became a teacher and magistrate.
Birkenhead's father was a sergeant-major who became a
barrister and Mayor of Birkenhead, while Simon was the
eldest child of a congregational Minister. Hailsham was
perhaps the only one from a really wealthy family and he
married into the aristocratic Graham family.

Buckmaster, who came from the most plebeian
background of all Schuster's Lord Chancellors, had been
Attorney-General in the Liberal Government and received
the Great Seal on May 27, 1915.

Schuster took up his post of Permanent Secretary in July,
1915. Within a few months he was contributing his views
when important decisions had to be made. J.H.M. Campbell,
KC, an advocate of the old school with a reputation in Ireland
but not popular with Judges in England, was anxious to
obtain promotion. He had been Solicitor-General and

Attorney-General for Ireland and wanted to be Lord Chief Justice for Ireland or failing that a High Court Judge in England. He pressed his claims widely and vigorously, persisting in his demands to the Lord Chancellor, Buckmaster. Much correspondence ensued and on January 12, 1916, a long letter from Schuster to Buckmaster was shown to the Prime Minister, Asquith. In no uncertain terms Schuster stated that Campbell was unfit for the position he sought:

> "Campbell's business is most unfortunate. You know of course that proposals (or alleged proposals) as to Campbell have been common gossip at the Bar ever since the formation of the present government, and members of the profession have constantly expressed to me the sense of indignation that any such appointment would arouse a storm exceeding in intensity that which followed Ridley's appointment years ago. The storm will break on the innocent head of the LC: but it would be the worst friendship to the PM to allow him to suppose that it will not damage him also. Even if C were allowed to hold an office for which by universal consent of his fellows he is unfit, any appointment which is obviously political at this moment would be a scandal with the resulting harm to the judicial office, to the Lord Chancellor, and to the Prime Minister himself. For really there is no possible defence. It is by no means clear that a vacancy in the KB ought to be filled at all. To fill it, by the appointment of an unfit man, selected not for his own political services (as has happened before) but as a political manoeuvre and to do so by means of an additional charge of £3,500 of the Consolidation Fund at a moment such as this - surely this is outrageous.
>
> "Forgive me if I write strongly. I know you do not care for any injury to your personal position if it results in what you think to be right. But the whole administration of the Law and Public Service are at stake. With what faith can we, after this, bring

forward proposals for economics affecting clerks at the courts?"[1]

Notwithstanding Schuster's strongly worded letter Campbell was, within two years, appointed Lord Chief Justice for Ireland.

The War and its Aims

Buckmaster's term of office (one year and seven months) was wholly in wartime and the conduct of the war gave him great concern. He had decided not to appoint any new KCs for the duration as so many members of the Bar were in the Services. He was amongst the members of the Cabinet who were uneasy about Kitchener's autocracy, and when the proposal to send an expedition to Salonika arose he circulated a memorandum to his Cabinet Colleagues on October 15, 1915.

This memorandum was a well argued plea for concentrating all efforts on the Western Front and doing nothing to weaken our forces there. On the first day of the battle of the Somme British casualties were 60,000. Albert Napier, who was chief clerk in the Lord Chancellor's Office at that time and later succeeded Schuster as Permanent Secretary, saw Buckmaster staring out of his window at a long column of troops crossing Westminster Bridge on their way to the front. He was muttering to himself, "Hateful, hateful".[2]

1. Buckmaster's Papers. R.F.V. Heuston. *Lives of the Lord Chancellors 1885-1940.* Clarendon Press, 1964, p.272.
2. *Ibid.,* p.279.

The war was not progressing well and towards the end of 1916 there was dissatisfaction with the Asquith Government. A split developed in the Liberal party between the supporters of Asquith and those of Lloyd George. Haldane wrote to Buckmaster (Haldane papers, December 6, 1916): "Asquith is a first class head of a deliberative council. He is versed in precedents, acts on principles, and knows how and when to compromise. Lloyd George cares nothing for precedents and knows no principles, but he has fire in his belly and that is what we want."

This did not convince Buckmaster; in December 1916 Asquith resigned as Prime Minister and with him Buckmaster and several other Ministers. Although they need not have done so, they followed that action because they felt they could not serve under Lloyd George, the incoming Prime Minister. On leaving office and being replaced by Finlay, Buckmaster received the following letter from Schuster:

December 10, 1916

Dear Chancellor,

Thus I may address you for the last time for some months. I don't like to bother you with a letter, but I must write a few lines to express what cannot be said face-to-face, that is my deep regret at your termination of office, and my very sincere and lasting gratitude to you. I have much cause for indebtedness to you - your generosity in taking me into your office, untried and unknown to you; your constant backing in every difficulty, your forbearance of stupidity and persistence, your unfailing kindness and readiness to think the best of the little I could do; your readiness to consider and enter into every scheme for improvement and reform. I hope and believe that in your regained freedom you will not lose interest in the Office or its officials. In war-time it is difficult to do much, and at any time economy and diligence are drab and uninteresting virtues for the practice of which constant encouragement is needed from outside. I hope you will remember how much is to be done so that when you return to office we may have already advanced and under your guidance may accomplish the remainder.

May I, without presumption, add a word on greater matters? My great fear is lest your party by demanding a definition of our aims, may be represented as a peace party, and so lose its influence just when it is most needed. Free trade, humanity, a respect for settled principles of law, a regard for the rights of others, whether nations or individuals, are the principles which are at stake both in our war with Germany and in our domestic struggles. They are now definitely committed to your care. I am afraid lest in the heat which must arise from the events of this last week and from any such policy as we discussed, the people at large and even your own followers may forget, and you may be involved in a general fog of controversy in which peace and pro-Germanism may look like the same thing. I express myself badly. Please forgive this intrusion, and believe me yours,

Most sincerely and gratefully,
Claud Schuster[3]

One can only surmise that Buckmaster discussed with his Permanent Secretary the all pervading topic - the progress of the war and that their views were conjoined. That is borne out by the last paragraph of the letter in which Schuster intrudes into politics by suggesting that the Liberal party should not appear to be too soft on Germany.

---

3. *Ibid.*, pp.285-6.

Relationship with Schuster

Buckmaster's father started life as an agricultural labourer, educated himself and became interested in politics. Buckmaster himself was born in a small house near Clapham Junction. With this background, not surprisingly he joined the Liberal party - in late Victorian times it was the party of reform. Buckmaster had many radical ideas often before his time. He believed in birth control, the abolition of capital punishment, female suffrage, broadening the grounds for divorce, and improving the housing conditions of the poor. He admired much of what the Labour party stood for and was encouraging when his friend, William Jowitt (Lord Chancellor in 1948), decided to join it. Indeed, in 1924, he was considered for the Woolsack by Ramsay MacDonald who eventually chose Haldane as his Labour Lord Chancellor. He was a great orator who spoke from just a few notes. Socially he was a member of the Garrick Club and was friendly with members of the political Opposition such as Balfour.

He was Schuster's first Lord Chancellor. How much did his influence affect Schuster? They were together in wartime. They both had their only sons serving in France. In discussing the progress of the war they were probably in agreement that efforts should be concentrated on the Western Front. Schuster may have had a hand in the memorandum dictated by Buckmaster in October 1915 referred to above. They may have had much in common, but Buckmaster was a reformer, Schuster a traditionalist.

Buckmaster out of office was required to sit as a Law Lord in the House of Lords and on the Judicial Committee. By

February 1923 he was evidently finding this work a strain and he informed Schuster by letter. Schuster wrote back in his role as the administrator who wanted to keep the wheels of justice turning:

> "Naturally your letter gave me both pain and anxiety. Consider my position. You taught me to have a zeal for justice and a deep interest in the prompt and effectual despatch of the business of the court. I know quite well that so far as you assist in attaining those ends, you are withdrawn from other activities, more pleasant in themselves, and even more profitable. But surely on all your teaching they are not more important. What matters more to a modern state than the maintenance of its supreme court in power and dignity? And, even from your own point of view, I cannot think that there is no sense of satisfaction in doing a thing, in itself worthy of the employment of the highest intellectual facilities, as superbly as you do this. After all, what is the situation? We turn to you in every difficulty, because speaking not otherwise than with respect of your colleagues, you are by far the best president of the court. The Chancellor cannot always sit. We cannot hope to have the benefit of FE's (Birkenhead's) attendance constantly. Upon whom else, other than yourself, can we depend, either to get through the shorter cases in a reasonable time, or to prevent a long case from stretching itself out into a public scandal? Even when the LC does sit, he feels very much that another Equity mind besides his own is much wanted for the Equity cases.
>
> "Everybody realizes the great judicial qualities which you possess: and I personally cannot imagine a more solid record of accomplishment than to have been recognised universally as you are, as the person most fitted to preside in the greatest of all tribunals."[4]

---

4. *Ibid.*, pp.300-1.

CHAPTER 7

Lord Finlay -
December 11, 1916 to January 14, 1919

Prolix yet Fair

Finlay, once a Liberal, was appointed Attorney-General by Salisbury, the Conservative Prime Minister in June 1900. He continued in that position until 1906 when the Liberals came into power. He had served the Government well and was highly respected in legal circles as a sound lawyer with an expertise in international law. Balfour, the Conservative party leader, and others felt that Finlay should be rewarded with a judgeship but they were no longer in power and it did not happen. Finlay recreated his practice specialising in the appellate courts. Following the retirement/resignation of Buckmaster in 1916, Lloyd George offered the Lord Chancellorship to Finlay on condition that he would not draw the pension of £5,000 a year to which ex-Lord Chancellors were entitled, because it was wartime and there were already four ex-Lord Chancellors living whose pensions had to be paid.

Finlay received the Great Seal on December 12, 1916. At the age of 74, he had come at last to the Woolsack. It was the greatest age at which anyone had been appointed (with the exception of Lord Campbell who was 80 in 1859).

Finlay's age was beginning to tell. On the Bench he was prolix and allowed others to be loquacious also. He was meticulously cautious, insisting in sending for all relevant authorities so that the Law Lords were soon surrounded by mountains of volumes. It was said that neither in pace nor in quality did he improve any tribunal over which he presided. But that was unfair. His judgments were invariably sound.

In the last two years of the war there was little for a Lord Chancellor to do other than to maintain the traditional machinery of justice. Heuston says:

> "In the despatch of the routine work of his department his Scottish prudence and unwillingness to hurry sometimes worried the agile Schuster, but that formidable civil servant was wise enough to know when to restrain his impatience."[1]

Judicial Appointments

Schuster had already shown that he could influence judicial appointments in Buckmaster's time (see Chapter 6). With the ageing Finlay he was even more persuasive. In 1917, a vacancy arose on the High Court Bench and Schuster's briefing to Finlay was such that Finlay could only accept Schuster's recommendation. In a memorandum to Finlay, he first offered his Chancellor a list of senior silks, but added that they were once papabili (able) but that they were now all too old. There followed a list of MPs who were also KCs but Schuster recommended one only:

> "Salter seems the most considerable in the eyes of the party and professionally it seems to me ... that if you wish to make an

---

1. R.F.V. Heuston. *Lives of the Lord Chancellors 1885-1940*. Clarendon Press, 1964, p.339.

appointment from the House of Commons it is difficult to look beyond him ... Of those who are not MPs you will have no difficulty passing over Marshall Hall, Powell, Langton, Ashton, Gregory, Compton, Schiller and Charles and it is not necessary for me to give the reasons ... There remain Gore-Brown, Talbot, Greer, Disturnal and Hawke."[2]

Of these Schuster favoured Talbot and Greer for the present vacancy but finally he noted that Roche would be the one regarded as the best by the Bar and he probably would not take a judgeship. Subsequently he put out feelers and reported that if an offer were made to Roche now, he would accept. He was appointed. Of the five referred to above who were short-listed by Schuster, all except Disturnal were later appointed to the High Court.[3]

Establishing Contacts

Schuster tolerated Finlay. The two men had some things in common. They were both linguists, Finlay was an expert in international law and Schuster with his continental background also had an interest in foreign affairs. But this was wartime, Finlay not being a member of the Cabinet, had little political influence. In June 1916 the trial of Sir Roger Casement took place. In 1917 there was an Industrial Unrest Conference and in the same year an attempted assassination of Lloyd George by the Wheeldon family. The Russian

---

2. LCO 2/601, September 20, 1917.
3. *Ibid.*

revolution also occurred in 1917 and must have caused great concern to the Government. However, there is no evidence that Finlay or Schuster had any influence on policy at that time. The period of Finlay's Chancellorship gave Schuster the opportunity to settle into the job and establish contacts and a framework from which he could exert his influence. Finlay was a close friend of Haldane and Haldane was chairman of the Machinery of Government Committee which was appointed in 1917. We know from the diaries of Beatrice Webb that Haldane was in the habit of holding meetings and dinner parties at his house in Queen Anne's Gate. At these gatherings, apart from Beatrice Webb, who in her own words said, "I tell them that I am discovering the land of Whitehall for the future Labour Cabinet",[4] the leading spirits included Labour MP Jimmy Thomas, Conservative MP Colonel Sir Alan Sykes, Liberal MP Edwin Montagu, Permanent Secretaries Sir George Murray from the Post Office and Sir Claud Schuster from the Lord Chancellor's Office. Sir Robert Morant was another who was often present.

With contacts like these Schuster rapidly found himself at the hub of the Executive wheel in a position to put his spoke in at almost every quarter.

Beatrice Webb comments that Haldane, Murray, Schuster and Morant were forever insisting that the working of Parliament makes sensible, leave alone scientific, administration possible, and that she tried to make them face the newer problems of combining bureaucratic efficiency with democratic control.

---

4. *Beatrice Webb's Diaries*. Ed. Margaret Cole. Longman, 1952, p.98.

Finlay and Birkenhead

Although Finlay had been appointed on the understanding that he would resign when required he was nevertheless surprised at the abruptness of his dismissal after the election of 1919. The first he knew of it was reading it in the press. He was made a Viscount and continued to sit as a Law Lord. In 1921, when Finlay was 79, Lloyd George wanted to appoint him Lord Chief Justice, but Birkenhead, Finlay's successor as Lord Chancellor, objected in two letters to Lloyd George, mainly on the grounds of Finlay's age and failing faculties. The wording of these letters suggest some input by Schuster:

> "Lord Finlay is approaching 79 years of age. He has in the past rendered the most eminent services as Attorney-General and has enjoyed the highest reputation as an advocate. You yourself thought that age unfitted him to hold the position of Lord Chancellor towards the end of 1918. Since then he has sat frequently in the House of Lords for the purpose of hearing appeals, and it is apparent to everyone that the great powers which he once possessed are now gradually leaving him under the burden of his advancing years. I have no doubt that even if he were willing to accept office on such conditions, professional opinion would condemn the appointment, and the public would inquire how it was that he who was too old to be Lord Chancellor in 1919 was not too old to enter upon the arduous office of Lord Chief Justice in 1921. But in addition, it would become apparent to the whole world immediately upon his assumption of his duties that he had reached an age at which he was unfitted to perform them."[5]

---

5. John Campbell. *F.E. Smith First Earl of Birkenhead.* Jonathan Cape, 193, pp.402-7.

This letter drew from Lloyd George an angry reply, in the course of which he said, "As to Finlay's capacity, Carson, whom you will admit is the most eminent advocate of his day, told me that the profession would regard his appointment with great satisfaction."

Birkenhead replied promptly on the same day:

> "The question has never arisen whether a Judge could properly be put under a condition to retire at the age of 80 because, so far as I know, no one has ever been made a Judge at an age which suggested such a stipulation. Campbell was 70 when he became LCJ but his vitality was amazing; he was, I think, a record. Carson has not practised before Finlay since the latter became Lord Chancellor.
>
> "I have sat with him continuously. I by no means say that he is unfit for judicial work but he is not the man he was and I do not think he could undertake the office of LCJ. The appointment is yours and if you appoint him I shall loyally co-operate with him but *I most earnestly hope that if you do you will make him LCJ without any condition* relying upon his age to terminate his tenure of office within a reasonable time. If any condition is imposed I am sure that we shall find ourselves exposed to the risks and difficulties suggested in my letter, the suggestion of which was the object of that letter."[6]

Lloyd George was evidently persuaded. Nevertheless he appointed as Lord Chief Justice Mr Justice A.T. Lawrence, aged 77. It was an unpopular appointment.

---

6. *Ibid.*

The Judicial Committee

Haldane and others believed that appeals from the Dominions and Colonies of the Empire to the Judicial Committee of the Privy Council were a means of keeping the Empire together. However, the Empire was beginning to come apart. Several Dominions wanted to assert their independence and did not see why appeals from British courts should not go to the Judicial Committee instead of to the House of Lords. There was interest in the whole idea during Finlay's time and he was in favour of it.

First there was the practical reason that no one could ever agree on who should pay for the Colonial Judges, who would sit, permanently or semi-permanently in London. Secondly the Dominions were not really interested in having their appeals heard by Judges from other Dominions. Thirdly, in the words Schuster put into the mouth of Lord Chancellor Finlay, the idea that English appeals should go to an Imperial Court was not acceptable because of the fusion of the legal professions in some Dominions. "I believe that such a change would meet with every grave opposition in the United Kingdom itself. If Australian solicitors can sit, why not English? I am strongly opposed to such a scheme."[7] Schuster's concern about the implications for the divided legal profession in England was, however, superfluous as Canada would not have the scheme at any price and that killed it. The decline of the Judicial Committee continued throughout the Schuster era. Nevertheless it still exists and has 50-70 appeals

---

7.   LCO 2/2464.

a year from New Zealand and smaller Commonwealth countries.

A Ministry of Justice

During Finlay's period of office, the thorny question of a Ministry of Justice arose. Haldane's Machinery of Government Committee reported and Schuster was required to brief Finlay on the reaction of his department. At the same time the Law Society was advocating a Ministry of Justice while the Bar was conspiring with Schuster to oppose any change. Schuster did produce a summary of Haldane's proposals while scarcely concealing his opposition to most of them. Paraphrased they were:

> "The Lord Chancellor should remain as a legal and constitutional adviser of the highest standing. He would be President of the (proposed) Imperial Court of Appeal but would be freed from the duty of frequent judicial sittings. He would cease to be the Speaker of the House of Lords. He would be responsible for all judicial officers and in making senior judicial appointments should consult a committee consisting of the Prime Minister, the Minister of Justice, ex-Lord Chancellors and the Lord Chief Justice. He should deal with all questions concerning legislation and should replace the Treasury as the channel of communication between departments initiating legislation and the Parliamentary Council's Office. All other functions should pass to a Minister of Justice who would in fact be the Home Secretary.[8]

---

8. LCO 2/3630.

CHAPTER 8

Lord Birkenhead -
January 14, 1919 to October 25, 1922

"Galloper Smith"

By 1919 Schuster was well installed at the hub of the legal
system. It was said later that some of his Lord Chancellors
were little more than ciphers who reigned while Schuster
ruled. Few of them came to the job with any political party
policy. Some had pet ideas of their own but lacked the time
or the energy necessary to put them into effect. From
whichever party they came they tended to be conservative
and traditional concerning the law. An inactive Chancellor
meant that Schuster could "rule" and he did; but when
Birkenhead was appointed the situation was different. The
character of the man, his ideas and energy, ensured that
during his Chancellorship things would happen.
Surprisingly, perhaps because the two men were very
different in character and lifestyle, a strong partnership
developed between them. In order to understand this it is
necessary to know something of Birkenhead's personality.

When Lloyd George peremptorily replaced the ponderous
Finlay with the rumbustious, hard-drinking Birkenhead, it
was no problem for the adaptable Schuster. He was ready for
more action than had occurred with his first two Chancellors,
and plenty of action took place. Birkenhead had acquired the
nickname of "Galloper Smith" when he had acted as Carson's

"galloper"[1] at a review of the Ulster Volunteers.

Always a brilliant orator, his "galloping" varied from a flow of persuasive rhetoric backed by sound reasoning to what many would say was bombastic nonsense. Nevertheless, for the most part, he was an energetic Lord Chancellor, combining a heavy workload with every kind of physical activity and most kinds of pleasure. Not surprisingly he died at the young age of 58. His appointment as Lord Chancellor caused raised eyebrows in many quarters, even in the Palace.

At the General Election of 1918, F.E. (as Birkenhead was referred to at the Bar) was returned for the West Derby Division of Liverpool, and Lloyd George offered him his old post of Attorney-General. In order to keep down the number of Cabinet posts that would mean that he would no longer have a seat in the Cabinet, F.E. was unwilling to accept such a blow to his esteem. Lloyd George then offered him the Lord Chancellorship. The King himself wrote to Lloyd George asking that the appointment be reconsidered on the ground that "His Majesty does not feel sure that Sir Frederick has established such a reputation in men's minds as to ensure that the country will welcome him to the second highest position which can be occupied by a subject of the Crown."[2] The King also stressed the youthfulness of the new Lord Chancellor who was 46 years of age.

The appointment was also unpopular with a large section of the public and with the Bench and the Bar. Nevertheless

---

1. NB: Military team: an aide de camp or orderly officer.
2. Second Earl of Birkenhead. *The Life of F.E. Smith, First Earl of Birkenhead* by his son. Eyre and Spottiswood, 1960, p.332.

F.E. received the Great Seal on January 14, 1919, and on February 3 he was created a Peer with the title of Baron Birkenhead.

Schuster's biography of Lord Birkenhead in the *Dictionary of National Biography* ran to seven pages. It included a description of his Master which cannot be bettered:

> "The brilliance of his first appearance, the rapidity of his wit, and the ferocity of his attack caused men to take a false view of his character and of his attainments. He was regarded as a swashbuckler, and courageous, but headstrong and superficial - in the courts, as the man for a crushing cross-examination or a speech to a jury rather than for a serious legal argument, and in the House for the brilliance, raillery, and rhetorical display of a partisan rather than for the measured view and wise counsel of the statesman. His appearance and manner of life contributed to this view. He was strikingly handsome, six feet one inch in height, of a distinguished figure, slightly marred by sloping shoulders. His clothes, although not in any way particularly out of the ordinary, gave the impression that he was over-dressed. The hat worn on the back of his head, the red flower in his button-hole, the very long cigar always carried in his mouth, made him a ready subject for the caricaturist. The great houses in which he stayed, the late hours which he kept, his fondness for gaiety and for gay people, for cards, for horses, and for all the bright and expensive things of life, confirmed the opinion that he was a reckless partisan, fighting hard for his own side, grasping at his own enjoyment and advantage, not a responsible or serious person either as a lawyer or as a parliamentarian. Furthermore, his sharp tongue, his aggressive demeanour, and the cynical attitude which he at times assumed made many enemies and not

only among his political foes."[3]

Schuster merely hints at what may have been a darker side to Birkenhead's character. He was prepared to make use of anyone who could help him in work or pleasure. In work he was a great delegator and no doubt Schuster was always prepared to act in his master's name. No harm in that; but Birkenhead also brought his own acolytes into the Lord Chancellor's Office.

Private Secretaries

In addition to his permanent officials he had two Private Secretaries of his own. One, the more orthodox, was Roland Burrows who was what we would now call a research assistant. He was a barrister whose function was to devil for Birkenhead and to draft his judgments. The other was an extraordinary but shadowy character Lt. Col. G.W.H.M. "Buns" Cartwright, who was officially the Ecclesiastical Secretary. He was useful to Birkenhead as a games player rather than a Secretary and was habitually at Charlton, Birkenhead's country house where he was always available as a fourth at tennis or golf. Birkenhead's children called him the "Games Master" and loathed him.

After Birkenhead's death in 1930, Cartwright devoted himself to cricket as player and secretary to the Eton Ramblers Cricket Club. When he died in 1977 his obituary

---

3. *DNB* 1921-30, p.784.

in *The Times* and the address given by Brian Johnston at a memorial service, spoke of nothing but cricket. It was a mystery how he lived for 50 years; he may have had a connection with stockbroking and John Campbell[4] suggests that he may have helped F.E. with his chaotic finances and that there might even have been an element of blackmail in his hold over F.E. In his later years Cartwright threatened to reveal certain dark secrets about F.E. He was certainly more than a secretary and was a constant companion for the last 10 years of F.E.'s life. Whatever scandal he could have revealed, he never did disclose.

The Lord Chancellor was responsible at that time for the appointment of clergy to some 700 livings. These advowson and benefices were far more in number than those in possession of the two senior Archbishops. These rights were no doubt exercised under the scrutiny of Schuster but it is surprising that he tolerated a man like "Buns" Cartwright in the position of Ecclesiastical Patronage Secretary. It is said that passionately fond of cricket as Cartwright was, his list of candidates for livings had against the names of the applicants, notes such as "good left-hand bowler" or "right-hand bat".[5]

There may have been some bias of a sporting nature in the way Cartwright did his job, but in a letter to Bishop Ryle dated May 18, 1922, Schuster was emphatic that ecclesiastical patronage was entirely free from political taint.[6]

---

4. John Campbell. *F.E. Smith Earl of Birkenhead*. Jonathan Cape, 1983, p.472.
5. *Ibid.*, p.473.
6. The plans are in Schuster's file LCD.

Absence of the Lord Chancellor Abroad

As Keeper of the King's Conscience the Lord Chancellor has closer contacts with the Monarchy than any other Minister and by ancient convention he is not allowed to leave the country without the Monarch's permission. The correspondence between Schuster and the King's Secretary show this peculiarity of the Constitution and the relationship with the Monarch.

In 1919 Schuster had to write to the King's Secretary requesting that Birkenhead be allowed to accompany the Prime Minister Lloyd George to Paris for the peace negotiations:

House of Lords, SW1
December 23, 1919

Dear Lord Stamfordham,

The Prime Minister has asked the Lord Chancellor to accompanying him to Paris very shortly for the purpose of discussing there the question of German offenders who are to be delivered up. The Lord Chancellor takes a strong view with reference to this list, and he thinks that in the circumstances it is essential that he should accept the Prime Minister's invitation and explain and enforce his view in Paris. He hoped that the result may be some reduction in the list, the numbers of which appear to him wholly extravagant.

The Lord Chancellor thought that the King should know beforehand of the necessity for the Lord Chancellor's visit. The letters placing the Great Seal in Commission in the event of any absence of the Lord Chancellor from the Kingdom, which were granted upon in case any necessity should arise, which is most improbable.

Yours sincerely
(Sgd.) CLAUD SCHUSTER[7]

Seven weeks later Schuster was writing again explaining the result of the visit. The letter shows that Birkenhead's attitude to the Germans was more lenient than that of the French. It also shows Schuster's concern for the health of his Lord Chancellor.

House of Lords, SW1
February 17, 1920

Dear Lord Stamfordham,

The Lord Chancellor wishes me to let you know the result of his visit to Paris, especially in regard to the fact that as a result of that visit, it will be necessary for him to visit Paris again.

As a result mainly of the negotiations carried on by him, the Allies have accepted his proposal that the Germans should be allowed themselves to try the persons whose names appear in the lists of those demanded by the Allied powers.

They have also accepted his proposal that a diplomatic hint be given to Holland, to the effect that if the Dutch see fit to intern the German ex-Emperor in some Dutch Colony at a distance from Europe, the Allies will not further press their demands for his surrender to them.

In order to see that the Germans honestly carry out their undertaking to try the accused persons, it has been agreed that an Inter-Allied Commission should be set up in Paris of which Monsieur Jules Cambon is President. The Cabinet express a unanimous wish that the Lord Chancellor should be the British

---

7. *The Times*, August 12, 1919.

representative upon this Commission, and having regard both to the pressure brought to bear upon him, and to other circumstances, the Lord Chancellor has been forced to acquiesce in this proposal.

In these circumstances, it will probably be necessary that the Lord Chancellor should in the immediate future frequently attend Meetings of the Commission in Paris. The Commission will meet on Fridays and Saturdays, in order to suit his convenience. The Lord Chancellor proposes in those weeks in which the meetings are held to leave London on Thursday night after the House has risen, and to return on Sunday.

He trusts that this arrangement will meet with the King's approval. It will not be necessary that any further Commission should be issued to provide for the conduct of business in his absence, as the existing Commission is operative until revoked, and although I am myself apprehensive that the Lord Chancellor must suffer from the excessive fatigue of these frequent visits, each of them involving at least one night journey, I do not think that any harm will result to public business.

Yours sincerely,
(Sgn.) CLAUD SCHUSTER[8]

This letter is endorsed "Approved G.R.I."

Birkenhead's Health

Always good value as an orator Birkenhead made one of his very best speeches when he was not fully fit. It was at the time when the situation in Ireland was coming to a head. Until the age of 48 he had been blessed with an excellent

---

8. *Hansard*. H of C. June 4, 1919, vol.116.

physique and in spite of his hectic - often dissolute - lifestyle, good health. Then in October 1920 he was struck with a serious and painful disease of the ear, supposedly caused by his diving into cold water from the deck of his yacht to amuse his daughter Pamela. He was an impatient patient; the pain made it impossible for him to work. Schuster was holding the fort. True to form he was a loyal adviser and good friend to his Lord Chancellor. He sought the sympathy of the King and in accordance with ancient tradition he asked the King's permission for Birkenhead to leave the country.

Schuster wrote to Lord Stamfordham on October 13, 1920:

"The Lord Chancellor has for some weeks been somewhat seriously indisposed. The origin of his trouble is obscure, but it appears to be attributable to the fact that he dived into very cold water shortly after the commencement of the Recess. As a result there has been and still is considerable suppuration in the middle ear. He has not had a day free from inconvenience and some pain and finds great difficulty in getting any sleep, which indeed only comes to him with the assistance of sleeping draughts.

"It was for some time feared that it might be necessary to operate upon him, but it is now believed that that danger is past and that in time the trouble may subside in course of nature. He is, however, still very unwell and very sleepless and is unable to attend to business except at intervals and then only for a short space of time. In addition, the fact that the time which ought to have been devoted to holidays and recuperation has been spent in this matter has greatly pulled him down.

"In these circumstances, his medical advisers have directed imperatively that he should go away for some three weeks or so, and it is proposed accordingly that he should go to the South of France accompanied by a doctor. He is very much grieved to be absent in the opening days of the Session, but he has consulted his colleagues, and both the Prime Minister and Lord Curzon have expressed a decided view that it is his duty to obey the advice which has been given to him, and not to risk the much longer absence which might be entailed by an attempt now to return to work.

"In these circumstances he will be greatly obliged if you will be so good as to lay the facts before the King, to express the Lord Chancellor's deep regret that he should be forced in this manner to absent himself from his duty, and to request the King's approval of his adoption of the course which his medical advisers direct him to take.

"The Chancellor's absence from the House will entail a delay in the progress of some departmental bills in whose passage he takes great interest. The main business, however, in this House during the coming Session will be in all probability the Home Rule Bill. The Lord Chancellor, however, is confident that unless some wholly unexpected change in his condition should supervene, he will be back in time to take charge of that Bill upon the Second Reading and in Committee."

The King made no objection to the Lord Chancellor leaving the country and endorsed Schuster's letter:

"Quite approve of his going away at once for a holiday and hope he will come back quite restored to health."

G.R.I.

(Royal Archives, Windsor Castle)[9]

By November 15, 1920, Birkenhead had returned from abroad and Schuster wrote again to the Palace to report on the Lord Chancellor's health:

---

9. John Campbell, p.474.

"The Lord Chancellor has completely recovered not only from the local malady in his ear, but also from the impairment in his general health which resulted from so many weeks of sleeplessness and pain. So far as the ear is concerned, there is no reason to apprehend any further trouble. Until the malady has entirely passed away there was some fear lest the power of hearing should be slightly lessened, but the Lord Chancellor tells me that he thinks that the ear is now more efficient for its purpose than before the illness. In general health the Lord Chancellor seems to be better than for a long time past. The enforced abstention from business has fulfilled some of the purpose of a rest cure.

"The Lord Chancellor is now full of energy, and is preparing to undertake the conduct of the Home Rule Bill in this House."[10]

The Irish Problem

The Irish problem has plagued British Government since the mid-nineteenth century. Asquith's Liberal Government passed a Home Rule Act in 1914 but this solved nothing. The rebellion in Dublin in 1915 again focused the Government's attention on Ireland but there was no easy solution. The Liberal Government was failing and the coalition was formed. Under that Government there were proposals ranging from complete Home Rule for Ireland, to making it a Dominion or Crown colony. Lloyd George suggested "Home Rule all round", ie, for Scotland and Wales as well as Ireland - devolution in other words. Finally the Government of Ireland Bill (which resulted in the Treaty of

---

10. Second Earl of Birkenhead, p.341.

Ireland Act 1921) was drafted. It provided for separate parliaments for North and South and for a Council of Ireland consisting of 20 members from each Parliament with a President to be appointed by the King. This Bill came before the House of Lords for its second reading on November 23, 1920. It was on this occasion that Birkenhead, although still not completely fit, made his brilliant speech.

Two days before, 14 officers had been murdered by terrorists in Dublin and he began his long and complex speech referring to this tragedy:

> "I should be blind indeed if I ignored the atmosphere of emotion and indignation in which all of us at this moment must approach the consideration of this question, and it will be necessary for us later to ask ourselves, as we frequently had to ask ourselves during the war, the difficult question: What is the true perspective which must be assigned to the appalling crimes to which the attention of the country was directed yesterday?"[11]

The part which reviewed the provisions of the Bill were made from full notes but when he spoke of the urgency in promoting conciliation his eloquence flowed. His theme was the hope and dream of peace. He fervently appealed for tolerance and understanding. He had little time to prepare this speech and in view of his state of health much of the formal briefing must have been done for him. Schuster would undoubtedly have had a hand in it.

---

11. *Ibid.*

A Contretemps with King George V

The convivial Birkenhead was a great entertainer and he was in his element as the host at a great banquet at the House of Lords in July 1921. King George V and 60 exalted guests were present. Evidently it did not please the Prime Minister, Lloyd George; he did not attend, pleading exhaustion. The arrangements for a function of that kind were the responsibility of the Clerk of the Parliaments under the direction of the Permanent Secretary. Schuster would have undoubtedly had a say in who the guests should be. Having been in post for six years he was by then a formidable civil servant; tactful, diplomatic - an invaluable counsellor and guide to his master. Any detailed practicalities of proposed legislation that Birkenhead put to Parliament were worked out by Schuster who was getting on well with his Lord Chancellor and gaining a high opinion of his varied qualities.

In the same year as he had entertained the King at the House of Lords the Lord Chancellor had a slight *contretemps* with His Majesty. The King had seen a press photograph of Birkenhead entering 10 Downing Street for a meeting on the Irish question. Michael Collins was also in the photograph, which showed the Lord Chancellor wearing a soft slouch hat and a rather bucolic suit. On the King's instructions Lord Stamfordham, the King's Secretary, wrote a note to Schuster saying that the King objected to Birkenhead wearing a soft hat for a formal occasion. Birkenhead was annoyed and wrote back to the effect that he usually wore a silk hat but many of his colleagues did not. On the morning in question he had come up from the country and had not had time to go home to get changed. He concluded the letter "... and after all in days far more formal than ours it was never the custom to appraise the adequacy or dignity of the Lord Chancellor in terms of headgear." Lord Stamfordham submitted Birkenhead's letter to the King with a memorandum and his proposed very tactful reply:

October 15, 1921
BUCKINGHAM PALACE

Humbly submitted

Acting on Your Majesty's instruction I wrote to Sir Claud Schuster a friendly, very unofficial, and almost a 'chatty' letter about the Lord Chancellor's dress as represented in the picture papers. He replied that he had shown my letter to Lord Birkenhead who would himself reply. I enclose his letter which I do not think is quite nice in tone, tho' whether it is intended to be jocose or not I am not quite sure. I do not altogether like the last paragraph. Your Majesty never intended to gauge the dignity or adequacy of the LC by his 'headgear'.

I enclose a copy of my answer in which I have *attempted* to smooth any possible wounding susceptibilities.

As to his reference to other colleagues, who have *not* been remonstrated with, not long ago I conveyed a similar hint to the Prime Minister thro' his P. Secretary. The worst offender is Mr Balfour but he is almost hopeless.

S.[12]
BUCKINGHAM PALACE
October 14, 1921

---

12. Second Earl of Birkenhead, p.396.

Private
Dear Lord Chancellor,

I am forwarding your letter just received to the King who will, I know, more than understand the circumstances which you explain under which the ubiquitous and tiresome snapshotters photographed you in country clothes, and will appreciate still more your expressed willingness to wear more frequently the hated hat!

Believe me His Majesty does not appraise the adequacy or dignity of his Lord Chancellor in terms of the altitude of his head-gear!

But it *is* because he holds in such high esteem that honourable and historical office, and, if I may presume to say so, the distinguished manner in which its duties are today fulfilled, that he does cling to these slight "ritual" observances especially on the occasion of the Irish Conference.

Believe me,
Yours very truly,
(Signed) STAMFORDHAM[13]

It is said on receipt of the reply Birkenhead made a furious telephone call to Stamfordham in which he said: "I don't like the King's brown bowler, but I'm not always ringing up to say so!" He replied in calmer fashion reluctantly accepting the criticism:

Lord Chancellor   HOUSE OF LORDS, SW1
October 15, 1921

My dear Lord Stamfordham,

Many thanks for your charming letter. Really of course I fully understand the importance of these things which seem

---

13. *Ibid.*

unimportant. In the snapshot I really thought that Michael Collins looked the more gentleman-like of the two but I fancy I was a trifle unlucky in the artist.

I showed Winston your letter and the enclosed photograph: he has been strutting about with quite unnecessary complacency ever since.

I value very much your assurance of the King's good opinion. Whatever the result may be I do at least labour incessantly in an office fuller than it ever was of anxiety and difficulty.

Yours very sincerely
(Signed) BIRKENHEAD

Lord Stamfordham felt that he was in a position to soothe the jangled nerves of the King with the following minute:

Humbly submitted
The Lord Chancellor is evidently appeased so all is well!

S.
15.10.21

His Majesty, although still disgruntled, appeared willing to accept the olive branch:

"His first letter was certainly *rude* but he seems appeased now. I only want him to keep up the dignity of his position. For a Conference of this kind he ought to be properly dressed."

G.R.I.[14]

---

14. *Ibid.*, p.397.

The Need for a "Restful" Holiday

On March 28, 1922 Schuster wrote to Lord Stamfordham seeking the King's permission for his master to leave the country for a Mediterranean holiday. Birkenhead had seen the King's oculist about his eyes and had been advised to take a restful holiday. Schuster wrote a most convincing letter saying that the Lord Chancellor had to leave England to get away from his responsibilities. He needed a period of rest and quiet in a warmer climate. "The state of the Lord Chancellor's eyes," he wrote, "appear to be the result of a deterioration in his general health, and that deterioration in turn is due in the main to the continuous overstrain of the last few years ..." That must have been written tongue in cheek as Schuster knew that Birkenhead's health was due to his lifestyle. On the other hand the reason for Birkenhead's absence may have been political. In the event he did not have a restful holiday. He went via the French canals in his motor yacht to Genoa where there was an international conference mainly concerned with relations with Russia and recognition of the Bolshevik Government.

At the same time Schuster had to deal with more mundane problems such as the replacement of the Lord Chancellor's State Coach with a motor vehicle; the renewal of the Great Seal and Purse and the question of army officers wearing swords in courts.

CHAPTER 9

Lord Birkenhead's Reforms -
Schuster's Hidden Hand

Land Law Legislation

In the preface to his biography of Lord Birkenhead, his son states: "I would like to place on record my gratitude to the late Lord Schuster, Permanent Secretary to the Lord Chancellor and loyal friend to Lord Birkenhead, without whose help I, as a layman, could not have written this chapter." He was referring to the chapter on the legal work of the Lord Chancellor. Lord Birkenhead made, or had a hand in, several important judicial decisions but his greatest achievement in his period as Lord Chancellor was his part in reforming the transfer of land by means of the Law of Property Act 1922 and the subsequent 1925 legislation. Birkenhead had the power and determination to insist on change that enabled Schuster to do most of the persuading and bargaining with his Chancellor's authority.

Schuster had a personal interest in reforming the law of real property. This is revealed in a letter to a colleague in 1920, in which he complains that he has the misery to be the owner of an undivided share in a block of buildings in Manchester which is already owned in 40 sections and on the occasion of the next death will run into hundreds. "The difficulty of managing the property and dealing with the tenants is immense," he wrote, "it is almost a commercial impossibility to effect necessary improvements and the lawyer's bill year by year swallows up an enormous proportion of the gross rental ..."[1]

Schuster in his Element

The means by which the legislation came into being reveals Schuster's hand in every move.

The law of real property in England and Wales in the nineteenth century, derived as it was from feudalism, consisted of a mass of technical rules known only to a part of the solicitors' profession. Reform was clearly necessary, particularly in regard to the large estates owned by beneficiaries under settlements, the result of which were that the land could not be sold without the agreement of all the beneficiaries. The Settled Land Act of 1882 had remedied this by giving the tenant for life the power to convey the fee simple, thus overreaching the titles of the beneficiaries who would then receive the capital values of their interests. In the 1890s, when conveyancing fees accounted for half the income of the average solicitor, the obvious way for further reform was to have a system whereby land could be transferred in the same way as stocks and shares. In 1897 public dissatisfaction with private conveyancing prompted the Lord Chancellor, Halsbury, to introduce a Bill which became the Land Transfer Act 1897 providing for the compulsory registration of the title of land, but only in the County of London. That restriction was due to the Law Society which had obtained a "county veto" enabling counties or urban

---

1. LCD files.

district councils to refuse to make registration compulsory. Universal registration was strongly advocated by the Chief Registrar of the Land Registry but he had been bitterly attacked by a militant group within the Law Society.

The Law Society's opposition to land registration had led to the appointment of the Royal Commission on Land Transfer in 1908. It reported in 1911 and endorsed the principle of compulsory registration with qualifications.[2] Haldane, the Lord Chancellor, presented Bills to Parliament in 1913, 1914 and 1915. None made any progress.

In March, 1917 a Reconstruction Sub-Committee was set up to consider post-war land policy. Sir Leslie Scott, for whom Birkenhead used to devil in Liverpool, was appointed chairman and Schuster was a member of the committee.[3] Scott had written to Schuster in 1918, "It surely must be possible to simplify 'the thing' somehow ... the public will insist on rough and ready registration by itself, if conveyancers would not provide a simple system to go with it."[4] His object was to assimilate the law of real and personal estate and to free the purchaser from the obligation to inquire into the title of the seller any more than he would have to do if he were buying a share or a parcel of stock. Compulsory registration would be extended to the whole country over a period of years.[5] Birkenhead inherited the problem when he came to

2. Cd 9981, 19,181, X1, p.1.
3. LCO 3/41 Land Transfer Sub-Committee LTSC Record of first meeting. January 21, 1919, p.2.
4. PRO, LCO 2/508.
5. John Campbell. *F.E. Smith. First Earl of Birkenhead*. Jonathan Cape. 1983, pp.484/5.

the Woolsack and immediately ordered Schuster to prepare his department for putting a Bill through Parliament. It was to have a rough ride.

In spite of general agreement that conveyancing must be reformed, there were many vested interests which made progress difficult. The committee was not receptive; the discussion centred on the evils of bureaucracy.[6] Scott argued for registration and gave political reasons. The committee accepted an undefined and limited extension of registration. Schuster added, "part of the political exigency rose from the fact that efforts to extend registration had failed in the past. If the committee failed also, we should be faced with conservatism on the one hand, and Bolshevism on the other." Middlebrook, a Leeds solicitor, sensibly pointed out that "Bolshevism was a revolt against landlords, not against any system of transfer."[7] Nevertheless the committee was persuaded to accept the abolition of the county veto.

Sir Walter Trower, the Law Society representative on the committee, remonstrated strongly. The most he would concede was a "period of probation where an amended Law of Real Property and the amended system of registration could be observed in fair competition."[8] Schuster was now in his element. He was in a position to show his diplomacy, negotiating skills and his ability to find a way to resolve a conflict by compromise. He wrote to Scott about Trower's suggestion of a period of probation:

---

6.   LTSC 10th Meeting, May 7, 1919.
7.   PRO, LCO 2/509. LTC 13th Meeting. June 24, 1919, pp.5-7.
8.   *Ibid.*, 16th Meeting.

"It is, of course, an absurd proposal, but if we could buy the support of the Law Society at that price, I think they [the other members of the committee] might not be content to pay it ... if we do not get their [the Law Society's] fairly active assistance in passing the Bill through both Houses, we shall find covert resistance and obstruction all round."[9]

On hearing of Schuster's hint that a "period of probation" might be acceptable, Trower asked for five years' postponement.[10] In the event the Law of Property Bill provided that no order for extension would be made within three years. C.F. Brickdale, the Chief Registrar of the Land Registry, wrote to Schuster, "a delay of a year or two is nothing to be alarmed at .. I think you have made a very good bargain."[11]

Schuster had done virtually all the negotiating to arrive at a compromise, albeit an uneasy one. Lord Birkenhead saw the opportunity to link his own name with an important piece of legal reform. Schuster wrote to the parliamentary draftsman: "The Lord Chancellor is very anxious to introduce the Bill before Parliament rises ..."[12] The Bill was a combination of two conflicting principles - a simplified system of conveyancing and compulsory registration. It abolished many ancient forms of tenure such as gavelkind and copyholds and contained the extension of registration after three years' delay in the terms of the Schuster-Law Society agreement. Birkenhead, in order to smooth the Bill's

9.   *Ibid.*, July 11 and 12, 1919.
10. *Ibid.*, July 12, 1919.
11. LCO 2/509. C.F. Brickdale to Schuster, October 16, 1919.
12. LCO 2/443. Schuster to A.E. Russell, May 16, 1919.

passage, informed the Cabinet that it was a technical not a political measure. However the Bill met opposition from the future Lord Chancellor, Viscount Cave, the Bar Council and of course the Law Society.[13] Benjamin Cherry, who was assisting both sides in the argument, explained the issue to Schuster as he saw it, "... the law will be made so simple [that] it will be possible to work it with second rate clerks ... This does not suit the conveyancing experts at Lincoln's Inn ... It is a case of conveyancing experts and reactionaries versus the public and solicitors."[14]

Birkenhead put the case for registration of title in strong terms in the House of Lords.[15] Schuster was under pressure to promote this view. He was not in a comfortable position because he was relying on Cherry's expertise - Cherry was the most eminent conveyancer of his day. Schuster well knew that Cherry had been commissioned by the Law Society to draft the Bill in the first place. Indicative of Cherry's dual role is a letter to Schuster in which he put as an aside query, "Have you heard that the solicitors in the Commons are prepared to vote for the Bill if you postpone the first compulsory order for 10 years instead of two (*sic*)."[16] Cherry then drafted amendments to the Bill extending the period of delay for registration to 10 years and recommended them to Schuster. Birkenhead, no doubt influenced by Schuster, decided to give way. He stated in the Lords, "Though I would indeed most gladly have avoided the delay of 10

---

13. Correspondence in LCO 2/445.
14. LCO 444. Cherry to Schuster, July 22, 1920.
15. HL Debates (Hansard) vol.41, cols.513-523, July 26, 1920.
16. LCO 2/444.

years, I am bound to recognise that a period of delay of five or 10 years is small indeed in the history of a nation, or even in the history of a system of land transfer."

The Bill was duly passed on June 8, 1922, and Birkenhead took the credit. The Act was just a prelude to the 1925 land law legislation. The intervening period was used to prepare rules and consolidating legislation; and it enabled Cherry to produce three textbooks. However, compulsory registration was still not countrywide; it was left to counties and boroughs to apply.

Although the London solicitors were more favourable to registration and registration remained confined to London and the suburbs, the Law Society due mainly to its provincial members had won the battle. The result was that in spite of the simplification of conveyancing made by the legislation they were allowed to increase their conveyancing fees by 33-and-a-third per cent in 1925 and retain their monopoly of land transfer. At Cherry's suggestion another huge increase of from 50 per cent to 350 per cent according to the value of dealings was allowed for registrated transfers provided solicitors accepted without objection registration in London and Middlesex. The heyday for the profession continued until 1974 when they lost the monopoly and the volume of conveyancing declined.

In the event Birkenhead's historic law reform measure was not as effective as he and Schuster hoped. The competing interests, viz, the conveyancers, the Bar, the landowners and the Land Registry had been handled by Schuster with some skill. The problem was that Cherry, professing to be an honest broker prepared for reform, was in fact using his considerable influence on behalf of the diehard conveyancers. Nevertheless the legislation for which Birkenhead received the credit was an important step forward.

Administration of the Courts

It was Birkenhead's drive which prepared the way for the property legislation of 1925 but it was on the administrative side of his position that he excelled. In this he was assisted by the loyal Schuster. Preliminary work was done for the Supreme Court (Consolidation) Act 1925 and the Poor Persons Procedure in divorce cases was revised. Schuster took a particular interest in matrimonial matters. Attempts were made to reform the antiquated circuit system but was defeated by the conservatism of local politicians who feared the loss of prestige which would result from the abolition of an Assize. The Judges too were obstructive. Schuster wrote, "... some Judges really do like their progress through the little towns with all the pomp and circumstance that can be mustered ..."[17] He added that Clerks of Assize and subordinates ought to be integrated into central office administration. He was assisted in standardising appointments and conditions of service of all staff by a Royal Commission Report on the Civil Service. As a result of this a Departmental Committee was set up; Schuster, inevitably, was a member. It was divided into three sub-committees to cover the county courts, the Supreme Court and the Probate

17. LCO 2/690.

Service. Minor changes were made to the Probate service, but the Supreme Court was resistant to change. One object was to standardise the appointment and conditions of service for clerks and other posts. Schuster was confident that the Lord Chief Justice, Lord Reading, and the Master of the Rolls, Lord Sterndale, would have agreed with his sub-committee's proposals. Lord Sterndale (a perfect Judge) always exercised his patronage to appoint King's Bench Masters after close consultation with the Lord Chancellor's Office. Lord Reading's successor, Lord Chief Justice Hewart, was likely to be very different. Later Hewart was to write to the Lord Chancellor, Cave:

"When the time comes for me to relinquish the office to my successor, whoever he may be, I desire to relinquish it entirely unimpaired and undiminished in any of the duties, rights or privileges, however apparently unimportant or uninteresting some of them may be thought to be."[18]

Schuster was keen to end the patronage and nepotism of the Judges. If his sub-committee's proposals were not accepted, he wrote,

"... in particular we should have a flood of sons of Judges' clerks and possibly of Judges' clerks themselves, and with all probability of the sons of butlers of these eminent persons ... I do not see how in present circumstances it would be possible to carry a Statute depriving the Lord Chief Justice and the Master of the Rolls of their clerical patronage."[19]

18. LCO 4/70.
19. LCO 2/938, para.38.

It had been noted at the time that five out of eight Clerks of Assize were the sons of Judges and their suitability was often questioned.[20] In spite of all the obstructions some progress was made. Retiring ages were imposed on Masters and Clerks and changes were made in their pension arrangements, but the patronage remained.

Over 50 years were to elapse before Assizes were replaced by the Crown Court by virtue of the Courts Act 1971.

County Courts

Throughout his career Schuster advocated an increase of jurisdiction for the county courts including the allocation of undefended divorce to them. In a letter dated May 13, 1919, to the Secretary of the Law Society, he wrote, "The proceedings of Parliament for the past few years are strewn with the wrecks of county court bills which have never reached harbour because they were overloaded."[21]

Schuster and Birkenhead decided that measures must be taken to improve the administration of the county courts and a Committee on County Court Procedure was set up in 1919 (the Swift Committee 1920, Cmd. 1049). It was agreed that the Treasury had mismanaged the county courts and on August 1, 1922 the responsibility for county courts was transferred from the Treasury to the Lord Chancellor's Office and Schuster became the Accounting Officer. The report of the

---

20. LCO 4/70.
21. LCO 2/234.

committee laid the foundation for the County Courts Act 1924 and for a drastic re-organisation.[22]

Until that time registrars (now District Judges) were minor judicial officers with a limited jurisdiction; they were also responsible for the administration of their courts including the appointment and payment of their staffs. Most of their remuneration came from the profits from fees of court and these could vary according to the amount of business. In wartime for example, court work almost disappeared in many areas. Registrars were appointed by the Judges and many also carried on with their practices as solicitors. The staff they employed were badly paid and the standard was low. They were often retained beyond the age when they were effective because they cost little and had no pension.[23]

The result of the reorganisation was that registrars in the main became independent of private practice and of violent fluctuations of income. Efficiency was increased with the object of devolving more work from the High Court to the county courts.

Appointment of Judges

Exceptionally Birkenhead appointed a county court Judge, Edward Acton, to the High Court. He happened to have been, like Birkenhead, a member of the Northern Circuit and a student at Wadham College, Oxford. Other appointments

---

22. LCO 2/234.
23. LCO 2/709, Memo by Schuster, March 26, 1923.

made by Birkenhead, of six High Court Judges and 10 county court judges, no doubt with Schuster's advice, were considered to be good and without any impropriety.

Accommodation in the House of Lords

Lord Irvine's problems concerning his accommodation in the Palace of Westminster in 1997 were a mirror of Birkenhead's time. The House of Lords had decided many years before that the Lord Chancellor should have an official residence in the Palace of Westminster.[24] The accommodation was extremely antiquated when Birkenhead took office and it was decided to modernise it by, *inter alia*, putting in a second bathroom. The question of the Lord Chancellor's bath excited much ribald fun and spurious indignation in the House of Commons which had not authorised the expenditure. The press made hay. Suggestions were made that the expense (£1,700) could have been used to build 20 cottages for aged workers and that the occupier should pay that sum out of his ministerial salary. On the other hand it was said that a second bathroom in a residence of 33 rooms was not an excessive luxury.[25]

In the event Birkenhead announced that he had never wanted to live in the place anyway and in fact he never did. His successor, Cave, was the first Lord Chancellor to benefit.

---

24. The plans are in Schuster's file LCD.
25. *The Times*, August 12, 1919.

Guardianship of Infants

Following the limited success of the campaign for women's suffrage in 1918, which gave the vote to women who were householders over 30 years of age, women's organisations turned to obtaining equal rights for wives to the legal guardianship of their children. The leading women's group was the National Union of Societies for Equal Citizenship (NUSEC) whose Parliamentary Secretary from 1919 to 1927 was Mrs Eva Hubback who later became the Principal of Morley College.[26]

A Guardianship of Infants Bill was introduced into the Commons in 1920 but was never debated and there were subsequent Bills before the Guardianship of Infants Act was passed in 1925. The Home Office finally took charge of the subject but the LCD via Schuster, was not reticent in giving its views to all concerned.[27] The debate on the matter continued until 1925 and it appears that Birkenhead had little to say about it, leaving the comments of his department to Schuster. His successor Lord Cave was opposed to any change. The progress of the debate under Cave's Chancellorship is covered in Chapter 12.

An Effective Partnership

Schuster probably enjoyed his time with Birkenhead more

---

26. See Chapter 12.
27. Dr Stephen Cretney, *Law Quarterly Review*. January 1996, vol.112, p.114.

than with any other of his Ministers. Completely opposite in character, as a team they were able to make progress in various ways. Birkenhead, the hard-drinking buccaneer with his profligate life-style wanted to make a name for himself. His attitude to life is immortalised in the *Oxford Dictionary of Quotations*: "The world continues to offer glittering prizes to those who have stout hearts and sharp swords." He believed that the motive of self-interest must be the mainspring of human conduct. His cynical comment was countered by a subsequent Lord Chancellor, Viscount Hailsham, who said, "... for the young it is not, oddly enough, the glittering prizes which attract the generous heart of youth; it is, on the contrary, the gleaming sword and the lust for battle."[28]

Because of his life-style, his pursuit of pleasure and sport of all kinds, Birkenhead had little time for mundane matters and so was prepared to delegate. His judgments and much of his writing was given to his private secretary, Roland Burrows, but political matters came to Schuster. This suited Schuster admirably. He could promote his own ideas on account of being backed by his Minister. Birkenhead for his part could use his position and often his brilliance as an advocate to persuade and convince where necessary. An example of this occurred when in 1921 Haldane publicly repeated his argument for a Ministry of Justice. As a result Birkenhead wrote a letter to *The Times* which (according to

---

28. Hansard HL Debates, vol.230, col.373. Quoted in R.F.V. Heuston. *Lives of the Lord Chancellors 1940-1970*. Clarendon Press, 1987.

Gavin Drewry) was drafted by Schuster,[29] pointing out that he entirely disapproved of any such proposal. In a book *Points of View* there is an article by Lord Birkenhead entitled "A Ministry of Justice". That article was drafted by Schuster, settled in consultation between him and Lord Birkenhead, and every word of it has his entire approval.[30]

In spite of his faults Birkenhead was a very talented man and not always a bombastic orator. He performed well in court, frequently giving unreserved judgments. In *DPP v. Beard* [1920] AC 479, he sat with seven Law Lords to determine the necessary intent required by the law to obtain a conviction for murder, and the effect of drunkenness making the defendant less or incapable of forming that intent. In Cabinet he had been described as having "almost taciturn wisdom in council" not unlike other Lord Chancellors.

29. Gavin Drewry, "Lord Haldane's Ministry of Justice - Stillborn or Strangled at Birth?" *Public Administration*, vol.61, winter 1983, p.396.
30. *Ibid.*, pp.398-9.

CHAPTER 10

The Fight for Women's Rights

The Intolerably Persistent Mrs Hubback

The 1914-18 War had added fuel to the claims of suffragettes, and in Birkenhead's time as Chancellor, there was continuous lobbying by the women's organisations to improve the rights of women. The resistance from the predominately male Establishment proved hard to break down.

Since 1857 the only ground for divorce had been adultery. In 1920 Lord Buckmaster sponsored a Bill which provided five grounds for divorce. Birkenhead made a wonderful speech in support of the Bill.[1] Yet Birkenhead, like Schuster, was never in favour of equal rights for women and their attitudes are revealed in the *Lady Rhondda* case (*Viscountess Rhondda's Claim* [1922] 2 AC 339), and during the prolonged discussions on the subject of the guardianship of infants.

Lady Rhondda was the daughter of D.A. Thomas, food controller during the 1914 war; he had been made a Viscount with the remainder that his daughter should succeed to the title on his demise. She petitioned the House of Lords claiming that she was entitled to receive a writ summoning her to sit as a peer. The statute on which the claim was based was the Sex Disqualification (Removal) Act 1919 which provided that a person shall not be disqualified by sex or marriage from the exercise of any private function. The petition was referred to the Committee of Privileges. Lord

---

1. *Hansard* (HL) March 24, 1920, vol.39, col.663 and *The Times*, March 25, 1920.

Haldane, who presided over the Committee, advised that the Act allowed women to sit in the Lords. The Committee, consisting of three Law Lords and four lay peers, reported in favour of the petitioner. However, when the report came before the Lords it was moved that it be referred back and the House accepted that motion. A committee on House of Lords reform was sitting at the time and Birkenhead remarked, "If we are to be abolished I think I would rather perish in the exclusive company of my own sex." On the rehearing by the Committee of Privileges 10 Law Lords and 12 lay peers voted against the petition and only two Law Lords and two lay peers voted in favour.[2] Birkenhead's judgment, rejecting the claim in the Appeal Court case which followed, ran to 32 pages in the *Law Reports*. Surely there was some input here by Schuster and Birkenhead's private secretary, Burrows? It was not until 1957 that peeresses were entitled to sit in the House of Lords.

The Lords took up a similar position in the case of Lady St Davids who sought to revive abeyant peerages. Schuster commented in January 1923, "She collects peerages as she might collect postage stamps."[3]

Background to the Guardianship of Infants Act 1925

Schuster's opinion of the *Lady Rhondda* case is not apparent

2. Second Earl of Birkenhead. *The Life of F.E. Smith, First Earl of Birkenhead*, by his son. Eyre and Spottiswood, 1960, p.418.
3. LCO 2/598.

from the records but his attitude on the rights of women, the topical question of the day, are revealed in the deliberations which proceeded the Guardianship of Infants Act 1925.

The subject arose on the tabling of a Private Member's Bill in 1920 by Mrs Margaret Wintringham, MP. The moving force behind the Bill was Mrs Eva Hubback, Parliamentary Secretary to the National Union of Societies for Equal Citizenship (NUSEC), who is said, "... involved him [Schuster] in wearisome correspondence with sundry women's organisations lobbying for them, in particular with the intolerably persistent Mrs Hubback."[4]

As described by his deputy, Schuster "had many of the prejudices common amongst Englishmen of his class ..."[5] and one of these in his early life was his attitude to the position of women in society. In the 1920s a change in his opinion can be noticed and this, in no small measure, was due to his contacts with the "intolerably persistent" Mrs Hubback. Tiresome she was at first but Schuster's irritation developed over some years into respect for this remarkable woman and her ability was recognised by the Department. So much so that her name was put forward by the Department in 1946 to be a member of the Denning Committee on Matrimonial Causes, although it was not accepted. She died in 1949.

She was born Eva Marian Spielsman of an affluent Jewish family in London in 1886. Until she went to Newnham College in Cambridge in 1905, she had moved almost entirely within a Jewish community. At Cambridge she made many

---

4. Dr Patrick Pollen. *Guide to the Records of the LCD*. HMSO, 1988.
5. *DNB*. 1951-1960, p.868.

non-Jewish friends including Bill Hubback, who shared her interest in the political and social questions of the day. They married in 1911, and he became a university lecturer in Liverpool and ultimately Manchester. Sadly he was wounded in the 1914-18 war and died as a result in 1917. Eva was left with three young children. She had a job as a lecturer at Newnham College until she moved with the children to London where she had friends in the Women's Suffrage Movement. At first she worked in the Information Bureau of the National Union of Women's Suffrage Society which, having achieved limited women' suffrage in 1918, changed its name in 1919 to the National Union of Societies for Equal Citizenship. She became the Parliamentary Secretary to the Union in 1920 when Dame Millicent Fawcett was the President.

The aims of NUSEC were:

1. Equal pay for equal work and equal opportunities in industry and the professions.
2. Reform of the divorce law and with the law dealing with solicitation and prostitution. An equal moral standard.
3. Pensions for civilian widows.
4. Equal franchise. An extension of women's franchise (limited at the time to women over 30, married, owned a house or lived in unfurnished rooms; over five million women were unenfranchised).
5. Equal Rights of Guardianship for both parents.
6. The opening of the legal profession to women including their right to become solicitors, barristers and magistrates.

Eva Hubback became Principal of Morley College in 1927 continuing to work for the NUSEC until she resigned in 1938.

The tremendous efforts she had made in pursuing the aims of the Society had achieved some success. Her methods in trying to mould the form of legislation which had originated in the minds of others into something nearer the aims of the Society are illustrated by Eleanor Rathbone, the President of NUSEC. She said in 1935 at Bedford College in the Fawcett lecture entitled, "The Harvest of the Women's Movement":

> "Another lesson we learned was the importance of being early in the field. If some legislative change is known to be projected which one wants to influence, it does not do to wait until the authorities have definitely made up their minds as to the form of change, much less until the Bill is actually drafted and may be difficult to amend without upsetting the balance of its parts. Get at the people responsible - the Minister or better still the officials or committees which advise him - while they are still in the stage of welcoming evidence and suggestions rather than of resenting criticism."

Eva Hubback certainly adopted that policy in her persistent importuning of Schuster.

The 1920 Bill sought to give equal rights to both husbands and wives in the parenting of their children. This was regarded as revolutionary at the time by most lawyers and Schuster was no exception. He, initially at least, regarded the Bill as so serious that it would drastically change family relationship and cause a breakdown in society.[6]

---

6. See S.M. Cretney. "What Will Women Want Next?" 112 *LQR*, January 1996.

Schuster - "A Fellow Conspirator"

The argument continued from 1920 to 1925 and what is significant is the extent to which Schuster concerned himself with the progress of the matter. Indeed it is perhaps an example of a civil servant, an official of the executive, venturing too far into the affairs of the legislature. The subject of family relationships at that time was within province of the Home Office where Schuster's old associate, Sir John Anderson (later Lord Waverley), was the Permanent Secretary. Schuster was determined that his views would count and it seems that the Home Office was prepared to allow Schuster to lead the opposition to the Bill. It did not progress, or was not allowed to, and by March 1, 1922, Schuster was minuting Birkenhead that it was "desirable to postpone for as long as possible the appearance of opposition to the Bill."[7] He noted that it was undesirable to annoy women who were the main backers of the Bill and that some members of the Cabinet were in favour. In the same month he was telling the Solicitor-General that the courts could not become involved in every family difference in every household and that his Department's main interest in the matter was to prevent the county courts or the High Court from having their time occupied by such matters. He could not accept the idea of joint responsibility for children; he thought that a household should be regarded as a single unit and that there should be one person to make the decision. Equal authority for parents was nonsense because "if two

---

7. LCO 2/757.

persons have equal rights a deadlock ensues whenever there is a difference between them."[8]

Mrs Wintringham's Bill had lapsed and other Bills were introduced. In evidence to a Joint Select Committee on the Bill on July 25, 1922, Schuster said that a court is concerned with the definite ascertainment of the rights of the parties. He could not accept that wives had rights within the family, "... there are no rights here. It is a question of discretion. To take a ridiculous instance, a dispute whether a child is to go to one school, or another - how on earth is the court going to deal with that?"[9] At that time it was difficult for a traditionalist to envisage that such questions could be dealt with routinely as they are in courts today. But with better reason Schuster was also concerned about the additional Judges who would be required to settle such disputes.

In January, 1923, the matter was referred to another Select Committee and a Schuster minute of March 23, 1923 to the Lord Chancellor, Cave, stated that giving both parents equal rights over their children would be "... to substitute a legal for a domestic forum in every household; to multiply the causes of strife, and to bring into courts, to the encumbrance of their proper business, a multitude of trivial disputes." Lord Cave, conservative as ever, hoped that the Select Committee would "condemn the Bill with praise" so that it would not progress further.[10] Schuster was prepared to pull all possible strings to support his Chancellor and stop the Bill. In 1923 he

---

8. *Ibid.*
9. *Ibid.*
10. *Ibid.*

asked the Home Secretary's Private Secretary to stimulate some private peer to put up an argument against the Bill and suggested that the Government spokesman, Lord Onslow, might stir up hereditary peers such as Willoughby de Broke or Stuart or Worsley, so that the House would see that the opposition was not merely official. Lord Onslow did in fact get up a "band of stalwarts" and Schuster said that the Lord Chancellor, Cave, hoped that Onslow would "continue this good work."[11] However, the serious opposition was coming from the officials of the Lord Chancellor's Department, the Home Office and the Health Ministry, supported strongly by Lord Cave. The Cabinet became aware of the official opposition and a small informal Cabinet Committee was appointed. In the meantime, Schuster had met the chairman of the Select Committee, Lord Wemyss and a member, Lord Askwith, who was a supporter of the Bill. Wemyss, quite rightly, thought that Schuster, a civil servant, had exceeded his authority in seeing Askwith; but Schuster merely commented that Wemyss was "very prickly and jealous of outside interference."[12] But opinions were changing. Schuster in his frequent meetings and correspondence with Mrs Hubback of the NUSEC had come to appreciate her arguments. A compromise was needed and negotiating compromises was Schuster's forte.

In July, 1923, Parliamentary counsel had produced draft clauses which eventually formed the basis of the compromise which became the Guardianship of Infants Act 1925.

---

11. *Ibid.*
12. *Ibid.*

In 1924 these draft clauses were embodied in a Government Bill regarded as a compromise Bill. The Labour Government was in power with Lord Haldane as Lord Chancellor. This compromise Bill did not concede that parents should have equal rights in respect of their children but it did provide that "... in deciding questions as to the custody and upbringing of a child, the court should have regard solely to the welfare of the child." Lord Haldane said, when introducing the Bill, "... the interest of the infant is to be looked at exclusively in judging what is right to be done."[13]

The First and Paramount Principle

It was Lord Cave, Lord Haldane's predecessor, who determined the final wording. He put down an amendment inserting the "first and paramount" principle. He argued that the welfare of the child should not be the sole consideration for the court to consider. There were other considerations such as the wishes of both parents and their conduct, the suitability of the mother to take charge of children, the responsibility of the father, questions of religion, etc. Consequently he proposed that, "... instead of saying that the sole consideration shall be the welfare of the infant, that the welfare of the infant shall be the first and paramount consideration, and that we should leave the Judge at liberty to consider other matters ..."[14] Lord Haldane accepted the

---

13. *Hansard* (HL). June 3, 1924, vol.57, col.794.
14. *Hansard* (HL). June 9, 1924, vol.57, col.349.

amendment. There was much discussion about this wording prior to the Children Act of 1989, Section 1 of which includes that, "... the child's welfare shall be the court's paramount consideration."

Schuster may have had some influence on the views of both Cave and Haldane. At an earlier stage he was claiming that the wording of Clause 1 of the original Bill had been "... hammered out inch by inch between ourselves and the promoters of Mrs Wintringham's Bill."[15]

Mrs Hubback was disappointed that the compromise had not resulted in parents having equal rights and she wrote to Schuster of their "... joint labours having been entirely in vain." Schuster wrote to her, "... a great disappointment to me that the turn of the events destroyed the Bill."[16] As he had worked hard on the wording of the Bill and as his affinity with Mrs Hubback had grown, he probably meant what he said.

In fact the Act contained many provisions which were of value to women and it was welcomed by many of the women's organisations and in pamphlet written by Mrs Hubback (September 1, 1924) she stated that, "in the opinion of many [it] will serve as a jumping-off ground in the future for the attainment of the full measure of reform required."

In the Annual Report of the NUSEC 1925-1926, there was a note, "your Committee would like to express its warm thanks to Sir Claud Schuster for the valuable help he gave for three years running in connection with the Bill in the House

---

15. Schuster to Greer. May 30, 1924. LCO 2/758.
16. *Ibid.*

of Lords."

It was not until 1973 that the Guardianship of Infants Act 1973 provided that parents should have equal rights and authority over the upbringing of their children. The Children Act 1989 went even further. It shifted the emphasis from rights to responsibility and made it possible for persons other than parents to apply for parental responsibility. It also made provision for such responsibility to be shared, for example between an unmarried father and a person with whom a child resides.

In 1928 academics were saying that in the previous two years the institution of the family, one of the pivots of the social system, had been subjected to drastic alteration by several Acts of Parliament, viz., Guardianship Act 1925, Summary Jurisdiction (Married Women) Act 1925, Legitimacy Act 1926 and the Adoption of Children Act 1926. It was also alleged that the parliamentary draftsmen had deliberately put devices into the Schedules which made it possible to defeat the objectives of the statutes.

Judicial Discretion to Order Reasonable Provision for Dependants

Concurrently with their campaign for equal parental rights, the NUSEC were also pressing for legislation which would enable the courts to upset wills which did not provide adequately for dependants. At the time a person of sound mind, memory and understanding could make a will disinheriting his wife and children, and they would have no legal redress. Even an eccentric will by which a man left his wife five pounds and his pet parrot, or because he hated all human beings had left all his property to a cat's home, could satisfy the test of testamentary capacity. The concern of the NUSEC was for widows and children who, because of capricious wills had been left destitute and forced to accept poor law relief. Supported by her formidable President, Eleanor Rathbone, Mrs Hubback was again the leader of the campaign. She had persuaded Lord Astor to put forward a motion in the House of Lords with the object of setting up a select committee and was having difficulty in getting support. On May 2, 1928, she wrote to Schuster asking him to spare her, "not more than three minutes soon"; by this time he had a cordial relationship with Mrs Hubback and he readily agreed to the request.[17] On May 11 she was making the moderate request in a letter to Lord Hailsham that she did not seek any, "... rash change in our law of testamentary freedom" but that something had to be done to protect widows - mostly from the lower middle class left entirely without provision. On May 18 she was telling Schuster that if any reform were made, in the light of the discouraging attitudes displayed in the House of Lords debates it would be what Lord Merrivale called, "a microscopic measure based on the [New Zealand] Testator's Family Maintenance Act 1900."[18]

Lord Astor was acting as the spokesman for the NUSEC and Schuster arranged for him to consult Sir Benjamin Cherry

17. LCO 2/1185.
18. *Ibid.*

who produced a lengthy memorandum on the subject. As in
the deliberations leading to the land law reforms effected by
the 1925 property legislation, it seems that Cherry was once
again acting as a double agent. He argued in the
memorandum against any restriction on the powers of
disposition. Possibly Schuster thought that Cherry would
persuade Lord Astor that the whole idea was a non-starter.
Cherry concluded his memorandum with:

> "Thus any proposal, involving a restriction on powers of
> disposition, must *prima facie*, be regarded with grave suspicion,
> and its adoption can only be justified where the object in view
> is paramount to all other considerations, and cannot be achieved
> by means of any other expedient."[19]

At this time the Representation of the People Act 1928 had
become law and the first general election in which the
franchise was open to women on the same terms as men, was
imminent. Reform on the subject of poor women being,
"bundled out into the streets after their husband's death,"
could attract women's votes. The NUSEC produced a
pamphlet and launched a determined campaign. Stanley
Baldwin, then Prime Minister, and Winston Churchill
received a delegation but did not commit themselves. Lloyd
George and Ramsay Macdonad, the leaders of the Liberal and
Labour parties, were strongly in support.

Sankey, the incoming Lord Chancellor after the election,
was sympathetic. Lord Buckmaster accepted that women
were in a condition of "economic subjection" but thought that

---

19. LCO 2/1185. May 10, 1928.

the courts would not exercise discretionary powers well. Hailsham was implacably against the whole idea and surprisingly Haldane was adamant that the State should not intervene in matters of wills; he said, "... if there is to be a tribunal set up, I would much rather set it up out of a Bench of Bishops."[20]

Eventually in 1931 a Bill was introduced by Eleanor Rathbone which was, as she had hoped, referred to a Joint Select Committee of both Houses. In spite of his, "grave suspicion" about the objects of the Bill, Cherry appears to have drafted it. On February 16, 1931 Schuster was describing the Bill as, "... carefully drawn, I think by Cherry; and like most of Cherry's work it is probably rather over-elaborate."[21] Reference to a Select Committee was the course favoured by Schuster, and Mrs Hubback was pleased with the progress it made. On March 4, 1931 she wrote a fulsome letter to Schuster thanking him personally and asking him to convey the thanks of the NUSEC to the Lord Chancellor, Sankey, "... for the help you both gave to the Wills and Intestacies Bill ... I felt doubtful at the time as to what the issue would be, and was delighted that the efforts of the Lord Chancellor prevailed."[22] Schuster lost no time in ensuring that the Committee was formed to his liking. He suggested to Lord Astor that Lord Thankerton should be chairman and on March 11, 1931 he wrote to Lord Astor, "... officially it is not the Lord Chancellor's job to settle names (for select

20. *Hansard* HL. May 16, 1928, vol.71, col.47.
21. LCO 2/1187.
22. *Ibid.*

committees) but he might be of some assistance to you in procuring suitable people to serve."[23]

Finally, the Committee unequivocally rejected the Rathbone Bill as being too complicated but it did recommend that a measure on the lines proposed would be worthy of serious considerations by Parliament.[24] Mrs Hubback and her colleagues had won an important victory, but the end was not yet in sight; this was just the end of the beginning.

Mrs Hubback, somewhat naively, had regarded Schuster as a fellow conspirator in the campaign. As in the campaign for equal parental rights for both parents, his approach to the question had been cautious, "... the subject is full of traps for the unwary ... [and] is so intricate and so new that it requires ... rather prolonged examination."[25] But as his rapport with Mrs Hubback developed, he became more sympathetic. Nevertheless he was careful, as a civil servant, not to express his opinion too openly. A Powers of Disinheritance Bill giving the courts absolute discretion was introduced in 1933 by Sir John Wardlaw Milne. J.F.W. Galbraith, KC, MP, was boasting that he had put down a very large number of amendments in order to put an end to the Bill. The result was that it was "talked out". Galbraith wrote triumphantly to Schuster on April 30, 1934, to the effect that he had succeeded in finally disposing of the issue. Schuster tactfully replied to Galbraith that he had, "... worked the business with extraordinary guile

---

23. *Ibid.*
24. Joint Select Committee Report on Wills and Intestacies (Family Maintenance Bill 1930-31) HC. 127, para.7.
25. LCO 2/1187.

and success.[26]

The debate continued; a body of opinion argued that the proposed measure would only concern the rich and that the ordinary working woman was not interested. Schuster agreed in a letter dated February 16, 1931, that the ordinary working woman was not very interested, but that the Bill excited, "a great deal of interest among that wing of the professional feminists who belong to the upper and middle classes."[27] Parliamentary counsel decided that the 1934 Bill would not do in its current form and Schuster having been sympathetic to the cause, then became concerned at the amount of litigation it might cause and stated that there was no substantial evidence of any need for alteration of the present law.[28] Another Bill was introduced in 1936; it was strongly opposed by Hailsham.

Schuster in writing to Simonds on October 29, was stating Hailsham's opinion that to discuss in open court a testator's reasons for disinheriting his wife or other dependants, "... would arouse forgotten scandals and embitter family life."[29] But Hailsham had suffered a stroke towards the end of 1936 and his statements after that date were either those of a sick man who was losing interest in the subject or were influenced to some degree by Schuster. The records show that Hailsham agreed, with some reservations, that the Bill should no longer be blocked, in particular that jurisdiction should be confined to the High Court. It was, save that an amendment provided

---

26. LCO 2/1188.
27. LCO 2/1187.
28. *Ibid.*
29. LCO 2/1189.

that the county courts were to be given jurisdiction over estates up to £600 in value. The Bill became the Inheritance (Family Provision) Act 1938 and another of the NUSEC's campaigns had finally succeeded due largely to the persistence of Eva Hubback with the help of her so called "fellow conspirator" Sir Claud Schuster.

Divorce Law

The Gorell Commission had recommended an extension of the grounds for divorce in 1912 but Bills presented by Lord Buckmaster in 1919 and 1920 did not progress. In the 1930s pressure from the public for change was revived, notably by A.P. Herbert, the MP and humorous writer. He had written a book *Holy Deadlock* calling attention to the need, in many circumstances, for divorce to be easier to obtain. The President of the Probate, Divorce and Admiralty Division, Lord Merrivale, was for ever resistant to change. The Government did not like the subject and dragged its feet. Schuster was prepared for change but his main concern was the working of the Poor Persons Procedure in divorce cases. He had constantly to remind the Law Society that, for the system to work there must be a sufficient number of solicitors willing to participate on a charitable basis. His interest in and knowledge of matrimonial affairs was apparent and he was appointed chairman of a Departmental Committee on Divorce in 1929 which recommended changes.[30] After many

---

30. LCO 2/1055. 79 Cmd 3375.

amendments A.P. Herbert's Bill finally reached the Statute Book as the Matrimonial Causes Act 1937.

CHAPTER 11

Lord Cave -
October 25, 1922 to January 23, 1924 and November 7, 1924 to March 29, 1928

The Consummate Conservative

By the mid-summer of 1922 the Coalition Government with Lloyd George as Prime Minister was showing signs of breaking up. Suspicious that honours had been sold for the benefit of Lloyd George culminated in the South African, Sir Joseph Robinson, having to withdraw his acceptance of a peerage in circumstances which reflected badly on the Government. The majority of the Liberal Party which supported Lloyd George met and decided that he must go. Birkenhead, a loyal supporter of Lloyd George, was scathingly contemptuous of his fellow Liberals and said so in no uncertain terms. The Coalition ended, and in the dissolution honours Birkenhead was granted an earldom. It was said that on his demission Birkenhead had recommended that Lord Cave should be his successor.

Although the subsequent election in 1922 resulted in a landslide victory for the Conservatives and Bonar Law became Prime Minister, his Government lasted little more than a year. As expected, the Lord Chancellor he appointed was Lord Cave who was to serve for two separate periods divided by Lord Haldane's short spell with the first Labour Government.

The circumstances of Cave's appointment are interesting. Sir Charles Mallett, who later wrote a biography of Lord

Cave, corresponded with Schuster following information he had received from Lady Cave. She was very close to, and supportive of, her husband. She was not an admirer of Birkenhead's way of life and maintained that he had had nothing to do with the appointment of her husband to the Woolsack. In the correspondence Schuster related that Birkenhead had liked and respected Cave, although they had had differences over the Law of Property Bill and the Irish problem. He surmised that Cave and particularly Lady Cave had remembered those differences. Schuster said that Lady Cave could not have any knowledge of what had happened. He was adamant that one day in the Lord Chancellor's room at the House of Lords, Birkenhead had discussed the matter with him. There and then in Schuster's presence, Birkenhead wrote a note to Bonar Law suggesting that his successor should be Cave.[1]

Schuster to the Rescue

Cave had been Conservative MP for Richmond in 1906 and had had a distinguished judicial rather than a political career, becoming a Lord of Appeal in 1919. He performed the Lord Chancellor's judicial duties in the House of Lords from 1922 to 1928, ie, during his two periods as Lord Chancellor and also when the ailing Haldane occupied the Woolsack in 1924. This he did at Haldane's request.

On July 25, 1924, during the time when Cave was

---

1. LCD files.

undertaking Haldane's judicial work, Lord and Lady Cave were required to attend a reception for the American Bar Association which had been invited over by the English and Canadian Bar Association. There were 2,000 men and 1,500 ladies to be received by Haldane and former Lord Chancellors. Haldane and his sister Elizabeth received for the first 15 minutes and thereafter 15 minute shifts the Caves, the Birkenheads and the Buckmasters continued until all had been received. Once the Birkenheads were 10 minutes late in relieving the Caves. Lady Cave wrote, "They did not arrive a minute too soon; we sank into armchairs at the back and were revived by sherry obtained from somewhere by Sir Claud Schuster." She also commented that Haldane was not so fortunate, all that could be found for him was beer.[2]

Constitutional Problems

Having been appointed by Bonar Law, within three months Cave found himself having to persuade him not to resign. Baldwin as Chancellor of the Exchequer had agreed that Britain should pay the United States £900 million to settle the debts incurred during the war. Bonar Law thought it was most unfair that Britain should have to pay this sum when she had received nothing from her debtors in Europe. On January 31, 1923 the Cabinet, without the presence of Bonar Law who had threatened to resign, met in the Lord Chancellor's room in the House of Lords. Schuster was

2. Sir Charles Mallett. *Lord Cave: A Memoir.* John Murray. 1931, pp.34/35.

present in a secretarial capacity. The Cabinet agreed that however bad the terms of the settlement were, it would be worse to repudiate the agreement and that the Duke of Devonshire and Cave should persuade Bonar Law not to resign. This they succeeded in doing. However, in the same year Baldwin became Prime Minister in succession to Bonar Law. The subject of protectionism then caused such a furore that Baldwin dissolved Parliament.

In the election of December 6, 1923 the Conservatives lost 117 seats. They were still the largest party in the House but without an overall majority. Cave had to advise the Government whether or not it should meet Parliament or resign at once. He advised that on the opening of Parliament the Government should be prepared to meet a "no confidence" amendment to the King's speech. The Government was defeated and the King sent for Ramsay MacDonald as the leader of the next largest party in the Commons.

This situation gave rise to several Constitutional problems which Cave, still Lord Chancellor and therefore the Constitutional adviser to the Monarchy, was called upon to answer. Schuster was an expert on the intricacies of the Constitution and the response, especially the phraseology in the correspondence, bear the hallmarks of his work

Cave was a die-hard Conservative and to him and many others, including Schuster, the idea of a Labour Government was alarming, but duty called. The first question was whether Ramsay MacDonald, not yet a Privy Counsellor, could he be appointed Prime Minister? The following answer was sent by Cave to Sir Maurice Hankey, the Cabinet Secretary:

House of Lords
9.1.24

Sir Maurice Hankey,

In my opinion no person should be allowed to kiss hands as Prime Minister or First Lord of the Treasury without first being sworn as a member of the Privy Council. It is the rule that every member of the Cabinet must be a Privy Counsellor, and take the oath of secrecy: and a *fortiori* the Prime Minister, who will be the *primus inter pares* and will advise the Sovereign as to the persons whom he is to take into this counsels, should be bound by the oath.

It is conceivable - although I know of no precedent for this course - that the King might commission Mr Ramsay MacDonald to submit names for a Ministry to be formed under his premiership, and postpone the ceremony of kissing hands until he has been sworn of the Privy Council, but in that case he would until he had kissed hands be in the position not of a Prime Minister but of a person negotiating for the formation of a government.[3]

The procedure suggested by Cave was followed. Thirteen Privy Counsellors including MacDonald were sworn in and immediately afterwards he was invited by the King to form a government. That night the King, George V, wrote in his diary: "I had an hour's talk with him, he impressed me very much; he wishes to do the right thing. Today, 23 years ago dear Grandmama died. I wonder what she would have thought of a Labour Government."[4]

There were now three large political parties in the House of Commons instead of two and this complicated any change

---

3. Royal Archives K. 1918 (131) 1.
4. H. Nicholson. *King George V*. 1952, p.284.

of government. Arising from that situation another Constitutional question was indirectly posed even before MacDonald had kissed hands. MacDonald had indicated in a magazine article that he could have Parliament dissolved at any time, and would accept office from the King on that understanding. This was presumably with the object of gaining more seats in a subsequent election. The propriety of this was questioned by Lord Stamfordham, the King's Secretary. Cave replied at great length, reviewing all the authorities on the subject and concluding that the Prime Minister does not have the right to a dissolution when he pleases. It is for the King to exercise his prerogative of dissolution on the advice of Ministers after considering all the circumstances.[5] This reply is printed in full in *Lives of the Lord Chancellors* by R.F.V. Heuston:

"A dissolution is rightly demanded in two circumstances only:

1. Where there is reason to suppose that the House of Commons has ceased to represent the opinion of the country.
2. When a large change has been made in the electoral conditions and it is proper that the newly enfranchised electors should enjoy their rights at the earliest possible opportunity.

"If a Prime Minister asked for a dissolution and the Monarch refused that would be unconstitutional unless another or other Ministers were to support the Monarch."[6]

---

5. Royal Archives K. 1918 (135).
6. Clarendon Press 1964, p.43314 (quoted from *Anson's Law and Custom of the Constitution*, 5th edn, 1922, vol.I, pp.327-9).

Heuston comments: "If it had not been for his years as a Member for Kingston, it is doubtful if Cave, bred at the Chancery Bar, could have produced such a convincing and lucid exposition of constitutional law and practice."[7]

This was surely not Cave's work but Schuster's. In words and phrases it is in the style of Schuster - he was always "fluent on paper" and constitutional questions were his speciality.

Indeed the memorandum he wrote at that time and another that he wrote in 1935 have been described as, "of impeccable orthodoxy".[8]

On many occasions Schuster was required to communicate with the King's Private Secretary, for example: when the King was unable to perform his functions because of illness; when he wished to express his opinion on current affairs; as well as when he sought advice on the dissolution of Parliament. As Schuster wrote in a minute in 1941:

> "It has, however, for a long time been the habit of successive Private Secretaries to the King to ask for a view of the Lord Chancellor on matters which are not directly the concern or function of the Lord Chancellor's Office, in accordance with a general but undefined idea that in matters which raise semi-legal or semi-constitutional points the Lord Chancellor stands in a peculiarly confidential relationship with the Crown."[9]

---

7. *Ibid.*, p.435.
8. *Guide to the Records of the LC*, p.288.
9. LCO 2/1131.

King George V's Attempt to Change the Law

In 1922 the King was disgusted and nauseated with the evidence published daily in the case of *Russell v. Russell* ([1924] AC 687) where the question for the House of Lords was whether evidence of non-access by the husband might be given in divorce proceedings which, if accepted, would have the effect of bastardising a child born in wedlock. In that case, and another, the King wanted the law to be changed so that the case could be heard in camera or that there should be reporting restrictions. In each case Schuster made a well-reasoned reply to the King's Secretary, Lord Stamfordham, which politely told the King he was not in a position to change the law.[10] However, Cave agreed that a Private Member's Bill could be brought knowing that it had little hope of becoming law. Schuster was not in favour of the Private Bill procedure. On later occasions he was to say that such a Bill was "a most outrageous attempt to pervert the course of justice" and that, "attempts, such as have never been made within my experience, to use [Private Bill] procedure to upset private rights for private purposes".[11]

Lord Cave's Second Term

In November 1924 when Lord Cave became Lord Chancellor for the second time, he was welcomed by the Judges. Lord

---

10. LCO 2/775.
11. LCO 2/1222.

Dunedin (Lord of Appeal in Ordinary) sent a letter which spoke for the rest:

> "It is not often that a galley-slave who has been emancipated comes back with pleasure to his old master; but so it is when I find myself once more under your rule. Not that I have anything to complain of my later superior. Really, however, Lord Chancellors are persons of whom I have sampled so many that I fear them not. The real persons who apply the lash when the slave 'sugars' at the oar are overseers Schuster and Neish (Sir C. Neish, Parliamentary Private Secretary to Lord Cave). I have, however, discovered how to secure mild treatment from them, viz. By fostering their just wrath against other colleagues - so my own life is tranquil."[12]

On his return to the Woolsack and the Lord Chancellor's duties Cave was popular in the Office. With Schuster's help he had no problems with the administrative side of the work. His appointments to the senior judiciary were generally approved. By appointing Henry Slesser, KC, who had been Solicitor-General in the Labour Government, to the High Court Bench, he showed that he did so without political bias. He made some alterations to the constitution of advisory committees for magistrates. Henceforth members of those committees were appointed for six years and half the committee were required to retire every three years.

---

12. Sir Charles Mallett, p.271.

1925 - A Memorable Year

1925 is memorable for the passing of the very important property legislation, the creation of which was begun in 1913 when Haldane was Lord Chancellor. He had reason to celebrate and perhaps the following comment by Harold Laski in a letter to a friend shows that he did so:

> "... another dinner with Haldane and a 'galaxy of Judges' - Dundedin, Sumner and Shaw, all Law Lords who had sat with five or six Lord Chancellors, plus Schuster, who had served five."[13]

It was during the Chancellorships of Haldane, Birkenhead, and to a lesser extent, Cave, that progress had been made in preparing the reforming property legislation. Cave had been critical of Birkenhead's 1920 Bill and caused some delay so that it was not passed until 1922. By the time the other seven statutes came before the Lords, Cave was Lord Chancellor, and it was thought that he might be obstructive. He was not, stating that because he had led the Opposition to the original Bill it did not mean that he would oppose all the Bills as amended. The Law of Property Act and six ancillary Acts were eventually passed in 1925 and came into force on January 1, 1926.

Also in 1925 improvements were made in the practice and procedures in the Royal Courts of Justice by the Supreme Court of Judicature (Consolidation) Act 1925. In the same

13. M de W Howe (ed.) *Holmes Laski letters.* "Laski to Holmes", 2 vols. 1953, p.764.

year by the County Courts Act 1924 the county courts were reorganised and the staffs became government servants instead of employees of local registrars. However, industrial trouble was brewing. In 1926 Douglas Hogg (later Lord Chancellor) prepared a Bill making general and "sympathetic" strikes illegal but Sir John Simon (also later Lord Chancellor) opposed it, maintaining that such strikes were already illegal and he advised his party that such a bill would be provocative. But there was provocation from other sources and the General Strike did take place causing turmoil in society and within the political parties. What Schuster thought at the time is not known.

During the same year Cave, it seems before his time, proposed a thorough reform of the House of Lords. He suggested that there should be a limit of 350 peers, some to be nominated and some to be elected from among themselves. That is an idea which may well have had Schuster's support but there was opposition from several quarters and no legislation was introduced.

Lady Cave describes the problems her husband had in piloting the Landlord and Tenant Bill through the Lords in 1927, and refers to his declining health. He was already exhausted after a hard year's work and he had to get the Bill through by Christmas. There were many questions from the peers and the debate continued over several nights. Cave told Lady Cave, "My noble friends are really rather difficult to satisfy". He was worn out and too tired to sleep, she said, and the Bill was passed in practically the same terms as those in which it was submitted. Lord Cave was never well again. Lady Cave recognised that her husband had been helped by

Lord Beauchamp and that Sir Claud Schuster understood what a great strain it had been for Lord Cave.[14]

A Legendary Figure

During his four-and-a-half years with Lord Cave, Schuster's stature and influence as a Whitehall mandarin had grown steadily. In 1926 he was able to say, "I am anything but busy",[15] but by this very nature it was impossible for him to be idle. He was prepared to delegate, eg, Napier was given the responsibility for county courts. Schuster spent one hour each morning with his Lord Chancellor; this light work-load enabled him to take part in committees and inquiries on a variety of subjects in the course of which he "... acquired a knowledge of men and business which made him formidable indeed, as well as a reputation for incisive and sometimes impatient interventions".[16] He concerned himself with so many subjects that it is not surprising that he made enemies. Napier's obituary states that:

> "... his method of obtaining his ends did not, however, always escape criticism and with the years an increasing dislike of opposition tended to strain his relations with certain members of the judiciary and heads of department with whom he was brought into contact."[17]

---

14. Sir Charles Mallett, p.38.
15. LCO 2/696.
16. Dr Patrick Pollen. *The Guide to the Records of the LCD*. HMSO, 1988, p.26.
17. *The Times*, July 29, 1956.

Notwithstanding that tendency he certainly had a good relationship with Lord Cave. Indeed, he was able to maintain good relations with his various Chancellors be they conservative, progressive or simply difficult to work with.

CHAPTER 12

Lord Haldane -
January 23, 1924 to November 7, 1924

"Statesman, Lawyer, Philosopher"

Haldane had been Lord Chancellor from June 19, 1912, to May 15, 1915, in Asquith's Liberal Government when he was forced to resign because of his alleged pro-German sympathies. The appointment of Claud Schuster as Permanent Secretary in the Lord Chancellor's Office by Haldane is chronicled in Chapter 2.[1] Well before his resignation Haldane had formulated his ideas on how the government of Britain and the Empire should be organised. He found the duties of Lord Chancellor with its mixture of political, administrative and judicial responsibilities, extremely burdensome. Moreover, the functions relating to "justice" in the abstract sense were divided between the Home Office and his own department. He was a great believer in the Empire and in the value of the Judicial Committee of the Privy Council as a means of holding it together.

Having a Ministry of Justice he thought, in his logical way, would tidy the whole machinery of government. But it was not to be.

Within five days of Haldane receiving the Great Seal as Lord Chancellor in the Labour Minority Government,

---

1. See also Jean Graham Hall and Douglas F. Martin. *Haldane - Statesman, Lawyer, Philosopher*. Barry Rose Law Publishers, 1996, pp.361-363.

Schuster had submitted to him a 45-page memorandum describing the present condition of the Office and the main work proceeding in it.[2]

Conscious of his master's ideas on a Ministry of Justice, Schuster included in the memorandum the following paragraph:

> "All the officers of the Department and the duties which they perform would form an integral part of the Ministry of Justice whether established under the Lord Chancellor or any Minister. They are coherent and homogenous, and their unification in this Department has already resulted in improved simplicity of organisation and economy."[3]

This suggests that in spite of his opposition to a Ministry of Justice, Schuster would have accepted all the responsibilities of such a Ministry provided it was still called the Lord Chancellor's Department and remained under his control.

The memorandum also charted the changes since 1915 when Haldane had resigned from the Office. There had been some additions to the staff, viz, an establishment officer, a Secretary of Commissions, five shorthand typists described as writers and a Mr R.W. Bankes who had been appointed as private secretary to both the Lord Chancellor and the Permanent Secretary. Reference was also made to the Ecclesiastical Secretary, that shady character, Mr G.H.M. "Buns" Cartwright, a crony of Lord Birkenhead (see Chapter 9).

---

2. LCO 2/938. Dated January 28, 1924.
3. *Ibid.*, para.9.

These additions to the staff followed the recommendation of the Sixth Report of the MacDonnell Commission on the Civil Service which recommended that all judicial patronage should be transferred to the Lord Chancellor and that control of all judicial departments should be placed in his hands.[4] The report observed that it "... may necessitate some further assistance being given to the Permanent Secretary, who has at present practically no staff to assist him in what are already very arduous duties."

In giving evidence to the Royal Commission Muir Mackenzie, Schuster's predecessor, had suggested the appointment of an Under Secretary to represent the legal departments in the House of Commons.[5]

That was something that Schuster always resisted. He did not want his department to be criticised in the Commons and it was not until Lord Mackay's tenure of office in 1989-97 that such a Commons representative was appointed. On the finance side Schuster had also expanded his empire. Due to pressure on the Treasury by Schuster, he, as Permanent Secretary, had become the accounting office for the Department and following the Swift Report on County Courts[6] he was also the accounting officer for that branch. The Civil Judicial Statistics had been transferred from the Home Office and all the staff of the Royal Courts of Justice were responsible to the Lord Chancellor.[7]

---

4. Cd. 7832, 1915.
5. *Ibid.*, Q.43-998.
6. Cmd. 1049. 1020.
7. LCO 2/938.

Haldane, however, was not in good health. Furthermore he held his second term of Office for 10 months only, due to the early demise of the minority government. The Labour Government had neither the time nor the power to affect any large-scale reforms. Haldane, however, found time to assist the progress of the Land Law legislation and the formation of a National Grid by the Central Electricity Board.

During the inevitable general election which followed, the "Zinoviev" letter was published by the *Daily Mail*. Zinoviev was the general secretary of the Communist International (the Comintern) and the latter purported to give instructions to the leaders of the British Labour Party. This demonstrated to the public that in spite of their professed moderation, the Labour Party were in fact revolutionaries. It is now generally accepted that the letter was a forgery - its provenance sometimes laid at the door of Conservative Centre Office. Haldane, and possibly Schuster, thought it was genuine.

Schuster's official working association with Haldane was brief but he had been for some years a frequent guest at Haldane's dinner parties. He knew him well and was qualified to pay him the following tribute after his death:

> "He was an ideal chief. He expected others to take responsibility, and he was ready and willing to devolve responsibility upon them. His temper was naturally sweet, unsoured by public obloquy. He attacked his duties with a boyish zest which he communicated to his subordinates. Always courteous, always considerate, he seemed to command affection, and in its

enjoyment he expanded. But he knew his own mind, he pressed on to his own goal, undeflected by clamour, undepressed by solitude, unfaltering in the face of death."[8]

---

8. C. Schuster. *Lord Haldane* (1928), p.33 (quoted by R.F.V. Heuston, *Lives of the Lord Chancellors*. Clarendon Press, 1964, p.237).

CHAPTER 13

Lord Hailsham - March 29, 1928 to June 8, 1929 and June 7, 1935 to March 15, 1938

Not an Innovative Lord Chancellor

When Lord Cave died on March 29, 1928, having resigned the day before, Baldwin offered the post of Lord Chancellor to Birkenhead. This was surprising as Baldwin was known to dislike Birkenhead, mainly for his lifestyle. Perhaps Baldwin expected Birkenhead to refuse the offer. This he did, on the ground that he was Secretary of State for India and had much more work to do in that capacity. He also disliked the ceremonial side of the Chancellor's work.[1]

Lord Hailsham was appointed by Baldwin. Like Lord Cave he had two periods as Chancellor, Lord Sankey's tenure of six years intervening. Hailsham was born into a well-established Scottish/Ulster family which had made its wealth from the sugar trade. Educated at Eton, where he had a distinguished career, he decided not to go to university. For several years he worked in the family business abroad and then joined the Army. After receiving an injury in the Boer War he was invalided home; he then read for the Bar. An early venture into politics proved abortive but his practice at the Bar flourished and by 1922 he was at the top of his profession. On the fall of the Coalition Government he was elected MP and within one month he became Attorney-

---

1. Second Earl of Birkenhead. *The Life of F.E. Smith, The First Earl of Birkenhead*, by his son. Eyre and Spottiswood. 1960, p.516.

General, a Privy Counsellor and a Knight.

When Hailsham was offered the Chancellorship, his son Quinten Hogg, argued with his father to persuade him to stay in the House of Commons where he could have continued his political career and very likely have become Prime Minister. On the day his father received the Great Seal the young Quinten sent his father a telegram, "Melancholy congratulations, Reform Lords." On his father's death Quinten became the second Lord Hailsham and on October 9, 1963, when he was 56 years old he disclaimed his peerage in order to make himself eligible to lead the Conservative party in the Commons. He did not achieve that position but he did become Lord Chancellor himself in 1979.

In 1928 Hailsham senior was at the height of his powers, but in spite of his ability he was not an innovative Lord Chancellor. In August, 1928, Baldwin asked Hailsham to act as Prime Minister while he was on holiday in Aix-en-Provence. During that time as acting Prime Minister it appears that he rarely went to 10 Downing Street. It is a matter of conjecture, perhaps little happened of importance to the governing of the country, but it could be that the Lord Chancellor's Office became the seat of the Government with Schuster as chief adviser to the acting PM.

Hailsham's first term on the Woolsack was short lived. The second Labour Government was formed in June 1928 and Sankey became the Lord Chancellor. When the National (Coalition) Government was formed in 1931, Hailsham hoped that he might take over the Great Seal again. However, MacDonald was Prime Minister and Sankey, his staunch supporter, was in too strong a position to be replaced.

Hailsham had to wait another four years until June 7, 1935, to become Lord Chancellor again. He was then 64 years of age and his health was beginning to decline.

The Trial of Lord de Clifford[2]

In December 1935, Hailsham presided over the trial of Lord de Clifford for manslaughter. It was the last occasion on which a peer was tried by his fellow peers.

Lord de Clifford had been involved in a road accident on August 15, 1935, at 3.00 a.m., when driving on the Kingston by-pass. The car he was driving collided with another car, travelling in the opposite direction. The driver of that car, Douglas George Hopkins, died as a result of the crash. The coroner's jury brought in a verdict of manslaughter, which was a felony. By an antiquated law a peer accused of felony had to be tried by his peers and Lord de Clifford was committed for trial by the coroner's jury (note: this power of a coroner's court was abolished by the Criminal Law Act 1977, s.56, and the right of a peer accused of felony to be tried by his peers was abolished by the Criminal Justice Act 1948). Schuster, in conjunction with the Clerk to the Parliaments, was responsible for the arrangements and drafting of the necessary legal documents. Each of the 800 peers was entitled to attend and, in fact, 85 did so, including the Lord Chancellor, Lord Hewart, LCJ, and two Law Lords, Atkin

---

2. William T. West. *The Trial of Lord De Clifford*, 1935 Revised (2nd) Edition, 1990, p.1. Also House of Lords Sessional Papers 1935-36, vol.VI, p.697.

and Wright. They were assisted by four High Court Judges. The trial took place in the Royal Gallery of the House of Lords. The prosecution was conducted by both the Law Officers and two Treasury Counsel. Hailsham presided, not as Lord Chancellor but as Lord High Steward. That office was once a great office of state but is now only appointed for special occasions. After the commission appointing him had been read, Hailsham left the Woolsack for a seat beneath the vacant throne where he received from Garter and Black Rod his white wand of office. The accused was then summoned to the Bar and the trial proceeded. Not surprisingly counsel for the accused obtained a ruling that there was no case to answer and each of the assembled peers in turn placed their right hands on their hearts and declared the accused "not guilty, upon mine honour". The Lord High Steward then broke his wand of office and the dignified and colourful assembly dispersed. As a traditional spectacle this must have been impressive but it was really a futile operation, correctly described as resembling a pantomime rather than a serious legal trial and which had taken a great deal of the time of Schuster and others in organising it.

Emergency Powers

In 1935 the invasion of Abyssinia by Italy alerted MI5 and the senior civil service to the power and ambitions of Italy and Germany. The probability of another world war was apparent to many but not to all in Government circles.

The Committee for Imperial Defence on which the service

departments and others were represented delivered an enormous collection of Defence of the Realm Act Regulations, which had been in force in 1918, to Warren Fisher at the Treasury. Fisher, somewhat horrified by all this out-of-date material, was advised by parliamentary counsel that a new code of Defence Regulations must be drafted with an enabling Bill and that an interdepartmental committee should be set up to prepare them. The Cabinet agreed; and what was more natural than that Fisher should ensure that his long-standing colleague and fellow-Wykehamist Schuster should be appointed as chairman of the Interdepartmental Committee? This appointment put Schuster in his element and illustrates the influence he had in most of the corridors of Whitehall.

The committee was called the War Legislation Committee with rising star Norman Brook (later Sir Norman, Head of the Civil Service) as secretary. The service departments and a dozen or so civil departments were represented.

Sir Harold Kent, a member of the Committee reported:

"It turned out to be a model piece of organisation. Schuster made a powerful chairman, through sheer prestige and personality, and was very good at shooting down, on proper occasions, the opposition to proposals from the chair. He soon acquired great faith in his secretary and gave him a free hand ... Lindsay (parliamentary draftsman) received his instructions from Brook, after Brook had squared the departments as well as he could, and he prepared drafts for the next meeting of the committee. Brook briefed Schuster, who seldom kicked at the drafting, and could be relied upon to do his homework."[3]

In that way were formed the laws (enacted as the Emergency Powers Act 1939) which, while restricting many civil rights, played an important part in maintaining security and helping the war effort in the six years from 1939-45. The work of Schuster and his committee must be recorded as a valuable achievement.

The Schuster committee had its lighter moments, usually at the expense of MI5. An argument rose over the Defence Regulation dealing with wireless telegraphy in which MI5 was quite rightly interested. The main provision was to the effect that no person should, without a written permit granted by the competent authority, make any sound transmissible by wireless telegraphy. When the regulation came up for consideration by the committee, satisfaction was expressed by MI5 and Naval Intelligence. There was an expectant hush, with all eyes on the chairman.

> "It looks like being a very silent war," said Schuster. There was a ripple of laughter around the table. "Of course," said the head of MI5, "we should only prosecute in really serious cases." "Oh no," cried Schuster, "not that again."

The head of MI5 came out of his strange world inhabited more or less exclusively by potential enemies and their spies and sympathisers. He looked for a moment at the other world of innocent persons pursuing their comparatively innocent avocations.

---

3. Harold S. Kent. *In on the Act.* McMillan, 1979, p.107.

"I suppose it won't do," he said, regretfully.[4]

The Abdication

The abdication of King Edward VIII in 1936 was not directly the concern of Hailsham as he had suffered a stroke and was absent from duty. He was nevertheless aware of what was going on and wrote to his son on October 7, 1936, to the effect that he was shocked and surprised to hear of the King's infatuation and that he had flaunted the lady so publicly (she was in the second Royal car).

On December 8, *The Times* commented that although all sympathised with the Lord Chancellor in his illness it was most unfortunate that the House of Lords should be without its chief legal adviser at such an important moment. Schuster had, over the years, gained a reputation for his knowledge of the Constitution and protocol and it is likely that he was consulted in the absence of his chief. It is understood that the departmental papers covering this event have been destroyed.

On December 10, 1936, the King abdicated. The Abdication Bill went through quickly and the time-honoured formula converting the Sovereign into a subject was pronounced by Jack Badeley, the Clerk of the Parliaments and a friend and associate of Schuster's.

Immediately a problem arose which enabled Schuster to exercise his influence upon a delicate situation.

---

4. *Ibid.*, 110.

George VI Bowled Over

In a memorandum annexed to his record of the Abdication crisis, George VI gives an account of an interview with Lord Wigram (who had been Private Secretary to George V and was Extra Equerry to Edward VIII) and Sir Claud Schuster (as representative of the Lord Chancellor who was ill). They had come to ask the new King's view on what the ex-King's future rank and titles should be. The question was urgent, the King was told, because the Director-General of the BBC was proposing to introduce the ex-King on the air as Mr Edward Windsor. The King said that this would be quite wrong but that before going any further it was necessary to know what his brother had given up by the Abdication. Upon Schuster replying that he was not quite sure, King George, who was normally represented as being completely bowled out at this time by his sense of his own inadequacy, gave a convincing exhibition of regal testiness as well as the solution of the problem:

> "I said, it would be quite a good thing to find out before coming to me. Now as to his name, I suggest HRH D of W[indsor]. He cannot be Mr E.W. as he was born the son of a Duke. That makes him Ld E.W. anyhow. If he ever comes back to this country, he can stand and be elected to the H of C. Would you like that? S replied, No. As D of W he can sit and vote in the H. of L. Would you like that? S replied, No. Well, if he becomes a Royal Duke he cannot speak or vote in the H of L and he is not being deprived of his rank in the Navy, Army or Royal Air Force. This gave

Schuster a new lease of life and he went off quite happy."[5]

Magistrates' Clerks

Schuster had for some time been in favour of the appointment of full-time magistrates' clerks, qualified as solicitors. He was adamant that part-time clerks, usually local practising solicitors, were bound to have conflicting interests from time to time. He pressed the Home Office to set up a committee on the subject. This was appointed in 1938. He unsuccessfully opposed the selection of Lord Roche as chairman on the grounds that he was too conservative.[6] Nevertheless the committee's report, which was not presented to Parliament until March 1944, recommended full-time justices' clerks and other reforms.[7]

In May, 1937, Chamberlain succeeded Baldwin as Prime Minister. Hailsham continued as Lord Chancellor but he was not in good health. On March 15, 1938, he was replaced by Maugham and was given the post of Lord President of the Council which was almost a sinecure.

A Change of Accommodation

For many years the Lord Chancellor and his officials had

---

5. John Wheeler-Bennett. *George VI*. Macmillan, 1958, p.295. Quoted by France Donaldson in *Edward VIII*. Weidenfeld and Nicholson, 1974, p.294.
6. LCO 2/1449.
7. Cmd. 6507.

their offices on the West front of the House of Lords overlooking Westminster Abbey. At some time in the early thirties the West front rooms were being refurbished which made it necessary for Schuster and his small staff to move out while the work was going on. They moved to rooms on the South East corner of the building and finding them to their liking they did not move back when the work was finished. They then had two fine rooms with a private office in between. Incomparably the grander room called "the Long Room" looks out over the river through magnificent long windows. The other room, smaller and cosier, looks out over Victoria Gardens, where Rodin's statute "The Burghers of Calais" can be seen. In the power game the size of rooms, quality of carpets and furniture are important. Schuster, quick to seize an opportunity, took possession of the grander room and left the smaller room for his Lord Chancellors. He managed to keep possession of his room until his retirement. During the time of Schuster's successor, Albert Napier, a certain Lord Chancellor decided he wanted the "Long Room" which overlooked the river and Napier had to move to the less imposing room.[8]

---

8. Information provided by former Permanent Secretary, Sir Derek Oulton.

CHAPTER 14

Lord Sankey - June 8, 1929 to June 7, 1935

A Six Year Stretch with Schuster

In 1919 Sankey was an eminent member of the Bar at the height of his career. Highly thought of by all political parties he tended to be conventional in outlook and had no political ambitions. Early in that year he was appointed chairman of a Commission on the Coal Mining Industry. The appointment was made by Birkenhead, the Lord Chancellor, no doubt on Schuster's advice. The experience it gave to Sankey caused him to take an interest in politics and be drawn towards socialism. Already friendly with Haldane he recommended the nationalisation of the mines as the only possible remedy for the problems in the coal industry.[1] His attraction towards socialism was such that in 1924 he was considered for the post of Lord Chancellor in the first Labour Government, although in the event, Haldane was appointed.

In February, 1928, Sankey was made a Lord Justice of Appeal and on June 8, 1929 on the election of the second Labour Government, he was selected by MacDonald to receive the Great Seal. He was 63 years of age.

Of all Schuster's Lord Chancellors, Sankey served the longest. Much of what he tried to do was thwarted. The weakness of the National Government from 1931 did not help; but he as not inactive. His proposals for the nationalisation of the mines was not accepted but his first

---

1. Report published June 20, 1919. Cmd. 82.

speech in the Lords was to introduce the Coal Mines Bill on its second reading.[2] He gave an excellent speech but the Bill only instigated minor reforms such as a reduction of the length of the working day.

One of Sankey's historic achievements was the Statute of Westminster frequently referred to as Sankey's Statute of Westminster. In fact, both Schuster and Cave had a hand in it. The important Statute, passed in 1931, put an end to the British Empire and substituted the British Commonwealth of Nations. Since the end of the War in 1918 there had been signs that the Empire was disintegrated and at the 1926 Imperial Conference the question of appeals to the Judicial Committee of the Privy Council became a burning issue.

The Judicial Committee Again

The brief to the UK delegation to the 1926 Imperial Conference was the responsibility of the Dominions Office and the Lord Chancellor's Department. A draft of the brief argued somewhat mildly that the right of Appeal from the Irish Free State courts should continue to lie to the Judicial Committee of the Privy Council and made such comments as, "new Judges appointed by the Free State Government appear to be excellent" and that there was no evidence that supporters of the former regime had suffered injustice. This was not to Schuster's liking. He and Cave toughened up making it clear that the right of appeal to the Judicial

---

2. *Hansard*. HL, vol.77, col.165.

Committee must remain.[3]

Understandably the Irish were offended and it was fortunate that the UK representative was the persuasive Lord Birkenhead who was able to sweet-talk the Irish into post-phoning the question until the 1930 Imperial Conference.

In Hailsham's time there had been some bad decisions by the Judicial Committee. The case of *Wigg v. Attorney-General of the Irish Free State* [1927] AC (674 PC) was catastrophic.[4] It concerned payments due to certain Irish civil servants. It was pointed out to Hailsham by the Registrar of the Committee that the court had misunderstood the meaning of "lump sum allowance" as well as the meaning of "a Treasury minute". It was generally agreed by Haldane, Cave and others that the decision had been wrong in law. Schuster arranged for the case to be reheard with a differently constituted court. To the embarrassment of all the new court confirmed the previous decision.

In 1930 with the Labour Government in power, Sankey was inclined to accept the equality of the Commonwealth countries and he believed that there could be an Imperial Court of Appeal which would be an international court within the Commonwealth. Schuster reluctantly conceded that such a tribunal might be necessary but it would lead to the end of the Judicial Committee.[5]

The Irish were determined to abolish appeals to a British tribunal and no agreement was reached. Sankey's Statute of

---

3. LCO 2/3465.
4. LCO 2/2464.
5. LCO 2/3465.

Westminster 1931 was the great hope; but it did not satisfy the Irish. In 1933 the Dail passed legislation abolishing appeals to the Judicial Committee. Two years later it was decided by the Committee itself, with Sankey presiding, that the Irish had the right to abolish such appeals (*Moore v. Attorney-General of the Irish Free State* 1935).

Canada too was becoming dissatisfied with the performance of the Judicial Committee and its judgment on an appeal concerning fishing rights did nothing to stop the Canadian Government wanting to control the right of appeal to the committee.

Attempt to Rewrite a Judgment

The case of *Croft v. Dunphy* [1933] AC 156 gave rise to what was described by Lowe and Young in the *Law Quarterly Review*, 1978, vol.94, p.255 as "An Attempt to Rewrite a Judgment".

The facts were that Dunphy, the owner of a Canadian ship, with a cargo of spirits sought the recovery of the boat and cargo after it had been seized 11½ miles off the Canadian coast by Croft, a Canadian customs officer. The judgment of the Supreme Court of Nova Scotia in favour of the customs officer had been reversed by the Supreme Court of Canada and was restored by the Judicial Committee of the Privy Council.

The customs officer clearly had authority under the Canadian Customs Act 1927-8 for his action. On behalf of Dunphy it was argued that the British North American Act conferred no general power on the Dominion Parliament to legislate extraterritorially.

The awkward situation arose from the following dictum of Lord Macmillan who delivered the Judicial Committee judgment:

> "Whatever be the limits of territorial waters in the international sense, it has long been recognised that for certain purposes, notably those of police, revenue, public health and fisheries, a state may enact laws affecting the seas surrounding its coast to a distance which exceeds the ordinary limits of its territory."

He concluded by stating that the British North American Act imposed no restriction on the power to legislate in customs matters and that the Judicial Committee saw no reason to infer it. These dicta were unnecessary: he would have been wiser to confine his remarks to the fact that it was an unquestionable principle of the international law that a state has a right to exercise its jurisdiction over its own ships both in its own territorial waters and on the high seas.

The situation was awkward for the Foreign Office because at that time British Government policy was to deny the legality of contiguous zones under customary international law. There had been disputes with the United States on this question which had been partly resolved by a treaty in 1924. It was feared that the US and other countries would take advantage of Lord Macmillan's *dicta*.

The judgment was reported in *The Times* (July 29, 1932) and on the same day the Treasury Solicitor wrote to the Foreign Office. The Canadian Government were most concerned (possibly because of its relationship with the US) and made representations to the Foreign Office. The Foreign Office took the view that the Government might be bound by this dicta and they decided to seek the alteration of the judgment.

After a preliminary meeting an interdepartmental meeting was called on September 27, 1932, which was attended by representatives of the Foreign Office, Admiralty, Board of Trade, Colonial Office, Customs, Dominions Office, Home Office, India Office, Lord Chancellor's Office, Ministry of Agriculture and Fisheries, Ministry of Health, Privy Council, Scottish Office Treasury and Treasury Solicitor's Department. All the representatives were civil servants.

The meeting was chaired by Sir Maurice Gwyer, the Treasury Solicitor. There was talk of a rehearing but it was said that there was no guarantee that the court would change its judgment. The major obstacle was that the judgment had already appeared in *The Times*. The Foreign Office representative suggested that if the offending passage (concerning the contiguous zone) did not appear in the more authoritative law reports, the impression would be given that *The Times's* report was wrong. After some further discussion in which it appears from the minutes that the Lord Chancellor's representative (Napier) took no part, it was agreed to form a small drafting committee to redraft the judgment as they thought it should have been delivered.

Schuster described his impression of the purpose of the meeting (in retrospect no reference given) in this way:

"It did not occur to me that it could be suggested that the Interdepartmental Committee was called together for the purposes of procuring an alteration in the judgment which had already been delivered. I thought that its object was to consider the situation and, in particular, the effect of the judgment upon the considered policy of His Majesty's Government. I could not attend. But in writing to Mr Napier, whom I asked to attend for me, I added, 'I do not see what the meeting can do or you can say'."[6]

The sub-committee drafted a letter to be signed by the Attorney-General and sent to Lord Macmillan the presiding Judge of the Judicial Committee, which included a proposed amendment to the judgment. The Attorney-General did not immediately forward this letter but a copy was shown to Lord Macmillan by Sir Charles Neish the Registrar of the Privy Council. Macmillan's response was somewhat chilly although he said he would not object to altering a "phrase or two, if that will give any comfort".

Sankey Displeased

In November, the affair came to the notice of Lord Sankey, the Lord Chancellor. There followed an exchange of correspondence between him and Neish in which Sankey referred to the "very serious situation"and "a very grave question is now at issue". Neish suggested that it was the practice of the Privy Council to alter a judgment at the request of one or other of the parties before it was actually reported. Sankey could not accept this and was obviously displeased. Neish then admitted that instances of amending judgments

---

6. *Law Quarterly Review*, 1978, vol.94, pp.255-275.

had been "mostly of a verbal character or of correcting some error of fact".

Sankey's final word on the subject is contained in a draft letter (the original is lost) which regarded the offending words about contiguous zones as *obiter dicta* which had little legal affect. He concluded:

> "No court would ever dream, after having given judgment, of altering it so that the decision should go the other way, nor would a court alter the language of a judgment which is part of the reasoning upon which the decision proceeds."

A memorandum by Schuster written at the same time plays down the role taken by the civil servants and glosses over the problem in his usual conciliatory manner. He wrote that the minutes of the interdepartmental meeting "no doubt" distorted the tone of the expressions used and continued:

> "The Treasury Solicitor informs me that the only question under consideration by the Interdepartmental Committee was the nature of the report, if any, which should be made to the Attorney-General, it being recognised that it was for the Attorney-General to decide whether any steps could or ought to be taken."[7]

As astute as ever Schuster came out of this affair unscathed. He had taken care not to be present at the interdepartmental meeting himself. He had ordered his deputy (Napier) to attend but not to do anything that could be interpreted as

---

7. *Ibid.,* p.275.

interference with the judiciary. According to the records Napier had complied in the best way possible by saying nothing.

The final text of the judgment was published on December 8, 1932. It was as originally reported in *The Times*. The Foreign Office were highly critical of the passage about the contiguous zone and requested that notes to the effect that the *obiter dicta* was irrelevant should appear in the *Law Quarterly Review* and the *British Year Book*.

This affair demonstrates that civil servants in positions powerful enough to influence policy must take care not to encroach upon the judicial function. It also shows that Sankey, as Lord Chancellor, was right to voice his concern and to defend the independence of the judiciary against the increasing power of the executive.

The *Croft v. Dunphy* judgment did nothing to prolong the jurisdiction of the Judicial Committee as the Supreme Court of Appeal for the Commonwealth. Nevertheless its jurisdiction did not decline substantially until after the 1939 war. In 1937 when the last edition of the leading textbook on the judicial committee was published, the author, Norman Wentwich, was still able to say, "The sphere of jurisdiction of the Privy Council now embraces more than one-fourth part of the world." Now of the Dominions only New Zealand retains the right of appeal to the committee, together with many of the smaller former colonies.

Hailsham, like Haldane, believed that it was of paramount importance that the right of appeal should be retained from all the Dominions and colonies in order to hold the Commonwealth together. Sankey and other Chancellors also liked the idea. In fact the confidence of the principal members of the Commonwealth in the Committee had been waning since 1918. At that time when Finlay was Lord Chancellor, Schuster had forecast that the idea of a Commonwealth together. Sankey and other Chancellors also liked the idea. In fact the confidence of the principal members of the Commonwealth in the Committee had been waning since 1918. At that time when Finlay was Lord Chancellor, Schuster had forecast that the ideal of a Commonwealth Court of Appeal to hold the Commonwealth together could not be achieved (see *ante*, Chapter 8).

An Ecclesiastical Appointment

The Lord Chancellor would not normally interest himself in these appointments which were made in his name. Schuster made the decisions aided by the Ecclesiastical Secretary in consultation with the parishioners. However, in March 1931, Sankey received a letter from the Bishop of St Albans complaining of an appointment. Sankey's reply is in Schuster's language. The directness of the questions, the sarcasm, the touch of humour, all smack of Schuster:

> "Your letter has caused me much perplexity, owing to the very strong language you use, and I regret that you view Mr Veitch's appointment with dismay and his going to Harpenden as disastrous. I cannot help thinking that the Harpenden's parishioners are a very difficult set of people. I offered the living to two of your nominees in turn. For your private information, the parishioners did not want either of them, but indirectly put

great pressure upon me to appoint another gentleman, who, however, could not take it.

"I am afraid it is very difficult to do anything in the circumstances, but before attempting it, I should like to know categorically what is their objection to Mr Veitch. I need hardly say that personally I have never seen and know nothing about him, except what I gather from his testimonials. Would you mind answering the following questions:

1. Is he too old?
2. Has he an unsatisfactory wife?
3. Has he too many children?
4. Has he too little money?
5. Is his Churchmanship too high, too low, or too Laodicean?[8]
6. Is his personal appearance against him?
7. Is his manner against him?
8. Is it thought that he is not a great preacher?
9. Are his politics unacceptable?
10. Is he not sufficiently learned?
11. Is he out of sympathy with young people?
12. Is his wife unable to play the organ?
13. Has he a poor singing voice?
14. Is he one of the 'vestmented' clergy?

You will, I know, think most of the foregoing questions impertinent and ridiculous, as I do myself, but they are simply those which I have accumulated from various parishes during my tenure, and I am sure that the objection of the parishioners to Mr Veitch must be due to one or other of these causes. If not,

8. Ie, having the fault for which the Church of Laodicea is reproached in Revelations, Chapter 3, V15: "thou art luke-warm, and neither hot nor cold."

I shall have to add a fifteenth to my list."[9]

Appointment of Judges

Sankey in his six years as Lord Chancellor, appointed five High Court Judges, 34 County Court Judges, two Official Referees and two Common Serjeants of the City of London. There was no criticism of his appointments, all of which would have been influenced by Schuster whose duty was to arrange and process all the necessary consultations. That he was the custodian of the papers relating to appointments is shown when in May 1933 the question arose of appointing Sir Cyril Atkinson to the High Court Bench. Atkinson was Conservative MP for Altrincham and his appointment would have caused a by-election. Sankey consulted Hailsham, his predecessor as Lord Chancellor and a Conservative, sending him a copy of a proposed letter to the Prime Minister. Hailsham wrote at length to Sankey stating that he agreed with the proposal to appoint Atkinson but that the Prime Minister should be asked if there were any grave political objections to such an appointment. He emphasised that this was not giving the Prime Minister a say in who should be appointed. His letter to Sankey included the following:

"... if I were in your place I should destroy every copy except one of the document [the draft letter to the Prime Minister], and lock the one remaining sample in the innermost recess of Schuster's

9. R.F.V. Heuston. *Lives of the Lord Chancellors 1885-1940*, Clarendon Press, 1964, pp.524/5.

most secret safe. It is quite astonishing how a secret like this gets out ..."[10]

Sankey was asked by his friend Professor Harold Laski, to consider appointing an academic lawyer to the Bench. He wrote to Laski saying that he had consulted four eminent lawyers on the question and all were against the idea. However, it had been suggested to him (by Schuster, no doubt) that he could ask an academic lawyer to go as Commissioner on Assize and see how he performed.[11] That was the customary method of testing the capabilities of a prospective Judge.

Schuster's Style

Sir Harold Kent has described a visit he made to Schuster's room accompanied by Sir John Rowlatt of the Parliamentary Counsels' Office. They had been "summoned to the presence" to discuss a point arising from the drafting of a Bill, the draftsmen were apparently raising some objection to the proposed abolition of grand juries. Sir Harold wrote:

"Rowlatt and I ... advanced across acres of carpet and were waved to chairs near the desk where Schuster was sitting. Rowlatt began to explain the point in what for him was a rather halting fashion ... Schuster did not seem over-impressed by the linchpin theory, nor, for that matter, by the baby and the

---

10. *Ibid.*, p.522.
11. *Ibid.*, p.524.

bathwater. He made those little impatient noises usually written as 'Tcha'. At the end he burst into a minor explosion, 'Nonsense, my dear boy. And with due respect for your father [a High Court Judge] he is for once talking though his August hat. I'm certainly not going to upset my Business of Courts Committee for this sort of high-falutin.' At that point the telephone rang. Schuster seized it and we listened to his side of the conversation.

Schuster: 'I can't hear yer. Well, who are yer? No, I'm dammed if I will.'

Schuster slammed down the receiver and the conversation was over. So also was our interview.

'Right', he said, 'Abolish the grand juries. The sooner the better'."

Sir Harold Kent goes on to say that the clauses concerning grand juries gave no trouble in Parliament, nor in the courts. Schuster's judgment was vindicated. The structure of criminal law remained unshaken.[12]

Remuneration of Judges

As Permanent Secretary, it was Schuster's duty to ensure that the courts were functioning efficiently. He expected the Judges to work; they were, while retaining their judicial independence, subject to his directions. Ancillary to this he was responsible for their conditions of employment and their pay.

A Select Committee had recommended a salary for County

---

12. Sir Harold Kent. *In on the Act.* Macmillan, 1979, p.150.

Court Judges of £2,000 per annum in 1878 and they had been lobbying for such an increase ever since. The delay had been caused by the 1914-18 war when they received a war bonus, and the difficult economic conditions thereafter. Schuster had written to Sir Warren Fisher at the Treasury in 1924 suggesting that the Judges' salaries should be increased to £2,000 but the time was unpropitious.[13] Then came the General Strike of 1926 and the financial crisis in 1931. There were many communications between Schuster and the Council of County Court Judges but the time for the increase was always "unpropitious". The result was that the County Court Judges did not receive their £2,000 per annum until 1937.

However, it was the pay of High Court Judges which caused Schuster the most trouble and almost resulted in a Constitutional crisis. Their pay had been static at £5,000 per annum since 1832 and the cost of living had increased substantially in the twentieth century. The Council of Judges began pressing for an increase in their salaries in 1920 and they received a sympathetic response from Birkenhead, who was particularly concerned with his own salary as he always spent more than he earned. He persuaded Austen Chamberlain that a large increase in salary was in order and it was left to Schuster and Warren Fisher to produce a memorandum for the Cabinet.[14] Due mainly to a change in government the proposed increase was not accepted and time dragged on while the economic situation deteriorated.

---

13. R.F.V. Heuston, pp.524/5.
14. LCO 12/40.

The economic crisis of 1931 caused the Government to decide to reduce the salaries of all public servants. The National Recovery Act 1931 and a related Order in Council cut the salaries of all public servants by 20 per cent. The intention of the legislature was to include Judges in this drastic measure. Their salaries, unlike those of civil servants, were and still are, charged on the Consolidated Fund in order to maintain the independence of the judiciary. Their remuneration is not dependent on a vote by Parliament like that of other public servants. For the Judges who had been hoping for a rise, a cut imposed by legislation was a shock to say the least. Their reaction was slow at first but it gathered momentum and became one of Sankey's most difficult problems during his Lord Chancellorship. Schuster of course was closely involved. Mr Justice Rowlatt threatened that he and others would resign as they could earn more at the Bar. The prospect of six resignations at the same time alarmed the Lord Chancellor's Office. Schuster wrote to the Treasury, "I very greatly doubt whether there are at the Bar six people fit to be appointed and ready to accept office."[15] The eccentric Mr Justice McCardie became a troublesome protester. He suggested that the Judges should have their salaries paid tax-free and he alleged that Schuster's salary had been almost doubled in the past 12 years.[16] The Prime Minister, Ramsey MacDonald, Sankey and the former Lord Chancellor, Hailsham, met together to draft a letter to the Judges. Schuster heard of it and managed to stop the "madness".

---

15. LCO 2/467.
16. LCO 2/1666.

There were rumblings amongst the Judges of Scotland and Northern Ireland. The Chief Justice of Northern Ireland had called a meeting of his colleagues and it was rumoured that the meeting wound up its proceedings by singing "God Save the King". Schuster said, "English Judges are in a mood where they are far more likely to sing, 'The Red Flag' than 'God Save the King'."[17] Amongst other protesters was Mr Justice Maugham, later Lord Chancellor, who produced a memorandum citing the Act of Settlement 1701 and the constitution of the United States and suggesting that Judges' salaries should be free of income tax but not supertax. Schuster was becoming increasingly frustrated with his charges. He remonstrated with Sankey: "As long as Judges go on talking about the Act of Settlement, which has nothing whatsoever to do with the question, it is very difficult to deal with people who do not seem able to see that we cannot introduce legislation dealing with them and leaving the police and unemployed untouched."[18]

A Deputation of Judges

The protests from the Judges increased throughout 1931 as their anger mounted. Sankey decided to set out his views in a long memorandum of January 5, 1932. This was put to the Prime Minister before he received Sankey together with a

---

17.   Robert Stevens. *The Independence of the Judiciary*. Clarendon Press, 1993, p.54.
18.   *Ibid.*, p.55.

deputation of Judges.

The memorandum, in which Schuster certainly had a hand, sets out the history of the affair quite fairly. It referred to the meetings Sankey had had with the leading High Court Judges including the Master of the Rolls. Surprisingly, in view of what happened two years later (see Chapter 18), Lord Chief Justice Hewart was not concerned in the protest; presumably he was ill. Sankey stated:

> "It is most unfortunate that the Lord Chief Justice has for many weeks been unable to attend to his official duties. Originally he wrote a letter in which he said, as far as I remember, that the Judges would cheerfully comply with the cuts which the Government thought necessary ... It is useless for me to disguise the fact that the Judges are ... rather bent upon giving trouble unless their demands are satisfied."[19]

Sankey related in the memorandum that originally the Judges had maintained that the Government had contracted by Statute to pay them £5,000 a year and that any reduction would be a breach of contract. Later they had shifted their ground. They claimed that although they admitted that their pay could be lowered by Act of Parliament, the Order in Council applied to persons in His Majesty's Service. Therefore the cuts in their salaries were illegal. Sankey admitted that they may have had a point but he could only make three suggestions in the memorandum, the Government could do nothing. It could pass an Act of Parliament reducing their salaries by £1,000 a year. Or it could accept their argument

---

19.   *Ibid.* Memo Schuster to Sankey, p.51.

and leave each Judge to offer what reduction he thought fit.

Sankey's suggestions were not accepted. Instead a compromise was offered by MacDonald whereby the Government would express doubts about the validity of the Order in Council as it applied to Judges and that they would voluntarily accept the 20 per cent cut for one year only. This offer was almost accepted but there were legal complications. Objections were made by the Chancellor of the Exchequer and the Auditor-General who wanted to see a legal basis for the compromise beyond the offer from the Prime Minister. The matter was referred to the Law Officers who found no legal basis on which to exempt the Judges from the salary cut. The Council of Judges decided to hold their hand for the time being but their members became more outraged than ever. Individual Judges protested in different ways. Mr Justice Rowlatt again wrote to Schuster threatening to resign. McCardie threatened to sue the Government for the part of his salary "illegally retained". MacNaghten in an interview with Sankey said that he had a mission to resist the power of the Executive. Sankey gives a full account of the interview referring to MacNagthen's "extravagant language" and that he was stating "a travesty of the truth". The interview ended by MacNaghten informing Sankey that he, Mr Justice Clauson and Mr Justice Luxmoore were about to sue the Crown by means of a Petition of Right.[20] The Government, Sankey and Schuster took this seriously. Who could hear the case?

The actual work of arranging for the attendance of the Law Lords to hear appeals is performed, under close supervision

---

20.   R.F.V. Heuston, p.513.

of the Lord Chancellor, by his Permanent Secretary. This might seem a routine matter, but in practice it is important and difficult, and occupies much time and thought. In the instant circumstances working arrangements for the hearing of a Petition of Right were especially difficult, as in other potentially sensitive cases.

Judges to Judge Judges?

For a Petition of Right to be brought a fiat granting it was required from the Attorney-General. Schuster was of the opinion that this fiat could not be refused. Assuming that it would be granted, it was suggested that the Judicial Committee of the Privy Council should hear the case and in a letter to the Attorney-General Schuster considered how the Council should be constituted.[21] Retired High Court Judges were possible candidates but some were too old, others biased against the Crown and some were known to believe that the cuts were illegal. In another letter Schuster considered the consequences of the Government losing the case. He wrote:

> "Should the Government lose, it would not be possible to have judicial salaries restored to the amount at which they stood before the Economy Act while the wages of the police, salaries of school teachers and the amount payable as unemployment benefit were still subject to reductions made under that Act."[22]

21. *Ibid.*, p.55.
22. LCO 2/1966.

Schuster came to the conclusion that the matter should be dealt with immediately by legislation. With legislation pending the Attorney-General would then have grounds for refusing his fiat for the Petition of Right.

A lengthy opinion was obtained from a leading member of the Common Law Bar named Hull. He came down on the side of the Judges mainly on the ground that they were not in the "service" of the Crown. Their relationship with the Crown was not that of master and servant because they could not be dismissed by the Crown alone. The Act of Settlement 1701 provided that a Judge could not be dismissed by the Crown but only by an address from both Houses of Parliament. By that provision the independence of the judiciary was preserved. MacNaghten was basing his Petition of Right on Hull's opinion and was not prepared to abandon it. On April 6, 1933, Schuster wrote to Sankey that he thought "... MacNaghten was definitely unbalanced by the excitement of the last few days. Whenever we tried to talk simple business to him ... he broke off into scraps of eloquence which I recognised as taken from Hull's opinion."[23] (MacNaghten was the son of Lord MacNaghten (the author of the MacNaghten Rules) but as a Judge he was not highly thought of.) It appears that the Cabinet had accepted Schuster's proposal as on the next day, April 7, 1933, Schuster wrote to Parliamentary Counsel saying,

> "The Cabinet are determined not to give way. On the other hand they think it is scandalous that such a question should be tried

---

23.   *Ibid.,* April 2, 1933.

185

before a Judge whose interests must necessarily be involved in the proceedings before him ... Legislation must be prepared at once ..."[24]

With the threat of legalisation and the passage of time many of the more orthodox Judges were separating themselves from the protesters but MacNaghten persisted although he had agreed to delay his Petition of Right. Having refused to pay both income tax and super tax he used that delay to try to embroil the Lord Chancellor in his dispute with the Inland Revenue. Sankey was furious and told MacNaghten he should feel free to bring his Petition of Right.[25] This caused Schuster to demand action from the chief parliamentary draftsman. He wrote:

"Begin with a recital which should be as long and as pompous as possible, asserting the independence and all the rest of it and negating any idea that the Economy Act or the Order in Council affected that in any way. I realise that this is extraordinarily difficult to do for I do not see how you can negative that which has never been asserted except by the Judges themselves. Then declare that notwithstanding all this they are affected by the cut."[26]

In fact, the Bill was not necessary. The Petition of Right was not pursued and the Government quietly dropped its Bill. However, the situation was still tense. On November 29, 1933, a Professor Morgan attacked the Government's position in

24. *Ibid.*
25. *Ibid.*
26. Robert Stevens, p.61.

The Times. Sankey and Hailsham composed a response which was tightened up by Schuster and the Attorney-General was then instructed to find a KC, MP, to send it. It went to *The Times* under the name of T.J.O. Connor, KC, MP.[27]

An Extremely Silly Bill

In the absence of a Government Bill, Lord Rankeillour brought out his own. Schuster described it as "extremely silly - you will notice that all it says is that no reference in any statute is to affect these people unless there is an express reference."[28]

Nevertheless there was support for the Bill in the Lords. The supporters alleged that cutting the salaries of Judges was "a breach of unbroken Parliamentary privilege of 231 years". High Court Judges were on a different footing from civil servants and members of the armed forces.[29] On the Second Reading it was that that they were not even in the same category as county court Judges and stipendiary magistrates.[30] Sankey, who tried to maintain a polite neutrality in order not to offend the Judges, suggested some amendments to the Bill and it passed the Lords as amended. Schuster, more forthright than his master and somewhat disgusted with his charges - the Judges - wrote in a letter to

27. LCO 2/1666.
28. *Ibid.*
29. *Hansard.* November 23, HL, vol.90, col.62.
30. *Ibid.*

Inskip (Attorney-General) that there were passages in the Bill about "rights" and "duties", as being in some mystical way a protection against socialism or fascism which had nothing to do with the controversy about Judges' salaries. In his opinion the Bill was so bad, that if it was likely to be passed, the Government would have to substitute a Bill of its own. Schuster found:

> "It's very difficult to exaggerate the contempt which I feel for the Bill. If it has meaning at all ... that meaning is mischievous."

Looking back at this convoluted conflict as a piece of legal history, it is clear that those Judges who protested were concerned about money rather than Constitutional principle and Schuster made it clear that that was his opinion.

The Bill did not proceed to the Commons and in 1934 the Judges' salaries were restored. In the same year Lord Chief Justice Hewart, who had taken no part in the salary dispute, made his attack on Schuster in the Lords and the intense interest aroused by that incident caused the subject of Judges' salaries to fade away (see Chapter 17 for an account of Hewart's attack).

Robert Stevens in his book, *The Independence of the Judiciary* ends his excellent chapter on "Schuster and the Judges" with the following two conclusions:

> "First the Judges - who, until the Utilitarian revolution in the mid-nineteenth century had been the second most important branch of government - had clearly become the third. This had the effect, second, of moving the debates away from power as such, towards status. Elites, conscious of ebbing power, have, throughout

history, taken similar stands."

In Professor Heuston's opinion, legally the Judges were right in claiming that the Order in Council did not apply to them. However, he thought them unwise to have taken the attitude they did when it was contrary to national policy.

CHAPTER 15

Sankey the Reformer
"Nepotism and Vested Interests in the Courts"

Attempts to Reform the Administration of the Courts

The report of the Royal Commission on the Civil Service in 1931[1] prompted Schuster to make a further attempt to reorganise his unwieldy judiciary dominated department. Soon after taking office he had realised that his aim must be to acquire for himself and his staff, to the exclusion of the Judges, the whole of the administration of the courts. His memorandum, written in Hailsham's time, shows how strongly he held that view:

> "... it may be safely asserted that no system of administration could be worse than administration by judicial officers. Any system which commits administration to the courts is likely to bring the courts into disrepute, since Judges have too little experience or skill to deal with such questions and is likely in the long run to bring the courts and the executive Government into violent collision."[2]

The Tomlin Royal Commission Report had recommended that departments should adopt a more business-like approach to their work, and thus it was not difficult for Schuster to persuade Sankey to set up a Departmental Committee on the

---

1.   Cmnd. 3909.
2.   LCO 2/1233.

Business of the Courts. Schuster's friend and ally, Lord Hanworth, Master of the Rolls, was the chairman and inevitably Schuster himself was on the committee. He was well able to air his long-held views on many subjects. Few of his ideas were accepted in his time but almost all have been put into effect since. On the subject of the Probate, Divorce and Admiralty Division, he wrote in 1933:

> "There is ... no reason for the continuance of a Division occupied with these three classes of subject except that it happens to exist ... There are many reasons why ... a reconsideration should result in the absorption of the Probate, Divorce and Admiralty Division in one great common law division ..."[3]

Shipping interests and the Bar practising in Admiralty prevented change in Schuster's time and it was not until the Courts Act 1971 that the Division was split up between Chancery, Family and the Queen's Bench Divisions. He had supported the idea of a business manager for the Supreme Court and put forward many procedural changes to expedite legislation. He had for years advocated fewer juries in civil trials and suggested changes in the procedure relating to the Prerogative writs. He had taken over responsibility for the county courts and wanted them to have increased jurisdiction including the hearing of undefended divorce cases. He was successful in providing that appeals from the county courts should go straight to the Court of Appeal instead of to the Divisional Court (Administration of Justice [Appeals] Act 1934).

---

3.   Minute by Schuster, March 22, 1933. LCO 2/3838.

Schuster's wish to reduce jury trials in civil cases was supported by the Hanworth Committee but the King's Bench Masters had other ideas. They drew up a set of guidelines which according to Schuster "... cuts down the effects of the section [of the Act] to an extent which never occurred to any of those who discussed the question before the Bill became law, and will frustrate the hopes, which had been formed by those who were party to preparing it ... it makes my hair stand on end."[4]

He did not have a high opinion of the Masters who were appointed under the patronage of the Judges and many were related to them. They regarded themselves as judicial officers and resented any administrative authority. The staff of the Supreme Court were also in a privileged position. They were not recruited like other civil servants. Ostensibly clerks were drawn from ex-solicitors' clerks but nepotism was common. Their working hours were 10 till 4 and they did not work during the vacations when the courts were not sitting. They tended to regard the courts as if they were there for the benefit of the Judges and not for the litigants. Moreover in any dispute with the administration, the staff could almost always depend on the support of the Judges. For example, a disgruntled clerk who had not received the promotion he thought he deserved could persuade a Judge to complain on his behalf. One can imagine Schuster's frustrations in dealing with this building in the Strand full of prickly members of the judiciary, under-worked staff and with a Lord Chief Justice like Hewart at its head, opposed to any change. Not

---

4.   Schuster to Bonner and Hanworth, October 17, 1933. LCO/1759.

surprisingly few initiatives for improving procedures came from the staff, from the Masters or from the Judges. Schuster was also ahead of his time in advocating the transfer of responsibility for the magistrates' courts from the Home Office to the Lord Chancellor's Department.[5] That transfer did not occur until 50 years after he had retired.

The Law Society

Schuster had always found the Law Society more co-operative than the Bar Council and he was generally in sympathy with its aims to make membership compulsory for all solicitors and to ensure that they maintained high standards in integrity. However, he did not favour the Society's scheme for a compensation fund financed by a levy on all solicitors. He thought it would be inadequate to meet some of the substantial defalcations which had occurred around 1928. He favoured separate clients' accounts and a compulsory annual audit,[6] but the Society members would not agree to any regulation of their accounting methods. Schuster then supported a Solicitors (Clients' Account) Bill in July, 1930, but the Society had a Bill of its own and a compromise was reached which resulted in the Solicitor's Act 1932. This enabled the Society to make rules regulating the professional conduct of its members and obliging them to keep separate clients' accounts. These regulations came to be

---

5.   LCO 2/3630.
6.   LCO 2/1567.

largely disregarded and there were more defalcations in 1938 which made further action necessary. Eventually the Society had to accept Schuster's demand for a compulsory annual audit of members' accounts and this became law by the Solicitors Act 1941. Schuster had been disappointed in the Society's attitude to unscrupulous solicitors and that it was difficult to find enough solicitors who would volunteer to support the Poor Persons Procedure.[7]

In Schuster's time the Bar was very much the senior legal profession and had the monopoly on appointments to the highest legal positions. The Law Society maintained that too many barristers were appointed legal assistants in government departments where the work done was appropriate to solicitors. In reply Schuster explained to the Society the determination of successive Lord Chancellors to uphold the Bar's monopoly.[8]

Law Reform

The idea of a government agency responsible for law reform was anathema to Schuster in Birkenhead's time because they both opposed a Ministry of Justice which would have that function. Later it seems that Schuster had had a change of heart. By 1927 when suggestions were made that the criminal law should be codified, a criminal law committee's attempt to codify the law of fraud was, according to Schuster,

---

7.   LCO 2/1756.
8.   LCO 2/1074.

"criticised out of existence".[9] Schuster did not favour codification and preferred reference to a standing committee. He envisaged a standing committee comprising Judges, members of the Bar and members of the Law Society as well as one or two persons from the outside world.[10]

No progress was made until there was a debate on the subject of law reform in the Commons in December 1932[11] after which Somervell, MP, KC (later Lord Somervell) wrote to Schuster suggesting the establishment of a Law Revision Committee. Schuster was still pessimistic, he replied:

> "... since the end of the Chancellorship of Lord Birkenhead (during which you will remember, we dealt with the Law of Property) no Chancellor has ever been in office for a sufficient time to permit any advance on such a subject. The times have also been very unpropitious and we have certainly not found in such attempts as we have made any disposition in the Bench or Bar to render assistance as was likely to encourage us."[12]

In spite of saying that, Schuster also informed Somervell that Sankey had already decided to form such a committee. Schuster's friend, Lord Hanworth, Master of the Rolls, was to be chairman of the committee but during 1933 he was still completing his chairmanship of the Business of Courts Committee and was not available until January 1934 when the Law Revision Committee under his chairmanship was set

---

9. LCO 2/963.
10. LCO 2/3565.
11. *Hansard*. HC, vol.273, col.1103.
12. LCO 2/3565. 24.2.1933.

up. It consisted of four Judges, five barristers, two professors of law, one solicitor and, inevitably, the Permanent Secretary, Sir Claud Schuster. Its terms of reference were "to consider how far, having regard to the Statute Law and to judicial decisions, such legal maxims and doctrines as the Lord Chancellor may from time to time refer to them require revision in modern conditions." The committee produced eight valuable reports before 1939 on such subjects as: the felony-misdemeanour distinction, evidence of spouses and larceny. Most of these were followed by legislation after much negotiation with the Home Office, whose co-operation was not always easy to obtain.[13]

Law reform has always been regarded as the Lord Chancellor's responsibility and until Sankey's time, apart from Birkenhead's efforts, it had been almost non-existent. What attempts had been made were usually frustrated by the inbuilt conservatism of the legal system. Sankey must be given credit for the advances made during his time on the Woolsack, assisted as he was by Lord Hanworth. Schuster, as the permanent member of the committee, which was serviced by his department, certainly made his presence felt.

Latterly the committee fell into desuetude until 1954 when it was revived by Simonds, when Lord Chancellor. But it was not until Lord Gardiner became Lord Chancellor in 1964 that the whole-time Law Commission was formed with a permanent staff and authority to propose reforms in all branches of the law.

---

13. LCO 2/1995.

Legal Education

A committee on legal education was set up by Sankey in 1932. Its objective was to establish an Imperial Law School which hopefully would help, like the Judicial Committee, to hold the Commonwealth together. Lord Atkin, the chairman, had been described by a former law lord, Lord Dunedin, as "clever, a good common law lawyer, but obstinate. If he has taken a view - quite unpersuadable". Schuster went further, he said, "... a very bad chairman, the last man in the world to keep a committee together and full of whimsies of his own ... It simply came to an end. I do not know why the chairman, in whose hands the matter practically lay, let it die, unless it was that there was no practical outcome."[14] Later he commented that, "anyone in the past who had touched the subject had burnt his fingers."[15]

14. LCO 2/1138. 2.6.1932.
15. *Ibid.* 20.6.1932.

CHAPTER 16

Clashes with Lord Hewart,
Lord Chief Justice 1922-1940

Delegation or Despotism?

Gordon Hewart was the son of a tradesman who succeeded in building up a high-class drapery business in Bury, Lancashire. Born in 1870, the second of seven children, he was a sickly child, given special attention by his mother. It soon became apparent that he was the most intelligent child in the family. From Bury Grammar School he went to Manchester Grammar and then, with a scholarship, to University College Oxford. He had a good academic career but with health problems he had to be content with a second-class degree.

He was attracted to journalism and decided to make that his profession from 1894. His interest in politics led him to the law and he was called to the Bar by the Inner Temple in 1902.

While building up his practice in the Northern Circuit he was fortunate to be briefed in a case which made legal history. At the Manchester Assizes in 1908 he succeeded in winning the libel case against the *Hulton Press* for Artemus Jones, a barrister later to become a county court Judge. The plaintiff's case was that he had been libelled by a fictitious article which alleged that a Mr Thomas Artemus Jones had been in Dieppe living it up with a woman who was not his wife. The highly respectable Artemus Jones was awarded £1,750 in damages. Hulton, the proprietor of the defendant newspaper, was so impressed with Hewart's performance that he promised to engage him on his behalf in future libel actions (*Jones v. E. Hulton & Co.* CA [1909] 2 KB 444).

Hewart's practice flourished; he was popular in the city and had contacts with a variety of business interests but remained on the radical wing of the Liberal party. He favoured Home Rule for Ireland, a free church in Wales, taxing landowners and votes for women. In 1912 he took silk and stood for election unsuccessfully in Manchester. The following year a by-election gave him his opportunity. The Labour party agreed not to enter a candidate and he was elected with the aid of the Labour vote.

Hewart in Parliament

In the same year, 1913, Hewart moved house and family to London. In Parliament he soon made an impression. He was an excellent speaker, able to use humour appropriately and became noted for his *bons mots*, eg, "the nineteenth hole is the one they call the alco-hole." Lloyd George, whom Hewart admired, became Prime Minister in 1916. He had been impressed by Hewart and offered him the Home Office. However, Hewart preferred to take the position of Solicitor-General and accept a Knighthood. His friend, F.E. Smith, later Lord Birkenhead, was Attorney-General at the time and it seems that the two worked well together. When Birkenhead became Lord Chancellor, Hewart stepped up to be Attorney-General and a member of the Cabinet. Lloyd George valued him for his presence and debating ability and he became Lloyd George's close confidant and adviser on legal and other matters. He would often send for Hewart at inconvenient times; he wanted to keep him available to help him while at the same time promising Hewart future promotion.

After some controversy Lord Justice Lawrence was appointed Lord Chief Justice only to read of his own resignation in *The Times* less than a year later.[1] So it was that Hewart in March 1922, became Lord Chief Justice of England, a position he was to occupy for 18 years. During his tenure he presided over many interesting and well-publicised cases. However, he was not a good Judge; he would take sides early in the proceedings[2] and that frequently antagonised counsel. Brilliant as he had been as an advocate, his assets as an orator and his rhetoric as a politician were not appropriate when emanating from the Bench.

Hewart on the Bench

According to R.F.V. Heuston:[3]

> "Hewart was perhaps the worst Lord Chief Justice of England since the seventeenth century. Although no imputation of corruption or dishonesty could be brought against him as against Scroggs or Jeffreys, on the Bench he rivalled them in arbitrary and unjudicial behaviour. The author of the famous dictum that, 'a

---

1. Robert Jackson. *The Chief.* Biography of Gordon Hewart. Lord Chief Justice of England 1922-1940. Harrap, 1959, p.141.
2. *Ibid.*, p.157.
3. R.F.V. Heuston. *Lives of the Lord Chancellors.* 1885-1940. Clarendon Press, 1964, p.603.

long line of cases shows that it is not merely of some importance but is of fundamental importance that justice should not only be done, but should manifestly and undoubtedly be seen to be done,"[4] was incapable of securing its observance in his own court. Towards the end of his career he was constantly in bad health and the routine administration of the courts began to suffer."

On his appointment as Lord Chief Justice, at the swearing-in ceremony he had been supported by Birkenhead, the Lord Chancellor, the Master of the Rolls, Lord Sterndale and many other members of the judiciary and the Bar. However, this rapid rise from his origin in trade was enough to make him enemies as well as friends. One who came to be regarded as an enemy by Hewart was Claud Schuster. A relationship in the nature of a feud developed between the two men. Paradoxically they had much in common. There was only one year difference in their ages. Both came to the law via Oxford, the Inner Temple and the Northern Circuit. Both were to become Treasurer of the Inner Temple, Hewart in 1938 and Schuster in 1947. Both came from Manchester and both tragically lost a son in the 1914-18 war. Both were small men but whereas Schuster was lean and wiry, Hewart tended to be rotund - they were soon to be in conflict.

Crown Proceedings

As Attorney-General Hewart had often represented the Crown in litigation and frequently relied on the fact that the

---

4. *R. v. Sussex Justices, ex parte McCarthey* [1924] 1 KB 256.

Crown - the Executive, ie, government departments in any form - could not be sued. He was well aware of the injustices this ban could cause and he became interested in the power of the Executive over the subject and how that power should be regulated by the Judiciary. Because of his interest in the question he had seemed to be the ideal chairman for the Crown Proceedings Committee set up by Birkenhead soon after his appointment in 1919. The terms of reference directed the committee to say whether or not the invulnerability of the Crown was justified and if not, to suggest remedies. Hewart soon found that he had a thorny subject on his hands. Almost every government department wanted to retain its protection from having lawsuits brought against it. The bureaucrats were scared and displayed their obstructiveness. The result was that in spite of his initial interest Hewart failed to act decisively and his committee became inactive.[5]

Schuster with his usual energy tried to progress the matter. There is much correspondence on the file[6] from Schuster to Hewart - then Attorney-General, and to the Treasury Solicitor, Sir John Mellor. Most of the letters begin, "The Lord Chancellor thinks ..." or "The Lord Chancellor is glad to learn ..." The Treasury Solicitor suggested that Schuster should chair a small committee which would set out the issues and report to the full committee. On December 1, 1921, Schuster replied that he was unwilling to take the chair as he did not possess either the knowledge or the authority. Nevertheless he accepted the chairmanship and proceeded to show that he

---

5.   *The Chief*, p.181.
6.   LCD files.

had both.

Schuster wrote at length to Lord Stamfordham, the King's Secretary, explaining that the Monarch would not be affected by Crown Proceedings legislation. There was a reply to the effect that the King was satisfied and appreciated that he had been informed. By early 1922 the small committee had prepared a draft Bill and put forward proposals and questions of principle for the full committee. On November 27, 1923, Schuster wrote a long letter to Sir Walter Trower, past President of the Law Society and a member of the small committee, explaining that the delay was due to the fact that some members of the full committee were against the Bill and that the chairman (Hewart, by this time Lord Chief Justice) was "not giving a lead". Progress was therefore disappointing. He concluded the letter by saying that the supporters of the Bill would have to adopt "Fabian" tactics.

On November 27, 1923, Schuster put up a memorandum to Cave, the Lord Chancellor, suggesting that Hewart should be told that "... he [the Lord Chancellor] no longer desires the opinion of the Committee as to the merits to change the law, but as to the details of the changes and the form in which the changes should be put ..."[7] On December 3, 1923, Schuster drafted a letter to go to Hewart, urging Hewart to make a report in order to allay the complaints by the Law Society and others.[8] However, a change of Lord Chancellor was about to take place and it was not until Haldane was on the Woolsack in January, 1924, that a letter as suggested by Schuster's

---

7. *Ibid.*
8. *Ibid.*

memorandum was sent to Hewart. On January 30, 1924, Haldane stated in the Lords that he hoped to put forward a Bill shortly. In 1925 there were questions in the Commons about the progress of the Committee. The answer, provided by Schuster, was that substantial progress had been made and that a report would be made later. In the event the report was not presented until six years after the committee had been set up and it merely recommended minor procedural amendments which were put into the Administration of Justice (Miscellaneous Provisions) Act 1933. The immunity of the Crown from litigation was not removed until the Crown Proceedings Act 1947.

Hewart's dilatory progress on the subject of Crown Proceedings was a continuing annoyance to the impatient Schuster from 1921 when Hewart was Attorney-General until the unsatisfactory legislation in 1933. But it was not the only subject on which the two men came into conflict.

Schuster Plans a Ministry of Justice

There were many other irritations for Hewart in the early 1920s. Committees were set up in 1922 and 1923 to recommend changes to the Assize system and the relationship between petty sessions, quarter sessions and assizes. Naturally Schuster was a member of these committees and his office was responsible for servicing them. They recommended changes which affected, *inter alia*, the Northern Circuit. Hewart believed himself to be the administrative head of the courts and he was annoyed because he considered that these committees were encroaching on his domain. Schuster had no doubt that he himself should be in charge of administration and did not conceal his view that Judges were not good administrators. The friction between them was developing into a running feud. As the years of the 1920s passed Hewart became obsessed with the idea that Schuster was scheming to have the administration of the legal system transferred to him and be put under a Ministry of Justice. The administration of courts, other than the magistrates' courts, had in fact largely been transferred to the Lord Chancellor's Office, but on the subject of a Ministry of Justice Hewart was completely mistaken. Although appointed by the premier advocate of such a ministry, Lord Haldane, Schuster throughout his career opposed any move towards a Ministry of Justice.[9]

It was Schuster's administrative efficiency that annoyed Hewart. Historically, at least until the Judicature Acts 1873-5, the Lord Chief Justice had control of the administration of the higher courts and now Schuster was concerned to make them more efficient. In addition Hewart rightly believed that Schuster was determined to maintain the powerful patronage that had been built up by his predecessor, Muir MacKenzie. This extended not only to ecclesiastical appointments and the selection of members of committees and inquiries but also to judicial appointments made in the name of the Lord Chancellor. Hewart's political background made him aware of the powers of other Civil Servants besides Schuster and

---

9.　Jean Graham Hall and Douglas F. Martin. *Haldane - Statesman, Lawyer, Philosopher*. Barry Rose Law Publishers Ltd, 1996.

with some reason he became concerned about the number of quasi-judicial roles that had been assigned to government departments during and after the War. He saw this as the Executive usurping the functions of the judiciary, eroding its powers, and therefore violating the principles of the Constitution. All his fears that the Constitution and the independence of the judiciary were being attacked were focused on Schuster. Schuster's seemingly powerful position, his direct and decisive manner, his confident attitude, made Hewart regard him with loathing. It rankled to such an extent that he was said to refer to Schuster in private as "Shyster" and "the hidden hand".[10]

"A Sinister Plot"

In 1927 Hewart's request for two more King's Bench Judges to be appointed was refused by the Lord Chancellor's Office. That was just another incident to fuel Hewart's simmering hatred for Schuster. Moreover with age he was becoming progressively more cantankerous. In court he was autocratic and irascible and his behaviour antagonised members of the Bar. In one libel case his interventions caused him to lose the friendship of the distinguished Serjeant Sullivan.

However, many others besides Hewart were becoming concerned about the tendency of the legislature to give government departments judicial powers and the authority to make delegated legislation. This tendency was regarded

---

10. *The Chief*, p.258.

as a threat to the Constitution and in particular a threat to the independence of the judiciary. Hewart decided to put his fears into writing and in the Autumn of 1929 he had published a small book entitled *The New Despotism*.[11] He expressed his fears in strong language. There was a sinister plot. There was "... a persistent and well contrived system, intended to produce, and in fact producing a despotic power ..." with the object of replacing the government departments above the Sovereignty of Parliament and beyond the jurisdiction of the Courts. He wrote:

> "It is not enough, therefore, that Parliament and the public should be unceasingly vigilant to observe and to destroy clauses in the Bills which, if they are enacted, have the effect of placing some departmental decision or other beyond the reach of the law. It is necessary also to be astute to preserve judicial independence against any assault however insidious. A good example of the insidious kind of assault is to be found in the scheme ... for the destruction of the profoundly important office of Lord Chancellor ... the scheme is to get rid of him, to parcel out his functions among various individuals, and in particular to assign the duty of making judicial appointments to a new Minister, who is to be named the Minister of Justice ..."[12]

Hewart went on to say that sooner or later the Minister of Justice would be a mere politician, not legally trained and, like other Ministers, a bird of passage. The decisive authority would rest with some permanent official. This official would

---

11. The Rt. Hon. Lord Hewart of Bury. *The New Despotism*. Ernest Benn, 1929, chapter 7.
12. *Ibid.*, p.104.

say if asked by a foreigner who selected the Judges in England:

> "I am the person who really selects them. The Minister of Justice is but a transient, embarrassed phantom, here today and gone tomorrow. But I am always here. Mine is the knowledge, mine the experience, and the task of the Minister is simply to ratify my decision."[13]

Hewart developed his argument by relating historical examples of attacks which had been made on the independence of the judiciary. His language became stronger - the scheme (for a Ministry of Justice) was an evil thing - sinister - odious, and manifold mischiefs would follow.

He could not accept that there was such a subject as administrative law. He expressed the opinion in Chapter III of the *New Despotism* that *droit administratif* is completely opposed to the first principles of the Constitution.

The Committee on Ministers' Powers

As early as 1922 Schuster had no doubt that the tendency to delegate legislative powers to administrative agencies and to the departments of State was there to stay. In giving evidence to the Royal Commission on Local Government he said that there is great deal of administration where the administrator is bound to exercise, or ought to exercise, a

---

13.   *Ibid.*, p.108.

judicial mind, although what he is doing is administrative and not judicial.[14]

Even before Hewart's book was published the alert Schuster knew what was coming. He had informed Sankey, and had written on his behalf to Neville Chamberlain, the Chancellor of the Exchequer who was acting Prime Minister:

> "... it is highly expedient that the Government should be beforehand in this matter and should have indicated its desire before such a publication stirs up further public excitement on the question."[15]

At the same time Schuster was drafting terms of reference for a committee to make an investigation.

There was support for Schuster in Whitehall and by the Government. By the time *The New Despotism* was published Sankey was ready to announce the names of the members of the Committee on Ministers' Powers. Schuster had made sure that the selection was to his liking. The members included his fellow Permanent Secretaries, Sir John Anderson (later Lord Waverley) of the Home Office and Sir Warren Fisher of the Treasury who was also Head of the Civil Service. With Schuster himself also on the Committee these three were the triumvirate who ran Whitehall between the wars. Harold Laski, the socialist intellectual, Sir Roger Gregory for the Law Society and Lord Simonds, a future Lord Chancellor, were also on the Committee. Lord Donoughmore was appointed

---

14. Royal Commission on Local Government 1923. Minutes of Evidence, Part 2, p.428, QS 6442-3.
15. LCO 2/1133. October 11, 1929.

Chairman, although he soon handed over to Lord Justice Scott. The Committee was appointed in October 1929.

The terms of reference were:

> "to consider the powers exercised by or under the direction of (or by persons or bodies appointed specially by) Ministers of the Crown by way of (a) delegated legislation and (b) judicial or quasi-judicial decisions, and to report what safeguards are desirable or necessary to secure the constitutional principles of the sovereignty of Parliament and the supremacy of the law."

Hewart received an invitation to attend before the Committee but he refused. He is alleged to have said to friends, "They've got my book, why should I appear - especially with Schuster on the Committee."[16]

A leading academic, Professor W.A. Robson, in giving evidence to the Committee, had an exchange with Schuster. Schuster put the following rhetorical question to Professor Robson:

> "Is really anything more required, in the kind of cases we are talking about now, than the application of an honest mind under the guidance of somebody else, who it is admitted, cannot possibly know all the things which are done but is responsible for seeing that an honest mind is preserved and a certain policy followed? How can you substitute for that a number of people?"

Professor Robson replied:

---

16. *The Chief*, p.215.

"There is a very large difference between a responsible body and this vast anonymity."

Schuster said that of course there was a difference. Professor Robson elaborated on the difference between a tribunal which can be seen, can hear both sides, can give grounds for its decision and whose decision can be reviewed by a higher tribunal and receiving a letter from a Minister stating that he has considered your representation and has made a decision. He said:

"... you imagine the papers have been handed round the department and that some underling has done it. There is a very large institutional and psychological difference between that and having a definite tribunal ..."[17]

However, in spite of Professor Robson's standing as a legal authority, his proposals were not accepted.

The Report of the Donoughmore Committee (Committee on Ministers' Powers) 1932 included the following:

"Mr W.A. Robson has put before us detailed proposals for the establishment of a system of administrative courts and administrative law independent of Ministers as the best remedy for the defects of the original system to which our terms of reference are directed. We have considered their expediency, but interesting as they are, we cannot recommend their adoption, in our own view they are inconsistent with the sovereignty of

---

17. Royal Commission on Local Government. Minutes of Evidence Part 2, p.66, Q996.

Parliament and the supremacy of Law."[18]

Predictably the Committee found that Ministers and civil servants had not abused their powers, but that safeguards were required. Parliament should only exclude the jurisdiction of the courts on exceptional grounds and Bills conferring law-making powers on Ministers should be accompanied by a memorandum of explanation showing that such a provision was necessary. The Committee's Report was regarded by some as a valuable state document, not surprisingly by the Chairman, Lord Justice Scott in *Blackpool Corporation v. Locker* [1948] CA 1 KB 349.[19]

---

18. Cmd 4060. HMSO. 1932.
19. *Blackpool Corporation v. Locker* [1948] CA 1 KB 349 - Court of Appeal, Scott, Asquith and Evershed, LJJ. This was a case of dealing with the provision of accommodation for the inadequately housed - within the purposes specified in Supplies and Services (Transitional Powers) Act 1945; according by Regulation 51 of the Defence (General) Regulations 1939, a competent authority, eg, the Ministry of Health may take possession of any land for the purpose, and by para.5 he may delegate that function to any specified person on class of persons, subject to such restrictions as he thinks proper. Scott, LJ, at p.367 states:
    "And yet the nature of delegated legislation is quite plain; and the senior officials of the Ministry had no excuse for ignorance. The report of the Ministers' Powers Committee (Cmd 4060 of 1932) which led to the appointment by the House of Commons of the present Select Committee on Delegated Legislation and the passing of the Statutory Instruments Act 1946 explains the whole subject quite clearly. I was chairman of the Committee at the time we had to consider our report and the drafting committee consisted of the present Lords Schuster and Simonds and myself; and I still think the Committee's description and analysis of delegated legislation is correct. It is shortly stated in para.2 in p.15 of the report. The word

For a time Hewart was satisfied that his book had made people aware of the danger to the Constitution and the threat to democracy that delegated legislation and quasi-judicial powers could be. But his obsessional hatred of Schuster remained and was to be manifested in an extraordinary climax.

Conciliation Impossible

On November 3, 1933, Hewart's wife died. She had been a devoted wife and mother for 40 years. Her devotion and support were the more important to Hewart as they had lost their eldest son in the 1914-18 war and their second son had received injuries from which he never fully recovered. Hewart felt the loss of his wife deeply; for a year he was rarely seen at social events. His grief and loneliness did not improve his behaviour in court and certainly did not mellow his attitude to Schuster. What is perhaps surprising is that on December 29, 1934, just over a year after his wife's death, he married for the second time. Even more surprising is that when he made his outburst in the Lords on December 11, 1934, which is described later, he was in the process of courting his wife-to-be.

His animosity towards Schuster continued to smoulder. This ill-feeling was well-known in legal circles and caused Schuster much concern. He had asked friends to intercede to

---

'legislation' has grammatically two meanings - the operation or function of legislation and the law which reflects therefrom ..."

try to improve their relationship. Even Sankey and his predecessors had attempted to get them to reconcile their differences. Hewart rejected all such approaches. His obsessive hatred boiled up again when he learned that it had been decided to set up a committee (or commission) to inquire into the state of the work in the King's Bench Division. Obviously Schuster was to be a member of the committee and Hewart quite rightly believed that he had been the instigator of it. At the same time trouble was brewing because of the unexpected death of Lord Justice Scrutton, a senior Judge of the Court of Appeal. His death caused a conflict which was begun by another Court of Appeal Judge, Lord Justice Slesser.

The Slesser Affair

Sir Henry Slesser was a Fabian Socialist MP who had been appointed Solicitor-General by Ramsay MacDonald in 1924. Subsequently he was made a High Court Judge and at the age of 46 a Lord Justice of Appeal. This unusually rapid advancement was thought to have been "jobs for the boys" by his political opponents. There may have been an element of political bias but Slesser was regarded as a reasonably good Judge who was respected by his colleagues in the Court of Appeal. That court sat (and still does) in two Divisions. The Master of the Rolls presides over Court No.1 (The Chancery Appeal Court) and the most senior of the other appeal Judges presides over Court No.2 which deals with Common Law Appeals.

Lord Hanworth, the Master of the Rolls, had been, on his own admission, "uneasy" sitting on Chancery Appeals although Slesser, sitting with him, said that he had had a happy relationship with him. This was spoiled by subsequent events. What happened is best related in Schuster's own words:

> "He [Lord Hanworth] was uneasy in the appellate chair from the Chancery Division and saw, on Scrutton's demise, an opportunity to preside in the Common Law Court. This would have meant that Greer, who was then unfortunately unwell, would have had to preside over the Chancery Appeals, or when he was away, which was then beginning frequently to be the case, I should have to be Chairman.
>
> "I am inclined to think that this was the genesis of a proposal (which subsequently, I regret, cast a cloud over our friendship [with Hanworth] that the Chancellor, for the first time in the history of the Appeal Court, should appoint a vice-president to preside there instead of the senior Judge. The idea was perhaps less objectionable in the case of a new appointment, but most insidious when it operated to exclude a sitting Chairman."[20]

On November 28, 1934, Slesser wrote to Hanworth, Master of the Rolls:

> "... After my evident failure to persuade you of the justice of my contention that I should receive the same treatment as my predecessors and not be singled out for innuendo of incompetence, I decided to consult my old friend, the Lord Chief

---

20. *Rt Hon Sir Henry Slesser*. Later Lord Justice of Appeal. Hutchinson, 1941, p.256.

Justice [Hewart], a very senior member of the court.

"He is of opinion that no case whatever has been shown why, if and when I became Senior Lord Justice, I should not enjoy the same position as my predecessors, namely President of the Second Court. Moreover, he said that I had no right to prejudice the position of future Senior Lord Justices by stepping down.

"He also said that as President of the Courts of Common Law he had perfect confidence in my appellate work.

"As he is second senior member of the Court of Appeal I regard his views as conclusive. He advised me to refuse to sit if the occasion arose otherwise than in my rightful place; this advice I propose to act upon.

Yours sincerely, Henry Slesser."[21]

Hewart, scenting the hand of Schuster in the proposed break with tradition, was annoyed.

Hewart Harangues the House of Lords

Hewart's annoyance became real anger when on Friday, December 7, 1934 his clerk called his attention to a Bill he had found amongst Hewart's parliamentary papers. The Bill contained a clause enabling the Lord Chancellor to appoint any one of the Lord Justices of Appeal as Vice-President to preside over the Chancery Appeal Court. Hewart maintained that this was the first notice he had received that a Bill was to be presented in those terms. The Bill (the Supreme Court of Judicature Amendment Bill, 1934) also contained a clause

---

21. *Ibid.*

authorising the appointment of two more King's Bench Judges with the proviso that the positions could not be filled without a resolution of Parliament. That provision was also an innovation. Hewart was incensed that information, of great importance to him, should have reached him in such a casual way. In fact, Schuster had written to Hewart two months earlier but it was alleged that when he knew the letter was from Schuster he threw it into the fire unread (but, see below, he did acknowledge receipt of the letter). So with these two annoyances on his mind, infuriated, he called a meeting of Judges on December 10 and persuaded them to give him support. Then, on the morning of December 11 he bought a newspaper and read the headline which purported to forecast the effect the Bill would have. It was:

"Harassed Judges Meet in Secret, Five to do the work of Eighteen, Greatest Legal Hold-up for Years, SOS for Help."[22]

This was the last straw. Hewart's rage was driving him to drastic action.

On the same day he was sitting on a case of some importance concerning Parliamentary privilege (*R. v. Graham Campbell, ex parte Herbert* [1935] 1 KB 594). That was the case whereby the well-known humorist and MP, Sir Alan Herbert, tried to show that the House of Commons was breaking the law by selling intoxicating liquor without a licence. In the House of Lords, Sankey was due to move the second reading of the offending Bill not expecting any controversy. Hewart

---

22. *The Chief*, p.262.

knew he had to be there. On the licensing case he had, as usual, made up his mind early and he dealt with it in a hasty and perfunctory way[23] and proceeded to the House of Lords in high dudgeon.

He had rarely attended the Lords because of his court commitments and had never spoken in a debate. He entered the Chamber in cold fury but had to wait before he could say his piece because a debate on another Bill was in progress. Few of the members knew or even noticed the grim-faced chubby little man who took his place on one of the cross-benches.

The debate in progress was the second reading of a Bill on the registration of osteopaths. During this debate Hewart could not resist giving his opinion about one clause. He made what seems to be a very reasonable objection:

> "My Lords, I certainly did not come here this afternoon for the purpose of speaking about osteopathy. But I have not merely listened to the speeches I have taken the unusual course of reading the Bill .... Clause 7 provides ... that 'an osteopath ... shall have the power to sign certificates of birth and certify the cause of death' ... Speaking as a lawyer I am staggered at that provision. Has anybody heard of a dentist or a midwife certifying the cause of death? ... I sincerely hope it [the Bill] may not be read a second time."[24]

When it came to the vote he duly voted against but he was in a minority and the Bill was passed to the Committee stage.

---

23. R.F.V. Heuston. *Lives of the Lord Chancellors*, p.520.
24. *Hansard*. HL, vol.95, December 11, 1934, col.212.

The next business was what Hewart had come to hear. Sankey rose to move the second reading of the Supreme Court of Judicature (Amendment) Bill. Clause 1 provided for the two additional Judges and Clause 2 for the appointment of a Vice-President for the Court of Appeal. He spoke as if these were mere technicalities, and the Lords dozed.[25] Immediately he had finished Hewart rose to speak. Normally an excellent speaker he was so furious that his words, tumbling out, could only be followed with difficulty by the reporters. However, the report in *Hansard* is clear enough to show that his speech was as violent an attack as has ever been in the Lords.[26]

He began by complaining that in November he had received a letter from the Lord Chancellor's Office signed, not by the Lord Chancellor but by a secretary [Schuster]. Other Lord Chancellors used to write to him direct but now it was always a secretary and that any reply to such a letter would, in future, be signed by his [Hewart's] clerk. The subject matter of the letter concerned the setting up of a Royal Commission [in fact it was a committee] with terms of reference to investigate the state of work in the King's Bench Division. He further complained that as Lord Chief Justice of England he was entitled to be consulted about the Commission and its personnel. He listed the membership of the Commission with a disparaging reference to Lord Hanworth, Master of the Rolls, and made a passing reference to Sir Claud Schuster, his arch enemy, who was also a

---

25. *The Chief*, p.262.
26. *Hansard*. HL, vol.95, December 11, 1934, cols.224-237.

member.

He then turned to the draft Bill before the House. He complained that as a mere matter of courtesy he, the Lord Chief Justice, should have been informed of the contents of the Bill. It was only by accident that his clerk had come across it a few days before amongst his Parliamentary papers. His anger was mounting. He spluttered and shouted. The smooth tranquillity of the Lords where formal and gentlemanly debate was the rule, had never been disturbed like this before. The House listened in silence. To those Lords who were not lawyers Hewart's complaints were difficult to understand; they were amazed and shocked to hear a speech so contrary to the traditions of the House.

He launched into an attack on Lord Hanworth whom he believed, quite wrongly, to be the instigator of the clause which had offended Slesser. He thought that Hanworth, as a friend and colleague of long-standing, should have kept him informed of what was being proposed.

He then began to deal with Clause 1 concerning the appointment of Judges, "What are the objections of this clause? There are 20. At this hour I will mention two. It puts into the hands of Government whips the decision as to what shall be the composition of the King's Bench Division."

It was also a departure from tradition. But it was Clause 2 which angered him most. He praised Lord Justice Slesser who had sought his advice:

"Lord Justice Slesser is a Judge in whom I, at any rate, have complete confidence; a scholar; a lawyer. I have fought him at the Bar. I listened to him for many years on the Bench. I have known him and sat with him since as Lord Chief Justice ... This Bill by

Clause 2, enables the Lord Chancellor to appoint a Vice-President of the Court of Appeal which means that any one of the Lord Justices of Appeal could preside. That is to say, the Lord Chancellor or one of his secretaries' secretaries, by a stroke of the pen, could say that the person to preside in the Second Court of Appeal is So-and-So ... What has Lord Justice Slesser done that that affront should be put on him?"[27]

His tone became almost menacing and after referring to his book, *The New Despotism*, he said:

"I have not been for 12 years Lord Chief Justice of England with my eyes closed ... When Lord Birkenhead was Lord Chancellor a little scheme was put before him whereby the Lord Chancellor was to cease to exist, all judicial patronage was to be taken from the Home Secretary, and all the powers were to be invested in a new person to be called, after the continental fashion, a Minister of Justice. And that scheme had strong backing from some entity the origin of which I do not know, the personnel of which I do not know, called the Lord Chancellor's Department.

"It is perfectly obvious why. If that is done it will no longer be necessary to have in this country a lawyer as head of the judiciary. You might have a successful merchant, and that person would be ignorant of the personnel of the Bar. When a vacancy occurs he would have to turn to somebody to ask whom he should appoint. That person would be a permanent official of the Lord Chancellor's Department. The plan persistently carried on, is as clear to me as my own face in the mirror."

To any lawyer it was obvious that the "permanent official" referred to was Schuster. Towards the end of Hewart's

27. *Ibid.,* col.236.

harangue it was clear that the House was very alert and that he was getting some support. He concluded with a threat saying what he would do at the committee stage if the second reading of the Bill was passed:

> "When the committee stage comes on, if these, forgive the expression, odious features are not removed, then I shall adjourn my court every day in order to be present here to take part in fighting the obnoxious part of the Bill not only clause by clause, but, as I used to do in happier days in the House of Commons, line by line and word by word."[28]

This outburst had caused a sensation. Nothing like it had happened before in living memory, nor has it happened since - a public quarrel between very senior Judges involving a top civil servant and the Lord Chancellor. Sankey had been taken by surprise, he was unable to reply. Lord Hanworth, the Master of the Rolls, started to defend himself but on a proposal by Lord Ponsonby, the Labour leader, it was agreed to adjourn the debate.

The debate was resumed on December 14, 1934. It was opened by Lord Reading who said that he had experienced no such difficulty as Hewart when he was Lord Chief Justice. He regretted the powerful speech delivered by Hewart. Disturbing statements had been made. Judgments should be suspended until the whole case had been heard. Was the strong comment on Clause 2 of the Bill because Slesser had been appointed by a Labour government? Hewart interposed, "I did not make that suggestion. The suggestion I made was

---

28.   *Ibid.*, col.237.

that a large part of the public might well think that it was so." Lord Ponsonby pointed out that only a small minority of Lords had the capacity to understand the debate between these high judicial authorities. The Bill was ill-prepared and there should be another adjournment.[29]

Lord Hanworth, having made a short statement on December 11, wished to say more. He spoke as if he had been deeply hurt by Hewart's allegation that he had been responsible for Clause 2 of the Bill. He said with some interruptions from Hewart:

> "... I had nothing to do with the genesis of this clause ... I acted in friendship when I spoke to Lord Slesser and that I came to this House without knowledge that I should be charged by the Lord Chief Justice with having interpolated that clause ... I can only ask your Lordships to treat me with the courtesy with which, so far, you have always treated me, and ask of you to believe me."[30]

Defence of Schuster

Lord Hailsham, the Secretary of State for War and Leader of the House, began by explaining the close and cordial friendship he had had with Hewart. He had admired and enjoyed his speeches. There were the traditional toasts mutually given between himself, as Leader of the Bar and Hewart as Lord Chief. He went on to make a convincing defence of Schuster.

---

29. *Ibid.*, December 14, 1934, col.366.
30. *Ibid.*, col.376.

Hailsham said that he had understood Hewart to say that Clause 1 of the Bill (concerning the appointment of Judges) was in pursuance of the plot to set up a Ministry of Justice and that Clause 2 was one of the things that were paving the way. He had understood Hewart to allege that there was a plot hatched by Sir Claud Schuster and those working under him to substitute a Minister of Justice for the Lord Chancellor in order that they might have a say in who should be appointed to judicial offices. He continued:

> "... I am bound to come here and tell your Lordships that I can show that that is an absolute delusion, that there was no such scheme ever hatched, and that this is all part of a plot to get rid of the protagonist [Hewart] against this new bureaucracy because he has the courage to stand against these permanent officials, is a complete mistake."[31]

He went on to relate the history of the idea of Ministry of Justice. It began, he said, with Lord Brougham in 1836 and then became active again when Lord Haldane was Lord Chancellor in 1913. In 1918 in response to proposals from Lord Haldane and the Law Society, the leader of the Bar Council prepared a report with the help of Schuster who was then Permanent Secretary to the Lord Chancellor, which report utterly condemned the idea. In addition Schuster prepared a memorandum for Lord Chancellor Finlay which set out the pros and cons but was clearly biased against the proposal. In 1921 when Lord Birkenhead was Lord Chancellor he wrote a letter to *The Times* in response to a

---

31.   *Ibid.*, cols.381-382.

public statement by Lord Haldane in which he advocated a Ministry of Justice. This letter which was drafted by Schuster, stated that Birkenhead entirely disapproved of such a scheme. In 1922 Lord Birkenhead had an article published entitled *A Ministry of Justice*. Again this had been drafted by Schuster and was categorically against the idea.

Hailsham pointed out that Schuster had been fighting against a Ministry of Justice ever since he had been in the Lord Chancellor's Department. He went on to praise Schuster as the author and instigator of many law reforms; his energy and devotion to duty had enabled such reforms to succeed. He regarded it as his paramount duty to defend a civil servant who was debarred from defending himself or taking any part in a public controversy. Hewart had made a "... scathing and a sensational attack upon the head of the Lord Chancellor's Department, my friend Sir Claud Schuster." The charge, he said, that a plot had been hatched in 1919 to replace the Lord Chancellor by a Minister of Justice so that civil servants should have more power particularly with regard to judicial appointments, was completely without foundation. Also it was inconceivable that Schuster was behind such a plot. Hewart interrupted to say that he had not used such words (he interrupted at least eight times during Hailsham's speech). Hailsham read from the verbatim report of Hewart's attack to prove that he had done so.[32]

He described Hewart's charges as allegations of "dark design" by Schuster. Hewart interrupted again to say that he had never used such words. But Hailsham immediately

---

32. *Ibid.*, col.380.

justified his description. He suggested to the House that that was the correct interpretation of what Hewart had said. Lord Ponsonby intervened asking why the necessary explanations had not been made to Hewart in conference instead of on the floor of the House. Hailsham replied irritably:

> "Although that is more immediately a question for the Lord Chancellor, I think the obvious answer is because, as far as I know, the Lord Chief Justice did not discuss this with the Lord Chancellor until he made his speech on the floor of the House."

Tempers were rising, Hewart snapped back to the effect that he had not been aware of Clause 2 until the Friday before, then it was only by accident that his clerk had found a copy of the Bill in with his parliamentary papers. There was no time for him to see the Lord Chancellor because he was busy with Appeal papers on Saturday and Sunday and he was in court on Monday. Hailsham replied that in Hewart's position he would have arranged to see the Lord Chancellor after court on Monday at 4 o'clock if there was no other suitable time. Hewart's reply to that was, "not if you had been treated as I have been during the last three years."[33] [34]

---

33. *The Chief*, pp.266/7.
34. The following is a comment by Quinten Hogg, Lord Hailsham of Marylebone, Lord Chancellor, and the son of the Lord Chancellor in this debate:
    "The Judges themselves are not always their own best friends. I speak not of occasional lapses from good taste or common sense - failings to which all of us are subject from time to time when under stress - but of the sad disease to which I sometimes give the name Hewartitis." (*A Sparrow's Flight*, Memoirs of Lord Hailsham of St

Hailsham concluded by praising Hewart:

"We have all seen on Tuesday that the force and vigour of his intellect are unabated, that he still retains that matchless eloquence and power of persuasion which many of us knew and admired in days of old ..."

A Most Painful Occasion Continues

Then Sankey rose to give his considered reply to Hewart's charges. He began:

"That speech took me entirely by surprise. It amazed me. I had no notice of what the Lord Chief Justice proposed to say. He never communicated with me and I had not the slightest idea of the nature of the attack which he was going to make. I regret that he did not give me even five minutes of his invaluable time when very much of this debate might possibly have been avoided."[35]

He noted that Hewart's attendance in the Lords on the previous Friday was, to the best of his knowledge, the first time he had been there and that the House would have been pleased to have his assistance on some of the law reforms which had been passed.

Hewart did not disagree. He had always had a certain contempt for the House and had made disparaging references about it. It is said that when asked by a friend if he often went

Marylebone, Collins, 1990, p.422.)
35.   *Hansard*. HL, December 14, 1934, vol.95, col.402.

to the Lords he replied:

> "No, not often ... I did go the other day. The first man I ran into was a man who had been gaoled for issuing a false prospectus, and the second was a man who had been fined heavily for company irregularities. I said to myself, 'This is not the House of Lords. This is the House of Frauds'."[36]

Lord Sankey then praised Hewart's ability as an advocate:

> "He is one of the most brilliant advocates of modern times, and even now at times he cannot forget the advocate. I could have wished, however, that his speech the other night had been rather more temperate in tone, and that he had been a little more careful in his facts and had charged his memory rather more closely before he began to speak."[37]

Sankey briefly explained the intentions of the Bill and then passed on to mention the "feud":

> "... It is clear that the Lord Chief Justice's remarks were an attack on the Lord Chancellor's Department. Let us not mince words - it was an attack upon Sir Claud Schuster, who has been Permanent Secretary to the Lord Chancellor since 1915 and has served under no fewer than seven Lord Chancellors. I had known ... long before I came to this House ... that the Lord Chief Justice did not see eye to eye with Sir Claud Schuster."[38]

Hewart said, "Did you?"

---

36. *The Chief*, p.267.
37. *Hansard*. HL, December 14, 1934, vol.95, col.403.
38. *Ibid.*, cols.403/404.

Sankey continued by saying that the two men were both eminent public servants, both men of great knowledge and great experience of administration. But, he said, they both have decided views on administration and with two men like that it was inevitable that they would disagree from time to time. This, he continued, did not make the life of a Lord Chancellor a bed of roses. When he first became Lord Chancellor Schuster had told him that he regretted the attitude of the Lord Chief Justice towards him and begged Sankey to try to heal the rift between them. He was still hopeful that the relationship could improve. He praised Schuster highly, referring to him as a great permanent official, and how he was grateful for the advice and judgment he had received from him.

This praise would not have surprised Hewart who believed that Sankey was in Schuster's pocket. Sankey stated that it was contrary to all parliamentary practice and to the whole spirit of the Constitution to make attacks on permanent officials. He then dealt with the charges Hewart had made. He referred back to the letter written by Schuster with Sankey's approval which was sent to Hewart on October 25, 1934. Hewart interrupted (he made 10 interruptions to Sankey's speech) to say that he had just received a copy of a letter marked "secret" dated October 25 that afternoon. Sankey said he was going to read the letter. This brought the remark from Hewart, "It announces a decision, it does not ask for an opinion." Sankey read the letter, signed by Schuster, which clearly explained the proposals of the Government. Hewart's interruptions at this point caused Sankey to say sharply, "Listen!"

Hewart's response in a disgusted tone was "Decisions!"[39]
Sankey agreed that the decisions were for two extra Judges
and a committee. He had hoped he said, that he might have
had the Lord Chief Justice's approval or criticism but was
disappointed in the answer which was:

October 26, 1934

Dear Claud Schuster,
    I thank you for your letter received this morning, and have
read it with much interest.

Yours sincerely,
Hewart.

PS: I observe the word "Secret" and it shall remain so.

Sankey explained that a week after receiving the letter he
arranged an interview with Hewart during which they had
discussed the appointment of the Judges. In fact, Hewart had
suggested a name which was that of one of the Judges to be
appointed. They had also discussed Hewart's objection to the
requirement for a resolution of the House of Commons. With
regard to the committee or commission to examine the state
of work in the King's Bench Division to which Hewart was
vehemently opposed in Sankey's opinion:

"What is the use of discussing the future of a man who says he
does not wish to have anything to do with an inquiry at all?"

Sankey had been walking up and down while making his
speech and was sounding more and more irate. The Ministry

---

39.   *Ibid.*, col.407.

of Justice plan was just moonshine, he said. "Hear, hear!" said Hewart ironically. "It's pure moonshine that is troubling the Lord Chief Justice," said Sankey. "I am delighted to hear it," said Hewart mellowing somewhat.

Sankey had mentioned that the Master of the Rolls was the President of the Court of Appeal.[40] Hewart retorted, "I thought by Statute the Lord Chancellor is President." Sankey was irritated, "I said the President who sits there day after day and week after week. Quibbles are not of any use in a case like this." The debate had been going on for three hours. Listeners and speakers were becoming exhausted, tempers were cooling.

Sankey stopped pacing up and down and resumed his usual dignity.[41] He declared that in the interests of the administration of justice the trouble should not be allowed to go further. He objected to the proposed adjournment because there was an urgent need for two extra Judges in the King's Bench Division.

When he sat down the former Lord Chief Justice, Lord Reading, stepped up with a compromise which he had the authority and experience to suggest. He proposed that if the Government wished to appoint a Vice-President for the Court of Appeal the appointment should not be made in the lifetime of any member at present sitting. Thus neither Lord Slesser nor any other members would be prejudiced.[42]

Lord Merrivale said:

---

40.   *Ibid.*, col.410.
41.   *The Chief*, p.268.
42.   *Hansard.* HL, December 14, 1934, vol.95, col.11.

"... To everybody who has ever been concerned with the administration of justice in this country this has been a most painful occasion. Certainly nothing of this kind has happened in the more than 50 years that I have been associated with the law."

He appealed to Hewart to accept that there had been a misunderstanding and that no sort of personal discourtesy had been intended towards him.

Lord Wright expressing some sympathy for Hewart also hoped that he would accept Lord Merrivale's appeal. During his career, and even on this occasion, Hewart had attracted a great deal of affection from his opponents as well as from his friends. He replied saying he was touched by the kind expressions which had been made about him by the noble Lords.

Emotional, as he always was, Hewart had almost the last word in the debate. He again referred to the letter of October 25 marked "secret" and said:

"It is quite true that that letter having been marked 'secret' was immediately put into the fire, and its contents not disclosed to any other human being in the smallest degree. I would point out that what the letter communicated to me was a decision. I was never asked to express a view ..."

Then having repeated his complaints about the King's Bench Commission and its personnel, he became more conciliatory. He said that he had understood Sankey to have said that he wanted to play the part of a peacemaker, he accepted the idea that a Ministry of Justice was dead and that he would not give it another thought.[43] His last words were:

> "A debate of this kind does not tend to edification. It is not good for the Law Courts, for the Bar, or for the public. I have no desire to prolong the controversy. On the contrary I have an overwhelming desire to prolong and perpetuate friendships. Blessed are the peacemakers. Let us all make peace and get on with our work."[44]

The Bill as amended was read for a second time and then an amazing thing happened. Sankey, Hailsham, Hanworth, Merrivale, Reading and several other peers left their seats and surrounded Hewart. They shook his hand, held him affectionately by the arm, slapped him on the shoulder. Among the throng another figure appeared and in the confusion Hewart found himself shaking the hand of Sir Claud Schuster.[45]

Was this the end of the "feud"? Unfortunately not. The relationship improved for a time but soon deteriorated and continued over the years. Schuster became progressively more autocratic although as efficient as ever. It was difficult for both contrasting characters to forget the past.

On February 22, 1939, Hewart opened *The Times* and read the names of the newly appointed silks for the year. Silks are appointed by the Lord Chancellor after he has taken advice from many sources. Hewart had not been consulted and had not seen the list before. Such a thing had not happened for

---

43. *Ibid.*, cols.418-419.
44. *Ibid.*
45. *The Chief*, p.269.

17 years. Hewart told his clerk that in his view this was once again evidence of Schuster's campaign against him.

By 1940 he was not in good health and he said he would resign in the near future. Nevertheless a month later he was shocked when told by telephone from Downing Street that Churchill expected his resignation forthwith. In this abrupt end to Hewart's career, can we see the hand of Schuster?

CHAPTER 17

Lord Maugham -
March 15, 1938 to September 3, 1939

A Surprise Appointment

Maugham's appointment as Lord Chancellor at the age of 71 surprised those in legal circles. It also surprised the politicians as he had had no political experience. Maugham himself always confessed that he had no idea how his name had been placed before the Prime Minister (Neville Chamberlain); but those entitled to judge expressed the view that Claud Schuster had much to do with it.[1] That will never be known for certain. However, we do know that in 1938 Schuster had been in post for 23 years and had worked himself into a position where he could influence all legal appointments. It is also known that Maugham (brother of Somerset Maugham, the author) was a friend of Professor Harold Laski who in turn was in close communication with Schuster. However, as against the notion that Schuster caused the appointment to be made is the fact that in a letter dated October 13, 1947, to the widow of Lord Caldecote, the Lord Chancellor, Schuster suggested that Caldecote should have received the Chancellorship when Maugham was appointed.[2] If Schuster had recommended Maugham it seems that he may have regretted it. The simple explanation may be that at the

---

1. R.F.V. Heuston. *Lives of the Lord Chancellors*. 1885-1940. Clarendon Press, 1964, p.553.
2. *Ibid.*, p.6068.

time Caldecote was Minister for the Co-ordination of Defence and that Chamberlain felt that he could not be moved from that critical position.

Another surprise is that in his autobiography Maugham does not make a single mention of Schuster by name.[3] He describes in some detail his duties as Lord Chancellor as if he carried them out in isolation. During his short tenure he must have worked hard. He steered several important Bills through the Lords, notably, the Inheritance (Family Provision) Act 1938, the Limitation Act 1939, the Official Secrets Act 1939 and the Evidence Act 1938 which dealt with the important question of hearsay evidence. In addition to the normal administrative responsibilities of his position, he was responsible for making elaborate arrangements to remove the courts from London in time of war. No doubt that function and many of his other responsibilities were delegated to Schuster. He must have been of great assistance to Maugham so one would expect to find some reference to, or acknowledgement of Schuster, in his autobiography. Schuster is believed to have said that he got on well with all his 10 Lord Chancellors except one - Maugham could have been that one.

A Difference of Opinion

Schuster's relationship with Lord Maugham certainly deteriorated after the outbreak of war in 1939. Maugham had

---

3.   Lord Maugham. *At the End of the Day*. Heineman, 1954.

been a strong and articulate supporter of Chamberlain and the Munich settlement. Schuster would have differed from him on that subject but when Maugham resigned on September 3, 1939, he did so for certain reasons and with certain intentions which later were disputed by Schuster. Maugham gave as his reason for resigning his age (nearly 73) and that during wartime a younger man should be appointed. He expressed the hope that he might resume his work as a Lord of Appeal at the next opportunity. A vacancy arose when Lord Macmillan became Minister of Information and Maugham returned to his position of Law Lord. According to Schuster and Caldecote, Maugham had given Schuster an assurance that should Lord Macmillan cease to be a Minister and wish to return to his duties as a Law Lord, Maugham would resign in his favour. When this did happen Maugham refused to resign saying that he had only agreed to resign at the end of the war. This incident supports the suggestion that Maugham was the Chancellor with whom Schuster was not in tune.

CHAPTER 18

Lord Caldecote -
September 4, 1939 to May 13, 1940

Honest but Uninspiring

As Sir Thomas Inskip, Lord Caldecote, unlike his predecessor Lord Maugham, had had a long political career, and been both Solicitor-General and Attorney-General. His appointment as Lord Chancellor was by way of a reward for long service. It terminated after only eight months when, on the fall of the Chamberlain Government in May 1940, Schuster telephoned shortly before the nine o'clock news to say that it was about to be announced that Simon was to succeed him on the Woolsack. He was demoted to his old post of Secretary of State for the Dominions. Demotion was inevitable because of his support of Chamberlain in the policy of appeasement to Hitler. Five months later he became Lord Chief Justice.

He was regarded as an honest but uninspiring Minister and achieved little during his short reign as Chancellor. Schuster had a good opinion of him as is shown by a letter he wrote to Lady Caldecote on October 13, 1947, two days after her husband's death:

> "I have always thought Tom the very model and example of what a lawyer in public life should be. He was not, I suppose, without a decent ambition, and desired to put his great gifts of character and sound judgment and industry at the service of his country. But, as it happened, I saw most of him at the great crisis of his life, at the time of the debate on the Prayer Book, when he was forced into the Ministry of Defence, when he had to abandon the idea

of becoming Master of the Rolls, when he became and when he ceased to be Lord Chancellor, when he, almost reluctantly, was persuaded to sacrifice the rest and retirement which he desired and to become Chief Justice. On all these occasions his own personal advancement and prestige were the last things which, for him, counted in the decision. *The Times* says that he was lucky. I have always thought him the opposite. If he had received the Chancellorship, as was his due, when Maugham was appointed; if he had become Chief Justice earlier in times when he would not have been hampered by war conditions, he might have had, indeed I am sure he would have had, in either office a long and fruitful reign. In each case fate was against him. And in addition he had to bear, as he did in silence, the burden of reproaches from ignorant people for the impossible task set him in the Ministry of Co-ordination of Defence."[1]

This is an example of Schuster's ability to put on paper words which are appropriate to the occasion. In this case he was saying what Lord Caldecote's widow would have wanted to hear.

The debate on the Prayer Book referred to by Schuster in the letter took place in the Commons in December 1927. Caldecote (then Sir Thomas Inskip, Solicitor-General) was a devout Anglican Christian, President of the Lord's Day Observance Society and several other Christian organisations. There was an impasse between Church and State as the new Prayer Book was thought to go too far towards placating the Anglo-Catholics and was unacceptable to the predominantly Protestant House of Commons. Caldecote made an

---

1.   R.F.V. Heuston. *Lives of the Lord Chancellors*. 1885-1940. Clarendon Press, 1964, p.606.

impassioned speech against the proposed changes and the new Prayer Book was rejected. Schuster, the expert on compromise, was then appointed chairman of a committee which managed to solve the problem.[2] A neutral appointment perhaps as, although he came from a Christian background, Schuster had no strong religious belief and he had Jewish ancestry.

Wartime Legislation

The outbreak of war in 1939 was not unexpected and for some months beforehand *ad hoc* committees had been considering the implications of war for the courts. War zone courts were organised in 11 regions, each with a High Court Judge as President, to be in operation when a region was designated a war zone. Schuster had been reluctant to accept these arrangements and had felt that the original Home Office proposals were "too drastic".[3]

On the subject of civil liabilities it was thought necessary to provide a form of protection for debtors which was more efficient and fair to all parties than the 1914 moratorium. Schuster was appointed chairman of a Cabinet sub-committee with the following terms of reference, "to consider the problems arising from the inability of persons, owing to war conditions, to fulfil their contractual and other obligations, and in particular to consider the complaints already made to

---

2. LCO 2/1348.
3. LCO 2/3412.

MPs and government departments." The complaints had come especially from evacuated areas such as coastal towns. The sub-committee made six reports. At first the thinking was that the common law principal of frustration would be sufficient and there was opposition to the complete moratorium declared in certain evacuated areas. It was decided that leases and contracts, mortgages, etc, could not be rewritten by the courts but the courts could be given powers to suspend and modify.

The Schuster sub-committee's solution was put into effect by the Liabilities (Wartime Adjustment) Acts 1941-4. This was decided as, "a kind of preventative and remedial bankruptcy without stigma".[4] It was administered by a Liabilities Adjustment Officer, usually the local county court registrar, and had a similar effect to a scheme of arrangement. This useful procedure was not used as much as it should have been during the war and was terminated soon after. However, it has a legacy, in that of late there has been encouragement to use, and a revival of, administration orders in the county courts.

From 1939 there were many allied forces in Britain, eg, Dutch, Norwegians, Poles, French, etc. The Allied Forces Act 1940 was passed which gave jurisdiction to the allied authorities over their own forces but reserved the jurisdiction of our civil and criminal courts. Two years later when American troops arrived the huge numbers and immense power of the United States ensured that they were treated differently. A committee was formed, naturally presided over

---

4. LCO 2/1400.

by Schuster, which prepared the drafting of the USA (Visiting Forces) Bill. This provided that no criminal proceedings would be prosecuted in the United Kingdom against members of the military and naval forces of the United States of America. It did not affect any powers of arrest, search, entry or custody exercisable under British law with respect to offences committed or believed to have been committed against the law. But persons arrested under such powers were to be handed over to the military authorities of the USA. The Bill was passed by Parliament with little argument on August 6, 1942.

CHAPTER 19

Lord Simon -
May 13, 1940 to July 27, 1945

"Cold Remoteness"

Schuster's last Lord Chancellor was in post for five-and-a-half years, only six months less than Sankey. He had been a contemporary of Birkenhead for a while at Wadham College, Oxford, and the two men were friendly rivals in politics and at the Bar. The raffish outgoing Birkenhead was fond of teasing the eminently respectable John Allsebrook Simon. At a college dinner, when Simon was making large sums at the Bar, Birkenhead began his speech, "Sir John Simon, whose presence here this evening is costing him a thousand pounds ..." Simon was not amused but he forced himself to pretend to be. He was almost completely lacking in humour, a cold fish, the complete opposite of the ebullient Birkenhead.[1] He made no attempt to cultivate the public; indeed along with Chamberlain as one of the appeasers of Hitler in 1938 he could not hope to be popular. His cold remoteness could be put down to his upbringing as the son of a non-conformist Minister and the numbing effect of being left a widower with three children while still under 30 years of age.

For the adaptable Schuster the change of Minister presented no problem. Moreover this was war-time; Simon

---

1. Sir Maurice Bowra. *Memories 1898-1939* (1966), pp.140-2 (quoted R.F.V. Heuston, *Lives of the Lord Chancellors 1940-1970*. Clarendon Press, 1887, p.38).

was not a member of the War Cabinet and the time was not opportune for reform of the legal system. However, he did secure the passage of two statutes which made necessary advances in the cause of justice at that time. They were the Law Reform (Frustrated Contracts) Act 1943 and the Law Reform (Contributory Negligence) Act 1945. Both these Acts were influenced by leading academic lawyers - Arthur Goodhart and Percy Winfield. But Simon firmly adhered to the traditional policy of excluding academics from judicial appointments.[2]

In 1941 he said:

> "I do not want to see the judicial bench filled with people who are no doubt terrifically learned but are living in complete seclusion and have no contact with the world."[3]

He carried out that intention by making several good judicial appointments, doubtless with Schuster's aid. Of particular interest is that he appointed one Judge at the age of 45 who was to become the best known English Judge of the century - viz, A.T. Denning.

A High Court judgeship became vacant in the Probate, Divorce and Admiralty Division in 1942. The advice that Simon received from Schuster was typical of the latter's confidence or over-confidence. It also shows, perhaps, how by innuendo rather than by a direct suggestion he persuaded Simon to appoint his personal friend. This example of

---

2.   *Ibid.*, p.57.
3.   Report of the Select Committee on Offices of Profit under the Crown. HMSO, 1941, p.97.

Schuster's influence was not lost on both Bench and the Bar.

He first suggested that Simon might wish to consult Merriman - the President of the Division, and implied that that would not be of much use. He then told Simon of possible Silks on the Admiralty side, obviously with little enthusiasm for any of them. He mentioned a certain L N, "... but you may perhaps not think it is necessary to trouble yourself with any prolonged consideration of his name." He suggested others on the Admiralty side at greater length:

> "Of these men Trapnell, though, as I have already stated, he purports to practise in the court, has never really had any footing in it; if I had had to comment on Cartmael a short time ago, I should have said that he was not regarded professionally as the equal of his competitors, and it appears to be accepted that he is a poor advocate and not very good tempered. Recently, however, I have heard that he is a better lawyer than an advocate and that his faults of temper are largely due to diffidence. Seller's [*sic*] activities really lie elsewhere; Willmer, though by common repute the ablest of them all, is still very young, and incidentally is still serving actively in the Army. The choice, if it be made from among those practising in the court, therefore, appears to lie between Hayward and Pilcher. I do not think it appropriate to comment on their respective merits which you have recently had ample opportunity of judging. Pilcher is a personal friend of my own.
>
> "If you turn to Divorce side, the silks are: Middleton, Glazebrook, Barnard and Bush James, all of whom took silk in 1939.
>
> "I do not trouble you with any details about these men as I do not think that in any circumstances you would be disposed to

recommend any one of them for a judgeship."[4]

After advice like that from a very experienced permanent secretary, Simon naturally appointed Schuster's friend - Pilcher.

Magistrates as Inferior Judges

Schuster's leverage in connection with the appointments of Judges was even stronger when dealing with magistrates and the Home Office. He wrote a memorandum to Simon dated September 3, 1942,[5] the need for which was touched off by two incidents concerning magistrates. The first arose from an argument that a stipendiary magistrate named Langley had had with a witness who was a trade union official. In the exchange the magistrate had alleged that the man must be incompetent in his job. In fact, he was an experienced trade union official of some standing. A Labour MP had attempted to table a question in the Commons about the incident but his question had been refused by the Clerk of the Table.

In the other case a JP named Metcalfe had made a remark to the effect that frequently Welsh girls were convicted of prostitution. In the first case Sir John Anderson, the Home Secretary had interviewed the offending stipendiary, reprimanded him and ordered him to apologise. Three

---

4. LCO 2/3829. Quoted by Robert Stevens in *The Independence of the Judiciary*. Clarendon Press, 1993, p.42.
5. LCO 2/2769.

questions arose from these two cases:

1. Should the question in the Commons have been tabled?
2. Could a magistrate be dictated to by a Minister?
3. How could a magistrate be removed?

Schuster had received letters exchanged between the Clerk of the Table in the Commons and the Home Office and he wrote a five-page letter to the Home Office. It was well argued in his usual fluent style. He was dismayed both by the attitude of the House of Commons Clerk and by the Home Secretary. The argument against allowing the question was based on the tradition that the judiciary could not be criticised by the legislature. In this case Schuster argued that even though "judiciary" included the magistracy he believed that there must be a democratic right for an MP to table a question. Admittedly such action should be discouraged as the normal remedy would be through the courts but in this case the question should have been allowed.

Schuster was also shocked that his old friend the Home Secretary had, in effect, interfered with the judiciary by dictating to a magistrate. On the question as to how a magistrate should be removed, having consulted an expert, Graham Campbell, and disagreed with him, Schuster wrote that magistrates were appointed at the Crown's pleasure and could only be dismissed on a motion before Parliament. In the letter he also included his opinion on the position of High Court Judges. They are appointed by letters patent and could only be dismissed on an address from both Houses of Parliament. But he argued that such an address was merely a franchise to call the attention of the Crown to remove the patent (that opinion is probably still valid).

He referred to the origins of magistrates and that they were originally principally executive officers with judicial duties. Now that had changed and they were inferior Judges. In the same letter he also made some prophetic suggestions viz, that the Home Office should be responsible for the prevention of crime and should arrange for suspects to be brought before the courts. It should have oversight of the prisons and the probation service. The Lord Chancellor's Department should be charged with the arrangements of all courts. That, of course, is now the present position; it is surprising that it has taken so long to come about.

In the last paragraph of the letter he felt bound to ensure that the reader would not think he was suggesting a Ministry of Justice in the Haldane mould. He wrote:

> "The combination of these two functions [of the Home Office and the LCD] in one Ministry of Justice would, as I suggest, aggravate the present evil and reverse the tendency of recent years whereby a magistrate has become more and more a magistrate and less a thief-taker, and would turn a magistrate, to put the matter at its highest for the sake of illustration, into something rather like the French *juge de paix*."[6]

Appointing a Chairman

Schuster's influence was not limited to judicial appointments. The War-time Committee on Reconstruction Priorities

---

6.   *Ibid.*

decided that provision should be made for the victims of industrial disease outside the social security system. The department in charge of the subject was the Home Office and the Permanent Secretary proceeded to set up another committee. He wanted a chairman who was a legal expert of high judicial standing and naturally sought the advice of the Lord Chancellor's Office.

Simon's reaction was that he could not spare a Judge. This was what Schuster had been saying since 1920, when many political problems had arisen following the 1914-18 war. He deplored the practice of diverting His Majesty's Judges from their normal duties to the investigation of problems which Ministers found difficult to resolve. Simon wrote to Schuster:

> "It is very undesirable that a Judge, who is now discharging his judicial functions, should take the principal part in advising on this sort of question. The question is essentially one of politics and of administration."[7]

So Judges were out. Both Simon and Schuster began to consider academics and others. Simon suggested a politician; Schuster did not agree, he put forward two other names. In the event Morrison, the Home Secretary, appointed none of those suggested by the Lord Chancellor's Office. He appointed Sir Hector Hetherington, Principal of Glasgow University. Within a short time Hetherington withdrew as he was appointed to another academic post. Other academics were suggested by the Home Office for the chair of the

---

7.   PIN 12/85. Quoted in *The Independence of the Judiciary*, p.48.

committee, now called "The Committee on Alternative Remedies". Two in particular were Sir Arnold McNair, Vice-Chancellor of the University of Liverpool and A.L. Goodhart, the Professor of Jurisprudence at Oxford. Simon thought that McNair was an excellent choice and approved of Goodhart as a reserve. But McNair turned the job down; in a letter to the Home Office drafted by Schuster, Simon had changed his mind about both McNair and Goodhart:

> "As [McNair] has refused there is no harm in my saying that I really do not think a man with no experience of litigation, with an academic qualification which is largely in the realm of International Law, would have been a very good choice, though, of course, he is an excellent chairman, thorough and painstaking to a degree and a very nice fellow. I make this comment because I have a message on the telephone that one of the names you were thinking of was Goodhart, Professor at Oxford. Here again, the trouble is that he knows nothing about the workmen's compensation which is statute and not common law, and though he is a very good lawyer, primarily American, I really do not think he is the kind of choice you should make. Why do you not consider A.T. Denning, KC - one of the best brains at the Bar I think and certainly a very quick and active mind? An even better name, perhaps, would be G.J. Lynskey, KC of Manchester."[8]

That Schuster had prompted Simon to change his mind is borne out by a memorandum by a Home Office official to the Home Secretary, Herbert Morrison, after he had told them to write to Professor Goodhart appointing him as chairman:

---

8.   PIN 12/85 Simon to Bannatyne, January 1944.

"Bannatyne and I have since seen Sir Claud Schuster, and Sir Claud, while expressing admiration for the ability and character of Professor Goodhart, says that his talk and manner are so strongly Jewish that he feels sure he could not be counted on to control such a committee as we have in mind."[9]

Finally Sir Walter Monckton was appointed to be the chairman of the committee.

These examples show that nearing the end of his career as Permanent Secretary his power to influence appointments was as strong as ever. In a memo to Simon on March 18, 1942, he had the effrontery to write that the Treasury had not lived up to its promise that the Lord Chancellor's Office would have one "free floating" Knighthood in every Honours List.[10]

War Pensions

In addition to the legislation on civil liabilities, see earlier in this chapter, Schuster was also concerned with other wartime legislation on subjects such as war damage, wartime leases and pension tribunals. Pension tribunals had been set up after the 1914-18 war and in 1922 and 1924 there had been pressure to provide for appeals against the decision of the tribunals. At that time the LCO had resisted such pressure, but Schuster was deeply impressed by his experience of the depth of public feeling. He had "personally read the papers in every case in which there was a serious complaint made of the

---

9.   Memo from CAD, January 17, 1944. PIN 12/85.
10.   LCO 4/7.

decision reached by the tribunals ..." and was dismayed to find that in the next war the Ministry of Pensions, having already rejected 110,000 claims, nevertheless continued to defer the establishment of appeal tribunals and proposed to restrict appeals to those who had served a certain time in the forces.[11] The excuse given for the restriction and the delay was that it was impossible in wartime to find enough doctors to work the system of appeals.

11. LCO 2/938, 2/2646, 2/2780.

CHAPTER 20

Baron Schuster of Cerne in the County of Dorset, GCB, CVO, KC

A Legislator at Last

On June 26, 1944, Schuster had the singular duty of signing his own Patent with the usual "Schuster" creating himself Baron Schuster of Cerne in the Country of Dorset. He also signed the Writ of Summons commanding him to attend the House of Lords. He was to become a member of the legislature at last.

In 1944, just after Schuster had retired, Simon set up a committee under the chairmanship of Lord Rushcliffe to consider the facilities then available for giving legal advice and assistance to the poor, and to make recommendations for modifying and improving the existing scheme. Sir Albert Napier, Schuster's successor as Permanent Secretary to the Lord Chancellor, was a member of the Committee and, not surprisingly, Schuster himself, by now Lord Schuster, was also a member. The Committee reported in May 1945 (Cmd 6641) and most of its recommendations formed the basis for the Legal Aid and Advice Act 1949. Schuster and Napier had argued that a legal aid scheme should be administered by the Lord Chancellor's Department but eventually accepted that it should be administered by the legal profession with one exception. They also tried to persuade the Committee that legal aid should not be available in all criminal cases. The result was that one recommendation of the Committee was:

(5) The legal profession should be responsible for the administration of the scheme, except that part of it dealt with under the Poor Prisoners' Defence Act.

Val d'Orcia

Towards the end of 1944 Schuster was appointed Head of the Legal Branch of the Allied Control Commission (British Zone) in Austria. Whilst waiting for Austria to be liberated by the Allied forces he stayed with a friend in Tuscany, Marchesa Iris Origo, a British-born woman married to an Italian aristocrat, who was well-known as an author particularly for her biography of Lord Byron. She had been associated with the literary set in London before the war and Schuster had known her then. In the 1920s, having tired of a life of luxury and dilettantism, she and her husband had taken a large run-down estate in the Val d'Orcia, south of Sienna. They had worked hard to make the land productive, when the war came. She wrote of her experiences during the war and they were published as *War in the Val d'Orcia - A Diary* (Jonathan Cape, 1947). This diary tells how her little community of farming families became almost entirely self-contained and how they had to hide their supplies of oil, hams and cheeses, so that the Germans would not find them; and how they sheltered and clothed the fugitives escaping from the Germans who knocked at their door - whether Italians, Allies or civilians. She describes the bombing of the bridges in the Val d'Orcia, the rumours of Allied landings in Tuscany which never came and how when the fighting did come, the Germans turned them out. When they returned they had to reap what was left of the harvest, to clear the land of mines and rebuilt the shattered farms.

The diary ends on July 5, 1944 with:

> "The Fascists and German menaces are receding. The day will come when at last the boys will return to their ploughs, and the dusty clay hills of the Val d'Orcia will again 'blossom like a rose'. Destruction and death has visited us, but now - there is hope in the air."

In 1977 Iris Origo was awarded with the honour of DBE for services to British Cultural Services in Italy, and for her work for partisans and escaped British POWs during the war.

Schuster visited her several times in Italy and enjoyed her hospitality and company. As writers they had something in common. His forte was undoubtedly his description of the mountain scenery and climbing anecdotes but he had also written two novels. The first he wrote in 1923, *All's Fair* under the nom-de-plume J.F.C. Dolby (Hodder & Stoughton, 1923). It is a romantic story, set at the beginning of the 1914-18 war, about an English girl at a finishing school in Belgium who, when disguised as a young man, meets a wounded British officer, Sir Gerald Singleton. They plan to escape from the Germans and after many adventures Sir Gerald discovers that his companion is not a boy but a girl and he falls in love with her. Eventually they are captured and are taken to a chateau used as a German hospital. There the girl meets Dietrich von Aver, who falls in love with her.

This conflict ends in a duel in which Dietrich is killed. After many adventures Sir Gerald and the girl escape.

Eleven years later his second book was published under

255

his own name, *Sweet Enemy* by Claud Schuster (Cassell 1934). This was a historical romantic novel covering the period of the French Revolution, written in the first person by a John Grendon of Grendon Abbey in the County of Storcester. He fought in the Netherlands on the side of the Royalists and eventually organised French émigrés to form an army to support any insurrection that might occur in France. In the Vendée he had met his cousin Diane and fallen in love with her but she was married to Armand. As in the previous novel the two claimants to Diane have a fight and Armand is killed. Finally Diane promises herself to John for ever.

It is unlikely that either of these books had a wide circulation; a copy of *All's Fair* obtained from the British Library appeared never to have been opened. These romantic novels reveal a surprising aspect in Schuster's character. He was not just a writer of descriptive - albeit elaborate - prose. He could fantasize, he had feeling for love affairs and passion. In 1944 he had been widowed for eight years and he was known to be lonely and had contemplated remarrying. During the next three years his loneliness was mitigated by his work with the Control Commission, his activities with the Ski and Alpine clubs and in 1947 he was Treasurer of the Inner Temple. He enjoyed female company and certainly took great pleasure in his visits to Iris Origo, but she was 30 years younger than he and it is unlikely that his relationship with her was more than a close intellectual friendship. In 1946 he and his grandson Christopher stayed with her in the Val d'Orcia when they were on their way to Austria. Christopher got on well with his grandfather whom he describes as a most interesting travelling companion. He always had something interesting to relate about the scenery, the people they met and incidents concerning places they passed through. Grandfather Claud said almost the same about his father when they travelled together in the Alps when Claud was a young man.

Austria

Returning to Lord Schuster's work with the Control Commission in Austria, it was said that in spite of his age he tackled the unexpected with the zest of a young man. The following tribute was recorded in *The Times* of July 11, 1956, by Major Sir John Winterton:

> "May I say something of Lord Schuster's service with the Allied Commission for Austria? Lord Schuster joined the British element at the end of 1944, when he was already 75 years of age. He was responsible for raising the Legal Division and he got together a really first-class team which did excellent work, particularly during the difficult days of 1945 and 1946. Lord Schuster's vitality was amazing and his penetrating intelligence a delight to those who worked with him and for him."

Soon after he had left the Austrian Control Commission Schuster initiated a debate in the House of Lords on Austria. He had referred to Austria as a satellite state and was corrected (with some asperity he thought) by the Lord Chancellor. Austria was not technically a satellite state at that time. He and the Lord Chancellor, Lord Jowitt, a Labour appointee, frequently differed in debate. The question under discussion was what support the Government could give to Austria and how the country could be prevented from becoming a satellite state. Schuster speaking for the Opposition offered support for the Government's policy. At the same time he berated Lords Pakenham and Pethick-Lawrence for professing "again and again Socialist opinions".[1]

Debates in the Lords

Schuster did not limit his speeches to the subject of Austria. Having been raised to the peerage he was at last in a position to voice his opinions personally in the Upper House instead of just briefing others. His work on the Austrian Control Commission had occupied him until 1946 and in 1947 he was Treasurer of the Inner Temple. He played an important part in its reconstruction after the bombing of the war. At the age of 78 he was by no means finished; he now had a new lease of life. During 1948 and 1949 he took an active part in the debates in the Lords and it obviously gave him a great deal of pleasure. He was now in the Legislature, to which he had been so close for the whole of his working life. He revelled in it. The reports of *Hansard* show the pleasure he gained from taking part in the debates. They also reveal how on most questions he was a die-hard traditionalist. He had no hesitation in joining the Opposition (Conservative) Benches and he states his views with undiminished force and

---

1. *Hansard*. HL. March 3, 1948, vol.154, cols.409-412.

eloquence. He was never loathe to remind his peers that he had had experience of every branch of English law.

In the debate on the Criminal Justice Bill of 1948, he did just that. He made it quite clear that he did not believe that the death penalty should be abolished, that he still believed in "whipping" and that he was not enthusiastic about the probation system. He made a statement about the police which sounds naive by today's standards. He said that in Dorset at least, where he sat as a magistrate, "... no session of criminal court ever passes in which the police do not say a good word for the convicted prisoner. They are just as much the friend of the prisoner as the probation officer ... I have never known police officers do other than their best for the prisoner. They never do anything to make his case worse than he makes it himself."[2]

Later in the debate on the death penalty clause of the same Bill he made a waspish attack on the Labour peer, Lord Stansgate (father of Wedgwood Benn) accusing him of making the issue a party matter. He did not like change and abolition of the death penalty was too drastic a change. He said that Judges and lawyers have a regard for the traditions in which they are brought up, "They are slow to wish change, and very rightly so, until it has been tested."[3]

In the same debate he alleged that the Parliamentary Committee which had reported on the death penalty in 1930 had been selected purely on party lines and packed so that it would come to the desired conclusion. The Lord

2. *Hansard*. HL. April 27, 1948, vol.155, col.441.
3. *Hansard*. HL. June 2, 1948, vol.156, col.124.

Chancellor, Lord Jowitt, asked Schuster what grounds he had for that accusation as he had been responsible for setting up the committee. Schuster replied with names and descriptions of the personnel. This provoked the Lord Chancellor into saying, "I do not want to follow the last speaker, either in the tone or tempo of his speech except to say this: that I very much regret that he made his assertion with regard to the selection of the Select Committee - for Select it is - of 1930 ... it is a monstrous suggestion to say that such a Select Committee is packed ... I deeply regret that such an accusation should have been made by a member of your Lordships' House."[4]

Views on Borstal Training

As a justice who sat at Dorchester in the old Crown Court in which the Tolpuddle Martyrs were sentenced, Schuster had had experience of the borstal institution at Portland in Dorset. In the long debate on the Criminal Justice Bill of 1948, in addition to his other contributions he gave his opinion on the Borstal System.

He said that at one of his last sittings at Dorchester he dealt with cases where borstal boys had escaped from the institution at Portland and had committed several further offences such as shopbreakings in the town of Portland. His opinion was that the inhabitants of Portland should not be expected to suffer these crimes, implying that the borstal

---

4.   *Ibid.,* col.137.

system of training was too lax and that the boys should be confined more securely. The Sessions would send an escapee who had offended to prison, which many of the boys preferred, but the Prison Commissioners would then transfer them back to the borstal and so, he said, the vicious circle began again. He finally admitted that he did not know what the answer was but suggested that the Home Office experts should consider the problem.[5]

Scottish Law

In January 1949 we find him telling certain Scottish peers what Scottish law should be. It had been proposed that if a defendant served a period of probation satisfactorily he should not have a conviction recorded against him. Not surprisingly Schuster and others were very much against such a proposal.[6]

Courtesy in the Lords

Traditional courtesies characterise the debates in the Lords and members are always referred to as the noble Lord, the noble and learned Lord (a lawyer), the noble and gallant Lord (a soldier) etc. Schuster however tended to be over-polite to the point of being obsequious. His openings to most of his

---

5.   *Hansard*. HL. June 3, 1948, vol.156, cols.317-319.
6.   *Hansard*. HL. January 26, 1949, vol.160, col.178.

addresses would begin with an apology for speaking. For example on the second reading of the Legal Aid and Advice Bill, on which he had every right to speak as he had been on the Rushcliffe Committee and sub-committees which prepared the way for the Bill, he began, "My Lords, I fear your Lordships may think it is superfluous for me at this time on a warm afternoon to delay you further from giving your approval ... but there are several reasons which make it difficult for me to be silent." He would then conclude, "... with apologies for keeping your Lordships, I sit down."[7]

In the debate on the Marriage (Enabling) Bill on March 24, 1949[8] Schuster found himself speaking against the Archbishop of Canterbury. As he was inclined to do whenever he spoke in the Lords, he began with a lengthy preamble, expressing his fear in opposing such an eminent person as the Archbishop and apologising for having the emeriti to speak at all. For example:

> "I shall therefore take the liberty of being brief [he was rarely so], as I am taking the liberty of speaking at all. I address your Lordships with considerable fear when I see the serried ranks of ecclesiastical authority which are prepared to overwhelm me ..."

The point at issue was whether a man or woman should be allowed to marry his or her deceased spouse's sister or brother. In the event such a marriage did not become law until the Marriage (Enabling) Act 1960.

In a debate on a procedural Bill Schuster offered glowing

---

7. *Hansard.* HL. June 27, 1949, vol.163, cols.334-337.
8. *Hansard.* HL. March 24, 1949, vol.161, cols.708-10.

tributes to the Parliamentary draftsmen and expressed his gratitude for the assistance they gave to the Joint Consolidation Committees. He admitted that it was not usual for the House to give testimonials to civil servants but nevertheless he thought that it was appropriate on that occasion. On this subject, unusually Lord Jowitt Lord Chancellor, was in agreement, but he could not help giving a slight dig at Schuster. He said:

> "I particularly agree with what the noble Lord, Lord Schuster, said in one of his 'irregular outbursts' in regard to the assistance of civil servants."[9]

Justices of the Peace Bill 1949

In the debate on the Justices of the Peace Bill[10] describing himself as a Lancastrian by birth, Schuster said, "I know I am rather impertinent in speaking about this matter at all ..." but he made it clear that he preferred that the Lord Chancellor should be responsible for removing a justice rather than the Chancellor of the Duchy of Lancaster.

The debate continued on the subject of the reduction of the number of Borough Sessions and Winchester was threatened. The Wykehamist Schuster began with, "I am bound by every sentiment of piety to defend Winchester". His argument was that a town must have a population sufficient to provide an efficient advisory committee for the appointment of justices.

---

9.   *Hansard.* HL. April 28, 1949, vol.162, cols.155-6.
10.   *Hansard.* HL. October 25/26, 1949, vol.164, cols.1035-1287.

Winchester with a population of 26,000 was just about large enough. He went on to speak about his beloved Dorset. There sat in Dorchester (not Barchester, he said) two separate bodies - the Justices of the Peace for the borough of Dorchester and the Justices of the Peace for the petty sessional division of Dorchester. Neither had enough work to do. Schuster himself had travelled eight or nine miles from his home in Piddletrenthide to Dorchester for two or three cases. He suggested an amalgamation. The debate then turned to the size of the towns which should have recorderships. Once again Schuster clashed with Jowitt who interrupted him saying that he was under a misapprehension concerning the number of boroughs which had a population between 25,000 and 40,000. Schuster's reply was that he had possession of the document which had been supplied by Lord Jowitt and with studied sarcasm he said, "I admit that my powers both of reading and of expression are inferior."

Later in the debate he referred to the fact that the immediate effect of the Bill "... is to drive me from both my offices, and to separate me from the administration of justice and from the colleagues with whom I have worked with great pleasure for many years. I cannot but regret that, but I will endeavour to reconcile myself to the inevitable."[11]

Quite what he meant by that is not clear as he had retired from the Lord Chancellor's Department some five years earlier. He later described himself as an "inveterate bureaucrat".

In the same debate frequently mentioning his membership

---

11. *Ibid.*, col.1165.

of the Roche Committee (on justices' clerks) he strenuously defended the British administration of criminal justice - the adversarial system and the lay magistrates. He said, "... I consider it far better than the brain of man has ever devised elsewhere".

In the debate on the Justices of the Peace Bill, Schuster was the predominate speaker, which in view of his experience was quite justified. His contributions covered a wide field. He emphasised that he did not want to support any amendment which was unpleasant for the Home Office or its officials.

Ministry of Justice

The debate on an amendment to the Criminal Justice Bill 1949 which sought to transfer the responsibility for appointing stipendiary magistrates from the Home Secretary to the Lord Chancellor gave Schuster the opportunity to state his views on a Ministry of Justice. He said that he did not wish to grab more patronage for the office in which he had served long ago. He commented that it would be difficult to house more staff in the House of Lords and that putting half outside would make administration difficult [it was done nevertheless in 1970]. To Schuster it seemed that more responsibility for the Lord Chancellor's Department was a dangerous shift towards a Ministry of Justice and he felt he had to state his views forcibly and openly - something he had been unable to do during his career as Permanent Secretary when he could only influence his Lord Chancellors behind the scenes:

> "We have never had a Ministry of Justice in the country, and I
> hope we never shall. Why have we never had it? Because there
> has never been centred in any one pair of hands the power both
> to control, however indirectly, the judiciary, in any range, and,
> at the same time, the executive force of government in the shape
> of the police. There resides in the Secretary of State (ie, Home
> Secretary) - and rightly so - an indirect control over the police and
> an indirect control over prosecutions generally. I suggest that
> these should be severed from whoever has the control, the rights,
> indirect though they may be, over the appointment of judicial
> officers. I think there should be a deep division apparent to the
> public between those two functions."[12]

[The Lord Chancellor now has responsibility for
appointments of stipendiary magistrates. They are known as
District Judges from 2000.]

The subject surfaced again in 1952 when a letter from
Schuster was published in *The Times* (March 24, 1952). It was
in reply to a letter from a Mr Gardiner who had said, "we call
our Ministry of Justice the Lord Chancellor's Department",
Schuster referred to a paper written by Lord Birkenhead who
wholly opposed the formation of a Ministry of Justice. This
was noteworthy because at the outset of his Chancellorship
Birkenhead thought that the question deserved consideration.
He changed his mind. Similarly Haldane had proposed, in
the Machinery of Government Report 1918,[13] the
establishment of such a ministry. In the course of his second

12. *Ibid.*, col.1203.
13. Cmd 9230.

Chancellorship, according to Schuster, "he abandoned the idea and was for the rest of his life opposed to it".

Crimes of Violence

On March 23, 1950[14] at 6.34 pm Lord Schuster rose to give his views on punishment for crimes of violence. He began with an apology, "At this hour in the evening I hesitated a great deal as to whether I ought to occupy your Lordships' time, and especially did I think so after listening to the speech delivered by the noble Lord Ammon, with every word of which I agreed."

He spoke of his debut at the Bar in 1894 when as a very new and very white wig he had first entered the Crown Court at Liverpool and asked himself what changes had come about in the administration of criminal justice since then. Apart from procedural changes he said that there were four:

1. Heavy sentences had been cut down.
2. Corporal punishment had been abolished.
3. The probation system had been developed.
4. The provision of borstal institutions had expanded.

He was opposed to the abolition of corporal punishment on the grounds that it was a deterrent and that it forced Judges to impose longer sentences. He was against long sentences but also believed that too short sentences were an evil as they

14.   *Hansard.* HL. March 23, 1950, vol.166, cols.490-495.

did not give the prisoner time to benefit from the rehabilitation prison can give.

He gave some praise to the probation service but was not satisfied with the borstal system particularly with regard to the way escapees were dealt with. He again referred to the region he knew - Dorset, and the borstal institution at Portland. He concluded by stating his opinion that young offenders should be beaten.

County Courts

In the debate on the salaries of county court Judges Schuster was bound to have his say. He rose to speak with his usual apology, "My Lords, it is with some diffidence that I rise to speak on this Motion, in view of the number of eloquent and eminent people who already have practically exhausted the subject ... For very many years, under the direction of successive Lord Chancellors, I was myself intimately connected with the organisation of the county courts ..."

He went on to refer to county court registrars as, "a kind of inferior Judge" with administrative responsibility for his office and staff. He stated that their situation had been improved by the change for which he was largely responsible, when the administration of county courts was transferred from the Treasury to the Lord Chancellor's Department. He argued that the pay of registrars should not suffer at the expense of an increase for county court Judges. He did not think that "arguments which are based on the housemaid's baby" were likely to be successful with the

Treasury. Presumably that was another way of saying, "Hard cases made bad law".

In the same debate he brought up his experiences in Austria where Judges were hampered by very low salaries so that there was none of the firmness and disregard of personalities that we would expect in this country. In conclusion, his love of history and tradition and belief in the system of justice he had known and supported for so long, became apparent. He said, "The injunction of the Tudor Sovereigns to their Judges to consider the poor man rather than the rich has for a long time been completely unnecessary."[15]

Income Tax Acts 1952

In the Lords on February 5, 1952, Sir John Rowlett, parliamentary draughtsman and son of Lord Justice Rowlett was praised for his work on the complicated Income Tax Acts of 1952. Schuster, described at the time by Harold Kent as, "that old warhorse"[16] made his contribution:

> "I should be glad if your Lordships would allow me to delay for a moment the passage of the Bill, while I add my testimony to what has been said by my noble and learned friend ... This is indeed a massive Bill - so massive that when I tried to weigh it in the Lord Chancellor's Office a little while ago it broke the weighing machine ... it had 532 clauses and 25 schedules and

---

15. *Hansard*. HL. February 14, 1950, vol.165, cols.324-327.
16. Sir Harold Kent. *In on the Act*. Macmillan, 1979, p.215.

respects in whole and in part 60 Acts of Parliament. The successful preparation of the Bill was an effort such as Hercules might have made. Sir John Rowlett - my noble and learned friend has already outraged our parliamentary convention, and rightly so, by mentioning his name - brought great courage to the task, besides the high intelligence, the industry and the learning which we expect to find in the Office of Parliamentary Counsel. He brought also an impetuous ferocity of approach which is unusual in that state department."[17]

The Clerk of the Parliaments

"The old warhorse" was still having his say in 1953. In paying a tribute to Sir Robert Overbury, the Clerk of the Parliaments, he felt bound to mention the former Clerk, his old friend, Jack Badeley[18] with whom he had worked for many years.

Schuster began in his usual vein, "My Lords, I trust that I may be forgiven if for a few minutes I protract this debate. My excuse must be that my knowledge of, and my working with, Sir Robert Overbury extends to a far longer period than that of any other Member of the House: it began indeed 38 years ago ..." He went on to say that Overbury had begun his career in the Courts in the Strand and from there to the Table and thence to the "supreme place of the Clerkship of the Parliaments" [in fact he was not promoted to that position until 1949 which was after Schuster had retired and was when Jack Badeley had also retired].

---

17. *Hansard*. HL. February 5, 1952, vol.126, cols.1063-3.
18. Henry John Fanshawe Badeley (Lord Badeley 1949) Clerk of the Parliaments 1934-1949.

The Earl of Drogheda following Schuster spoke of, "... our much loved friend Jack Badeley", and described briefly the work of the Clerk of the Parliaments:

> "He is responsible for the administration of the staff of the House, and on him, more than anyone else, depends the happy working of the House. The staff of the House has been a happy one ever since I remember."[19]

Retired Services Officers' Pay

In what appears to have been his last speech in the Lords there was an uncharacteristic petulant tone. Speaking of his own pension, Schuster said that he was receiving far less than he thought he would receive because, "... we have fought a big, victorious but disastrous war, and we have had six years of Labour Government."

He complained that the government had given a definite promise to certain officers and now they had broken the pledge. It could be argued that it was a contract but he did not go into that. He obviously felt very strongly that it was wrong for a government to break a pledge and concluded by saying:

> "This is a pledge, and in its keeping by the Government, whatever government may be in power, all our people ... have a definite and intransient interest. When that principle is departed from, then I think that there is an end, not only of our

---

19. *Hansard*. HL. October 27, 1953, vol.183, col.1373.

public faith as between man and man, but of our position in the world."[20]

Schuster had become disappointed with the changes in society as much as with the change in government. He was beginning to feel his age.

Schuster and Coldstream

Napier succeeded Schuster and was in post for 10 years, when Sir George Coldstream became the next Permanent Secretary in 1954. He did not possess the dynamism of Schuster but he had a strong personality, stronger than that of Napier. Obviously he thought highly of Schuster and frequently consulted him when the problems of the Schuster era were revived. The Constitution and the future of the Judicial Committee of the Privy Council were subjects which had recurred throughout Schuster's time as Lord Chancellors and politicians thought of ways of holding the Commonwealth together.

Coldstream had written to Schuster on the subject just after Jowitt had become Lord Chancellor in 1945. He (or probably Napier who was then Permanent Secretary) evidently needed support in restraining the new Minister who:

"... has become enamoured of the old scheme to send the Judicial Committee on circuit ... There is, as I believe, no reason to suppose that a peripatetic body would be particularly welcome

---

20. *Hansard.* HL. December 15, 1953, vol.184, cols.98/99.

in the Dominions."[21]

Schuster's views on the impracticability of such a scheme have already been stated (*ante*, Chapter 11). Nine years later the subject of appointments to the Judicial Committee arose when Kilmuir was Lord Chancellor.

Normally Lords of Appeal were appointed to the Judicial Committee; Coldstream asked Schuster how it was that Parmoor (described by Hailsham as a "stupid as well as a tiresome man") had been appointed when Loreburn was Lord Chancellor. Schuster, having retired for 11 years, felt able to express his views as pungently as ever:

> "You will bear in mind that Sir Kenneth Muir Mackenzie [Schuster's predecessor as Permanent Secretary] was completely unscrupulous in interpreting a statute, and disregarded its provisions if they did not suit him ... Parmoor's appointment was disastrous ... Whatever was the statutory situation at the time of Parmoor's appointment, it has been completely changed by subsequent legislation, under which substantial salaries have been provided for men appointed *ad hoc*, not holding or having held high judicial office, or any of the judicial offices in the Dominions or Colonies specified in the original Act. Those new offices were invented to meet the case of India, and were intended to be held by one Hindu and one Moslem. I do not know how this has worked out since the scuttle ... to add the human touch of interest, this appointment was disastrous. Parmoor was for years a thorn in the flesh of successive Chancellors and of their unfortunate Permanent Secretaries. He wouldn't sit when he was asked to do so. He would sit when he

---

21.   LCO 2/7233.

was asked not to, and his colleagues, who anyhow disliked him, objected to sitting in a mob. He was, by this time, a disappointed and embittered man. He had expected to hold a Law Officership under the Conservatives; he had formed eccentric opinions on the merits of the War; and he hated Haldane, whom he regarded as the author of the War, in alliance with Grey. Hence he was always *mauvais coucheur*, and the unfortunate Secretary (who had to deal also with Loreburn) ... was in a difficult and dangerous position ... The other holder under the 1833 Act was that old rogue, Ameer Ali, who was well qualified to hold judicial office because his tender conscience would not allow him to give judgment against a Moslem, when engaged in litigation with an opponent of any other faith."[22]

Ten days later Coldstream gave the Schuster account of the Judicial Committee to Lord Chancellor Kilmuir in a memorandum dated December 16, 1954:

"The question was raised, somewhat half-heartedly, from time to time in the 1920s and 1930s, but never got anywhere. Lord Schuster (who understood so well the art of the practicably possible) told me that he had become convinced that the proposals for an itinerant Board would be unlikely to find favour with the Dominions and were likely to raise dissensions which were then at rest."[23]

Eleven years after Schuster's retirement, his disciple Coldstream had not forgotten what he had learnt. Indeed, in a letter dated December 22, 1966, to the Hon Mrs Betty Turner, Schuster's daughter, he was fulsome in his praise of

---

22. LCO 2/533. Schuster to Coldstream, December 7, 1954.
23. LCO 2/7237.

her father:

> "... I am glad to say that your father's shadow falls as strongly as ever and we often marvel at the power and lucidity of his memoranda and letters. What a great man he was!"

In her reply on December 30, 1966, Mrs Turner commented that her father would have been angry about the proposed abolition of hanging in the Criminal Justice Bill and suggested that he would have been unhappy about many of the liberal ideas and trends of the swinging sixties.[24]

India

Following the Imperial Conference of 1930 a Round Table Conference on India was set up with the object of deciding on a new constitution for the sub-continent. Sankey knew little about India and neither did Schuster but with his usual energy he quickly remedied his lack of knowledge sufficiently to brief his Lord Chancellor on some relevant subjects. This is revealed in a letter from S.F. Stewart (Sir Samuel Findlater Stewart, Under-Secretary of State for India 1930-1942) to Coldstream dated February 22, 1957. Stewart had been examining the Schuster papers which had been obtained from Mrs Turner. He noted that the biggest group of letters was a series which passed between Schuster and his distant cousin, Sir George Schuster, who was then Finance

---

24. LCO files.

Minister in the Viceroy of India's Council. George Schuster, as a financier, was interested in devaluing the rupee and in the question of whether the new constitution would give India more control over its finances. The subject matter of the correspondences was, in the event, only academic as the Government of India Act 1935 which resulted from the Round Table Conference did not affect the financial position. However in his letter, Stewart wrote about Schuster:

"It does, perhaps I should add, illustrate [Schuster's] attitude to his job as adviser to the Lord Chancellor (Sankey) who was the rather bewildered Chairman of the Indian Round Table Conference. Schuster made no claims to any expertise in currency matters but his capacity to get hold of a question and the pains he took to examine it, stand out. He wrote an elaborate note on the currency question for the Ld. Ch. Which, so far as I know, never emerged in the public discussions.

"The rest of the papers are a rather mixed bag, but all of them illustrate Schuster's quickness of mind, and, in the right cases, his helpfulness. The most interesting perhaps concerns his attempts, in Sankey's interest, to get to the bottom of the enigmatic Mr Ghandi. He got advice from various quarters, none of it, I believe, throwing a clear, or steady light on that very strange man. He was consulted by the Bishop of Chichester, who had made contact with Ghandi and wanted his own mind clarified. Schuster wrote to him more than once, very wisely and guardedly ..."

Stewart went on to say that he had been interested in the character sketches Schuster had made of the personnel of the Round Table Conference. He gave "a very clear, vivid, and penetrating sketch of Hailsham". Stewart had the impression that Schuster was keeping, for his own amusement, character sketches of all of the Lord Chancellors under whom he had served. That would have been of extraordinary interest; but, if he had produced such sketches, they were never published.

In the same letter to Coldstream, Stewart as Under-Secretary of State for India said that he had intended Schuster to go to India on the Davison Committee to examine the State's side of the question but Schuster had broken his leg in a skiing accident and was out of action so far as India's affairs were concerned.[25]

In his reply to Stewart's letter on February 26, 1957, Coldstream wrote about his former chief, "... he was far and away the most stimulating person I ever came in contact with, and it seems to me that you have picked on two of his most remarkable qualities; viz, his extraordinary quickness of mind, and his facility for not wasting time on anything not worth doing."[26]

Trollope and the Law

Shortly before his death Schuster had agreed to give a lecture on the literary works of Trollope at the Inner Temple. His extensive historical knowledge of the law and his passion for accuracy ensured that this was in the nature of a severe critique.

Neville Laski, the Master of the Library of the Inner Temple, noted in July 1956:

---

25. *Ibid.*
26. *Ibid.*

"Less than a fortnight before his death, when the manuscript of this lecture was given to me by Master Schuster, the final page was missing. On his attention being drawn to this, he promised to rewrite it and said that he would add some further matter referable to three minor novels by Trollope which had previously escaped his notice. Unhappily death intervened between promise and performance."

Schuster's lecture notes began with Trollope's prejudice against lawyers:

"There is one class of persons, and one form of human activity, to which the Trollope is definitely and invariably unfair. He exhibits throughout a hatred and contempt for the lawyer and his profession, and he continuously holds the law up to ridicule. Lawyers, though they were conventionally unpopular, especially in fiction, are in private life no more disliked than any other men. Perhaps some of their unpopularity is due to the fact that many novelists have been unsuccessful lawyers. But it seems strange that Trollope should have nourished such a venom. His father had been a barrister, and had failed to succeed. But Trollope himself, when he commenced as an author, had very little acquaintance either with courts of law or with those who practised in them."

He then proceeded to analyse five of Trollope's novels each of which contained a full length description of a trial in a criminal court, viz, *The Three Clerks, Orley Farm, The Eustace Diamonds, Phineas Redux* and *John Caldigate*. He said that in some of the novels the legal blunders were so gross, and so deeply affect the plot, that they invite severe criticism. In others they were trivial. He referred to *The Three Clerks*, which he described as a social document of some importance, in which the climax takes place in the Central Criminal Court. The book is marred, he said, by a complete disregard of the elementary principles of legal procedure - disregard which is not excused by the boast of ignorance. At the trial the character Alaric was charged with the crime of fraudulent conversion of trust property. Schuster maintained that at the time the selling of shares which were part of a settlement, although fraudulent, was not a crime.

He gave other examples of Trollope's "legal blunders" and commented that:

> "It is not the business of a novelist to teach law, whether substantive or procedural. He is not bound to a pedantic accuracy in his description of legal incidents or legal forms ... But if, like Trollope, he takes for his general theme the social manners and habits of an age, he is bound by his art so to present them that his readers receive a fair account of that which he describes."

(The above is taken from manuscript in the Inner Temple Library, for private circulation 1956.)

The Trollope lecture notes were prepared when Schuster was 86 years of age yet he had lost none of his ability to express in writing his opinions with clarity and force.

CHAPTER 21

The Most Powerful of Permanent Secretaries

A mandarin pursuing a relentless course as a back-room operator Claud Schuster, Permanent Secretary to 10 Lord Chancellors, was able to influence the course of important events for 24 years.

At the comparatively young age of 45 he found himself in charge of a small but unique department of State in a position to assume power. This he did to the limit - in grand measure. Not a great success at the Bar, he found his niche in the corridors of power in Whitehall. Having gained valuable experience in the Insurance Commission of 1911 under the tuition of Sir Robert Morant, from 1915 he began to make his presence felt. His department was dominated by the judiciary who had been accustomed to administering their own affairs and believed that the doctrine of the Separation of Powers meant that they could not be directed in any way by the Executive.

The same doctrine also meant that, unlike other departments of state the activities of the Lord Chancellor's Department could not be criticised in Parliament. It was not at that time subject to the scrutiny of select committees (since 1991 LCD has been subject to scrutiny by the Home Affairs Select Committee).

From his appointment in 1915 Schuster

"... had t o adapt his technique of a higher Civil Servant to a new environment in which Judges receive with circumspection any advice from an emissary to the executive. A Chancellor, although head of the judiciary, does not command Judges, but seeks their advice. Schuster's role was often to suggest who should be asked to advise, what should be referred to a committee, who should be invited to serve, and what should be done with the report."[1]

As for the Judges, the very nature of their positions made them highly individualistic - they could not agree amongst themselves. A Council of High Court Judges had been set up by the Supreme Court of Judicature Act 1873 and should have met annually but by 1919 meetings were rare. Schuster's opinion of June 23, 1919 was, "that the proceedings [of the Council of Judges] on each occasion have not been such as to encourage those present to come together again with any hope for any good result."[2] His natural desire for efficiency made him realise that, leaving the judicial function aside, the administration of the courts must be in the hands of the Executive. Twenty-seven years after his retirement the Courts Act 1971 finally achieved Schuster's aim. His legacy perhaps.

Having regard to his striving for efficiency, conflict with the Judges was inevitable. Minor disputes with individual Judges over pay, etc, were overshadowed by his clash with Lord Chief Justice Hewart. That dispute was largely due to Schuster's influence in the drafting of legislation. Did he exceed his remit?

He was able to extend the influence he had on his Lord Chancellors and use their authority to ensure that legislation was drafted as he wanted it to be. Hewart's explosion was

---

1. DNB. 1957-1960, p.867.
2. LCO 2/442.

sparked off by a clause in a Bill put there by Schuster.

As Permanent Secretary he was careful not to express political views on subjects unconnected with the law. However, when he retired his many eloquent speeches in the House of Lords and his exchanges with Lord Jowitt revealed his - in modern parlance - right-wing views. An autocrat, he had always been confident that his view of a problem was the right one. Towards the end of his career he became over-confident and impatient with the views of others; his dictatorial tone was inclined to offend. He was nevertheless respected and highly thought of by colleagues and associates. In the mountaineering and skiing fraternity he was revered as a steadfast climbing companion, an organiser and as a writer of vivid descriptions of the mountain scenery.

During his 29 years in office Schuster became the most powerful of the Permanent Secretaries between the wars although Fisher and Anderson ran him close. These three were the triumvirate who ruled Whitehall in that era and Schuster was regarded by the legal profession and other officials as the alter ego of each of his Lord Chancellors.[3]

As Albert Napier, Schuster's successor, wrote about his Minister:

"... the Chancellor being a kind of universal joint between Cabinet, judiciary and Parliament, there was hardly a public event which did not call for action of some sort on his behalf ..."

Schuster was the one to take action "on his behalf". Where

3. R.F.V. Heuston. *Lives of the Lord Chancellors 188-1940.* Clarendon Press, 1964, p.24.

an administrative decision was to be made:

> "Schuster presented the facts so clearly and above all so fairly, that the Chancellor could give a decision which was truly his own in the brief time available to him for departmental business."[4]

Truly the Lord Chancellor's decision it may have been but it was also the decision that Schuster had intended.

He was the chairman of eight committees and a member of dozen of other committees and sub-committees.

In over 300 pages of *The Guide to the Records of the Lord Chancellor's Department* by Dr Patrick Polden[5] Schuster's name is mentioned in almost every page in connection with subjects ranging from advice to the King, to legal aid, from international law to ecclesiastical appointments.

A Creator of His Own Niche

To sum up, we have a small, lively man, an autocratic character, always over-confident that his opinion on a problem was right, impatient with those who differed, who did not suffer fools gladly, and who never wasted time on what was not constructive. Having little authority in his own right, he used the authority of his Lord Chancellors to get legislation drafted as he wished, to make the judicial appointments he thought appropriate, to pack committees to obtain the kind of report he wanted and in many other ways

---

4. DNB 1951-1960, p.868.
5. HSMO. 1988.

to influence the processes of government. What is interesting is that autocratic and irascible as he could be in relationships with equals and subordinates, he could not have used the same approach to each of his Chancellors, most of whom had strong characters themselves. He surely did not have the servile charm of the suave Sir Humphrey Appleby in the *Yes Minister* series. It is more likely that his Chancellors were impressed by his quickness of thought, his directness and, as time passed, by his enormous experience of the workings of government.

An hour was set aside each morning for the Chancellor and Schuster to discuss current problems. There were decisions to be made and, like Sir Humphrey Appleby, Schuster knew how to guide his Minister towards the conclusion that he was confident was the right one. In this respect he was no different from other Permanent Secretaries. A carefully phrased memorandum with the pros and cons just slightly biased would probably have been submitted to the Chancellor. It may or may not have been read critically. The oral communication was more important. A decision as to whom to appoint as chairman of a committee could have been decided like this:

Schuster: As you know, Lord Chancellor, because of the recent corruption case the PM has decided to set up a committee of inquiry into Ethics in Business and the Department of Constitutional Affairs want us to provide a suitable Judge to chair it.

LC: But you told me that it is our policy not to spare Judges for such inquiries which are set up because the politicians cannot make up their minds what to do.

Schuster: Quite so, Lord Chancellor. In any case our Judges always think they are overworked and if we reduce their numbers we will be showered with complaints.

LC: That means we should look at senior skills.

Schuster: Yes, this inquiry is not of much importance to us but it could be a way of testing a candidate for a judgeship. There are AB, CD and EF but they are all elderly and I'm sure you will not wish to consider them.

LC: What about GH, he seems to be a very decent chap, I was with him on the Northern Circuit.

Schuster: No, Lord Chancellor, he's a failed Conservative candidate waiting for a safe seat. Appointing him would be political. IJ and KL are in the same category, the first is a Liberal and the latter was once a Marxist. Neither are judge material.

LC: What about an academic?

Schuster: It has been the policy of your predecessors to avoid academics whenever possible. They are too learned, they tend to be prolix. They examine both sides of the question to such an extent that they never come to a firm conclusion. Many years ago Professor X chaired some committee. It was a disaster, he was too clever by half.

LC: This is more difficult than I thought it would be.

Schuster: MN comes to mind, he was at Winchester and New College, I know him well - a good alpinist.

LC: What about OP, a good type and his wife is the daughter of the Earl of Gratwick?

Schuster: He has very strong views on every subject and what we want for a prospective Judge, is someone without any views on anything. QR is the right type, a good lawyer, but I am not sure that he could control a committee.

LC: ST was in my chambers; he was an excellent lawyer and has a good personality.

Schuster: We must avoid any suggestions of nepotism, Lord Chancellor, and anyway he is very junior as are UV and WX. YZ is a possibility for the future in fact we may want to give him a judgeship very soon and we do not want him to be tied up on a committee for a year or more.

LC: That seems to leave the only possibility as the good alpinist MN.

Schuster: Yes, Lord Chancellor.

CHAPTER 22

The English Gentleman

Schuster saw himself as very much the English gentleman. His love of, and facility with, English was evident in the three books he wrote about climbing, *Pleasant Pastimes* (1911), *Men, Women and Mountains* (1931) and *Postscript to Adventure* (1950). His belief in the British constitution, his love of foxhunting and the Dorset countryside, his passion for climbing and skiing in the Alps which were the vacation pastimes of the wealthy at that time - all these made him appear and behave as an ultra-loyal Englishman. His London address was 7 Camden Hill Court, Kensington, and he was a JP for the County of London and for the County of Dorset. He was an active member of the Alpine Club, the Oxford and Cambridge University Club and the Travellers' Club. Yet, being fluent in German and also speaking French and Italian, he was also at home on the Continent. For his liaison with the Belgian Government on various subjects he was awarded *L'Ordre de la Couronne de Belgique*.

In short he was a Christian Englishman of Jewish descent with a German name, who had thoroughly integrated himself into English society. His successor as Permanent Secretary to the Lord Chancellor described him as possessing, "... many of the prejudices common amongst Englishmen of his class."[1]

Prejudice he may have had - he was certainly a patriotic Englishman. It is said that he was anxious to rebut any

---

1. Sir Albert Napier. *Dictionary of National Biography* 1951-1960, p.868.

suggestion that he was of Jewish origin.[2] However, that may be apocryphal; he certainly made no attempt to change his name and it is more likely that he was determined not to give any preference in appointments, etc., to those of any particular denomination or class. His patriotism is confirmed by his opinions stated in the "open letter" summarised below.

An Englishman's View of the War

Early in 1915 an American ex-senator, Albert J. Beveridge, on a visit to Britain had had a conversation with Sir Claud Schuster, who was at the time serving on the National Insurance Commission, about the outbreak of war. Evidently, Schuster felt that he had not explained sufficiently the position of Britain and wished to clarify what, as he said, was "the point of view which I believe to be typical of the English middle class". He wrote a letter to Beveridge which was published as an open letter in the *New York Times* on April 18, 1915. It covered a complete half-page and was headed, "Prominent Briton, Setting out his Nation's Case, Says Englishman had No Belief that the Making of War on Germany would Cure their Own Economic or Political Ills, and that the Crisis found them in a State of 'Muddled Astonishment'."

He began his letter by describing the state of mind of the ordinary Englishman in July 1914. There was industrial unrest and the Irish question was as troublesome as ever but

2. Robert Stevens. *Independence of the Judiciary*. Clarendon Press, 1993, p.24.

the Englishman's thoughts were on his own affairs. The country was in a period of abounding prosperity. Schuster quoted figures showing that imports and exports had increased, the volume of shipping using British ports had increased. He conceded that there was jealousy between Britain and Germany as to foreign markets but he was confident that, "the Lancashire cotton operative would enable us in the future, as it has done in the past, to hold our own against any competitor." That was in spite of others predicting a depression in the cotton industry. "But no Englishman wanted war," he said, "but it did not cross the mind of any single human being of any class or shade of political belief that a cure could be found for any of such evils as there might be in the economic or political situation of this country by making war, and, least of all, so far as the economic questions were concerned, by making war on Germany." Schuster went on to explain that in 1913 Germany took from Britain £80 million worth of goods and sent us £60 million, and in 1912 she took from us £17,500,000 of cotton yarn and woollen goods. Making war on a country where there were millions of British pounds outstanding would be foolish in the extreme. He wrote that in July and August of 1914 when most people in Britain had booked their summer holidays in the coastal resorts, they were awakened to realize that there was a European crisis. Their reaction was one of "muddled astonishment". They had known that the Germans had been building up their fleet and that the Continental armies were much greater than theirs. There was still no sense of impending danger. They then heard of the assassination of the Austrian Archduke and had some sympathy with Austria. This was followed by a period of calm. The Foreign Office must have been uneasy but the outside world was not informed until Austria threatened Serbia. Serbia being an ally of Russia and Russia an ally of France it became apparent that the situation was serious but was still not really their concern.

However when the German army invaded Belgium all Britain was united to support brave little Belgium against mighty Germany. The justice of the war was not doubted by the mass of the people of England and their resolve was increased by the manner in which the war was conducted. Schuster wrote, "... the devastation of Belgium; the strewing of mines in the North Sea; the sinking of merchant ships and emigrant ships and the attempt to sink hospital ships; the outrages and burnings in Northern France; the bombardment of English open places and the murder of English women and children; the cruel treatment of our prisoners, even the wounded (evidence of which accumulates day by day)." He then appealed to the American readership; would they not be angry if such things had happened to them? Beveridge had suggested to Schuster that Britain was seeking war with Germany with the object of destroying her trade by force of arms and he could not see what Germany had to gain by a war with Britain. Schuster could not explain the German objectives. It could, he said, have been a mysterious unrest such as that which makes a hive of bees swarm or simply a collective insanity.

He then proceeded to explain in seven lengthy paragraphs what he thought must be the main causes of the war from the German point of view. These are summarised as:

1. The personal and professional ambitions of the leaders of the army and navy, who because of the size and strength of the forces which they commanded exercised a direct influence on the German government.
2. The personal position of the Emperor (Kaiser) who was jealous of the increasing popularity of the Crown Prince with the military party. He feared that he might be supplanted, if not on his throne, at least in the hearts of his people.
3. A national sense that the country and its inhabitants were not sufficiently valued for their culture and achievements by the rest of the world. Up to 1870 German thought promised to conquer the world. Unification under Bismarck's influence by 1870 gave them great material strength such as they had not realized before. Yet people still looked to England and especially to France for advanced methods of thought. The Germans felt that they were a young nation which was undervalued. Schuster wrote: "This feeling manifested itself in personal acts wherever you meet Germans over the Continent, in an uneasy self-assertion." They had grown rich rather suddenly and had defects associated with that process.
4. Whereas Great Britain had no economic advantage to gain by the war, Germany had much to gain. From 1807 it had exacted large monetary contributions from occupied territory, had plundered resources and needed continually expanding markets.
5. The German landowners had submitted to heavy taxation to finance the armed forces and had been persuaded that the spoils of war would alleviate the tax burden and the spectre of socialism would vanish.
6. Germany feared Russia which was recovering from the Russo-Japanese war and had access to finance from its ally France [evidently the Revolution of 1917 was not foreseen].
7. The Germans intended the war to be a Balkan war against Russia and Serbia with the prospect of advancing into the

Middle East. It was hoped that France and certainly England would be little interested in a squabble in the Balkan peninsula. The lack of interest of France would hopefully result in the breaking of her alliance with Russia.

In addition to these reasons Schuster added: "the careless teaching of professors and military historians that war is a godlike thing and that the Germans are the greatest people upon the earth, and you have a result which is good enough to account for the present situation."

He concluded his open letter by considering the prospect of winning or losing. "If we are beaten we shall go down in what we regard as the worthiest cause in which a nation can fall. We believe that if we go down the cause of liberty throughout the world will suffer. Assuredly the result will not be a period of peace; nor will Germany's domination endure forever." But he did not seriously think that the Allies would be beaten. At the time (March 1915) Germany had occupied almost all of Belgium and some of the richest parts of Northern France; her spirit was unbroken and her people had not considered the possibility of defeat. Nevertheless the comparative military powers of the contenders was changing and Schuster somewhat optimistically believed that the united power of the Allies would soon overcome the German forces. His concluding paragraph was:

"We have every confidence in the strength and loyalty of these Continental nations which are embattled on our side. We think that both the fleet and the army have proved themselves worthy. But beyond all this we have 'great allies' - and a determination that 'government of the people, by the people, and for the people, shall not perish from the earth'."

This open letter, published in a leading American newspaper, makes some striking impressions. First, it was unusual for a civil servant who would be barred from writing to a British newspaper, to occupy a complete half page in a journal such as the *New York Times*. Did he have the authority of the Foreign Secretary, Sir Edward Grey? Secondly, it is remarkable that much of what Schuster wrote could have been applied to the situation at the outbreak of the Second World War. Thirdly, in writing the letter, hoping perhaps for American intervention and for Germany to be overwhelmed, he would not have foreseen the extent of the terrible slaughter that was to take place during the next three-and-a-half years. The ghastly thought that his only son could be killed in action just a few weeks before the armistice was signed in 1918, must have been far from his mind.

The loss of his son, Christopher, affected the Schuster family deeply. They were devoted to him; grandson Christopher (named after his deceased uncle) recalls his grandmother bursting into tears at the thought of her son's death 17 years after it had happened. His mother, Elizabeth, tried to make up for the loss by being both a son and a daughter to her parents. She became too masterful, domineering and almost masculine. Unfortunately these characteristics caused her marriage to Theodore Turner, KC, to break down. This disappointed Schuster, who liked his son-in-law - he had enjoyed arguing with him on law-related subjects. The breakdown of the marriage began from about 1938. From that time, Theodore Turner stayed in London while his wife and children were living at Piddletrenthide (Dorset). There was subsequently a divorce which resulted in grandfather Schuster acting as a father figure for the three children. He was working in London, but visited Piddletrendthide whenever possible during the nine years he owned the house. Grandson Christopher says that Schuster loved small children, had a good sense of humour and liked having his leg pulled. He encouraged the children to talk to him. Christopher remembers an occasion when the three children were having a meal with their grandfather when he suddenly left the table to telephone their mother to say "these children won't talk to me". For all that the children developed a great love and respect for Schuster. When Schuser took up hunting again in the form of foxhunting at the age of 64, he did so, it is said, in order to accompany his small granddaughter, Jennifer and his grandsons, Christopher and Michael. He wanted Christopher to go to the Bar and was disappointed when he did not do so (he had a fine academic career in education becoming headmaster of Stowe School). But he was pleased when Michael did go to the Bar and no doubt would be delighted to know that he now is a High Court Judge.

An Administrator of Genius

The most important influences in Schuster's life came from his position as an administrator closely associated with the legal profession. As a member of the Alpine Club (see Chapter 6) he enjoyed the companionship while climbing in the Alps of eminent lawyers and others, such as Lord Sterndale who was Schuster's idea of a perfect Judge and an ideal Englishman. Another climbing companion was Lord Sumner, an interesting man with radical ideas; he was a candidate for the Lord Chancellorship in 1915. Other climbers included Sir Henry Lunn, traveller and travel agent, and his son Arnold.

When he took up the position of Permanent Secretary in the Lord Chancellor's Office in 1915 at the age of 45, he was a Civil Servant of 16 years' standing. He moved swiftly and the agility of his body was reflected in the agility of his mind. He was a quick reader and thinker, fluent on paper and lucid in stating a case. His rapidity of thought was described in an obituary in *The Law Times*, July 6, 1956:

> "The particular quality which most contributed to make him an administrator of genius was his remarkable rapidity of thought, which enabled him to master unfamiliar technicalities in an astonishingly short time. Thus, for example, with no Chancery training behind him, he could, when the development of legislation required it, talk conveyancing with Underhill or company law with Topham and talk it in their own language."

Many who knew him in his last year have said that his vigour and rapidity of thought and judgment were the envy of much younger men.

As one would expect he was a person of wide culture and many interests. He had read (and remembered) all that was best in English and the classical languages. He detested modern (*post* Elliot) poetry and liked detective stories. He rarely listened to music but enjoyed playing bridge and watching athletics. In spite of often being outspoken, he was certainly not lacking in what would now be called social skills.

Although autocratic and somewhat frightening in manner he, like many men of his temperament, appreciated those who could stand up to him. In his relations with his subordinates he commanded great loyalty and respect. In return he was loyal to them and was always ready to assume full responsibility for their actions. In the headquarters of the Lord Chancellor's Department today (2002) his name is still revered. A memorandum he wrote in 1942 setting out the forms of address for members of the judiciary, peers, clergy, officers of the Armed Forces, etc., is still in use by the staff. A former associate speaks of him with affection - "An excellent boss. He was autocratic but why shouldn't he be? He was always right."

A close friend (PM) wrote in *The Times*, July 4, 1956:

"But there was a gentler side to this shrewd judge of character; he recognised sincerity when he met it - as many of us fail to do - and he appreciated it fully. His literary sensibility; his love of natural beauty; and above all his power of sympathy and warmheartedness to those in difficulty were the outward signs of a truly fine nature. Though he disliked any mention of the word psychology, he understood many facets of the heart. Perhaps because he had endured so much grief himself he knew how to give to others the consolation which may - and should - be part of it. His loyalties once given, were unshakable and I can think of no fitter end to his life here than the *Wykenhamist* dinner, crowded with the shades of his beloved Winchester."

[He was taken ill and died at a Wykenhamist dinner on June 28, 1956.]

As Schuster grew older his dislike of opposition increased and this tended to strain relations with members of the judiciary and heads of departments with whom he came into contact. In his own office he would on rare occasions become impatient and would vigorously wind the handle of the ancient telephone equipment to summon an unfortunate member of his staff. When he was really exasperated he would press all the buttons and furiously wind the handle to summon all his officials. They all came running. In spite of such behaviour he was highly regarded by those who worked closely with him.

Schuster had certainly enjoyed life and perhaps because of that he did not like growing old. Sir Arnold Lunn wrote:

"One of his last remarks was: 'I'm just waiting for death.' When asked whether he believed that there was any life beyond the grave, he replied with a decisive 'No'. But among the mountains he sometimes recovered his hope that death was not the end."

Sir Arnold Lunn described him at the age of 86 two days before his death as still having something of the *jeune feroce* in him. Age had not impaired his penetrating mind nor the vividness of his personality. He still preserved the grasp of essentials so characteristic of the legal brain. Lunn said:

"The incisiveness with which he expressed his contempt for the insincere and the pretentious and for the third rate in life and literature might have been mistaken for intellectual arrogance but there was none the less a genuine strain of humility in his attitude to his fellow man. He never took praise for granted and

297

the friendly criticisms of his writings from those whose judgment
he respected both surprised and delighted him."[3]

---

3. Sir Arnold Lunn. *British Ski Year Book for 1957*, vol.xviii, no.38, p.283.

Bibliography

Bowra, Sir Maurice. *Memories 1898-1939*. 1966.

Campbell, John. *F.E. Smith. First Earl of Birkenhead*. Jonathan Cape. 1983.
Churchill, Winston. *My Early Life*. Leo Cooper. 1989.
Cole, Margaret (ed.). *Beatrice Webb's Diaries*. Longman. 1952.
Cretney, S.M. "What Will Women Want Next?" 112. *LQR*. 1996.

De W Howe, M. (ed.) *Holmes-Laski Letters*. 1953.
Drewry, Gavin. *Lord Haldane's Ministry of Justice*. Public Administration, vol.61, 1983.

Eve and Creasy. *Life and Work of John Tyndall*. 1915. (Chapter on Tyndall as a Mountaineer written by Schuster, Claud.)

Graham Hall, J. and Martin, Douglas F. *Haldane - Statesman, Lawyer, Philosopher*. Barry Rose. 1996.
Graham Hall, J. and Martin, Douglas F. *A Perfect Judge*. Barry Rose. 1999.
Grigg, P.J. *Prejudice and Judgment*. Jonathan Cape. 1948.
Grigg, P.J. *The People's Champion*.

Hennessy, Peter. *Whitehall*. Fontana Press. 1989.
Heuston, R.F.V. *Lives of the Lord Chancellors 1885-1940*. Clarendon Press. 1964.
The Rt Hon Lord Hewart of Bury. *The New Despotism*. Ernest Benn. 1929. Clarendon Press. 1964.

Hogg, Quinten. Lord Hailsham of Marylebone. *A Sparrow's Flight*. Collins. 1990.

Jackson, Robert. *The Chief. Biography of Gordon Hewart, Lord Chief Justice of England 1922-1940*. Harrop. 1959.

Kent, Sir Harold S. *In on the Act*. MacMillan. 1979.

Lunn, Sir Arnold. *British Ski Year Book*. MacMillan. 1957.

Origo, Marchesa Iris. *War in the Val d'Orcia - A Diary*. Jonathan Cape.
1947.
O'Halpin, Euan. *Head of the Civil Service - A Study of Warren Fisher*.
Routledge. 1986.

Mallett, Sir Charles. *Lord Cave - A Memoir*. John Murray. 1931.
Maughan, Lord. *At the End of the Day*. Heinemann. 1954.

Nicholson, Harold. *King George V. His Life and Reign*. Constable.
1952.

Polden Dr, Patrick. *Guide to the Records of the Lord Chancellor's
Department*. HMSO. 1988.

Salter, Lord. *Memories of a Public Servant*. Faber and Faber. 1961.

Schuster, Claud (JFC Dolby). *All's Fair*. Hodder and Stoughton. 1923.
Schuster, Claud. *Sweet Enemy*. Cassell. 1934.
Schuster, Claud. *Mountaineering*. Clarendon Press. 1948.
Schuster, Claud. *Pleasant Pastimes*. 1911.
Schuster, Claud. *Men, Women and Mountains*. Nicholson and Watson.
1931.
Schuster, Claud. *Postscript to Adventure*. 1950.

Second Earl of Birkenhead. *The Life of F.E. Smith, First Earl of
Birkenhead*, by his son. Eyre and Spottiswood. 1960.
Stevens, Robert. *The Independence of the Judiciary*. Clarendon Press.
1993.

Webb, Beatrice. *Our Partnership.* Drake and Cole. LSE and Cambridge University Press. 1975.

West, William T. *The Trial of Lord Clifford.* 1935.

Wheeler-Bennett, John. *Anderson, Viscount Waverley.* MacMillan. 1962.

Wheeler-Bennett, John. *George VI.* MacMillan. 1958.

Williams. *The Making of Manchester Jewry.*

Index